ITALIAN ECOCINEMA
BEYOND the HUMAN

NEW DIRECTIONS IN NATIONAL CINEMAS

Robert Rushing, editor

ITALIAN ECOCINEMA BEYOND THE HUMAN

Elena Past

INDIANA UNIVERSITY PRESS

This book is a publication of

Indiana University Press
Office of Scholarly Publishing
Herman B Wells Library 350
1320 East 10th Street
Bloomington, Indiana 47405 USA

iupress.indiana.edu

Manufactured in the United States of America

Cataloging information is available from the Library of Congress.

ISBN 978-0-253-03947-7 (hardback)
ISBN 978-0-253-03948-4 (paperback)
ISBN 978-0-253-03949-1 (ebook)

1 2 3 4 5   24 23 22 21 20 19

In Memory of Nino, Lucy, and Sydney
For Ray and Ana

CONTENTS

Acknowledgments ix

Note on Translation xi

On Location: Italian Ecocinema *1*

1 Hydrocarbons, Moving Pictures, Time:
   Red Desert 23

2 Location, Dirty Cinema, Toxic Waste, Storytelling:
   Gomorrah 56

3 Posthuman Collaboration, Cohabitation, Sacrifice:
   The Wind Blows Round 87

4 Silence, Cinema, More-than-Human Sound:
   Le quattro volte 123

5 Volcanoes, Transgenerational Memory, Cinema:
   Return to the Aeolian Islands 153

   Epilogue *190*

Bibliography 195

Index 207

ACKNOWLEDGMENTS

A N ACADEMIC PROJECT. A LABOR OF LOVE. A journey. A long walk through thick intellectual woods, sometimes dark and hopefully deep. Frédéric Gros (2014, 19–20) writes that books need to be able to walk, and they need to be conceived while walking: "Books by authors imprisoned in their studies, grafted to their chairs, are heavy and indigestible. [. . .] Think while walking, walk while thinking," he urges.

Although I frequently feel myself to be grafted to my chair, my notebooks are full of metro cards and train tickets, reminding me that this book relies on collaborations and ideas formed while moving about Italy, talking with friends, attending the conferences of the American Association for Italian Studies and the Association for the Study of Literature and Environment, conversing with a growing community of ecocritics in Italian studies, walking and thinking with my students in Detroit and Abruzzo.

In Italy, conversations with members of the cast and crews of the films in this study were transformative. Most of these contacts would not have been possible without the help of the gifted Giovanna Taviani, whose generosity during my stay in Rome I will always cherish. The names are numerous, and I hope that I am remembering them all: Carlo Di Carlo (*Red Desert*); Gennaro Aquino, Paolo Bonfini, and Greta De Lazzaris (*Gomorrah*); Pierangela Biasi, Roberto Carta, Mario Chemello, Anamaria del Grande, Katia Goldoni, Rocco Lobosco, and Fredo Valla (*The Wind Blows Round*); Paolo Benvenuti, Michelangelo Frammartino, Simone Paolo Olivero, and Marco Serrecchia (*Le quattro volte*); Antonino Allegrino, Antonio Brundu, Franco Figliodoro, Flavia Grita, Janet Little, Pietro Lo Cascio, and Antonino Paino (*Return to the Aeolian Islands*). There were additional members of the film community who offered insightful perspectives on how films in Italy are made, taking the time to share a coffee and a slice of cinematic life: nicol* angrisano, Iaia Forte, Paola Randi, Piero Sanna, and Piero Spila. Roberto Marchesini and Eleonora Adorni welcomed me at the *Scuola d'Interazione Uomo Animale*. I learned so much from all of these people, and from their artistry, candor, and generosity.

My work was supported by a Research Enhancement grant from Wayne State University's Office of the Vice President for Research. Wayne State's

Foreign Language Technology Center, led by Sangeetha Gopalakrishnan, and the Humanities Center, directed by Walter Edwards, generously backed various aspects of the project. The Biblioteca Luigi Chiarini of the Centro Sperimentale di Cinematografia offered an exceptional array of resources, and the staff there was knowledgeable and accommodating without fail.

Anne Duggan, Pierluigi Erbaggio, Victor Figueroa, Dana Renga, and Thibaut Schilt all read and offered discerning feedback on sections of the manuscript, as well as encouragement along the way. Damiano Benvegnù, Enrico Cesaretti, Alina Cherry, Raffaele De Benedictis, Matteo Gilebbi, Silvia Giorgini-Althoen, Jim Michels, Kate Paesani, and Monica Seger are exceptional colleagues, collaborators, and friends who enrich my thinking and my life via conversations over Skype, espresso, and happy hours. Writing days with Tracy Neumann kept me focused, no matter how crazy the semester. Francesca Grandi and Sara Amoroso made Ed and me feel at home in Rome. Robert Rushing, series editor at Indiana University Press, and Janice Frisch, acquisitions editor, have made it highly rewarding to work with the Press, and the anonymous readers of my manuscript were insightful and extremely helpful.

Millicent Marcus taught her graduate students the importance of sisterhood in the academy. I am indebted to her for showing us an affirmative, sustainable intellectual path. Deborah Amberson, Giovanna Faleschini Lerner, and Serenella Iovino tirelessly support and respond to my work, shape my thinking, and make me grateful every day that academics is a collective endeavor. My sister Mariana Past looks out for me in the most generous of ways, intellectual and affective. My parents Al and Kay Past inspire me with their writing projects and ask enthusiastically about mine. My partner Ed Slesak has walked many miles with me as I worked on this project, and sometimes he carried me, too.

Parts of Chapter Four were published in Italian in *Animal Studies: Rivista italiana di antispecismo* 11 (2015): 56–76, in an article titled "Il cinema e il suono del silenzio: *Le quattro volte*." Some of Chapter Five appeared in *L'analisi linguistica e letteraria* XXIV.2 (2016): 135–146 with the title "Volcanic Matters: Magmatic Cinema, Ecocriticism, and Italy." My thanks to the editors of the journals for allowing me to reprint my work here.

NOTE ON TRANSLATION

PUBLISHED TRANSLATIONS OF WORKS IN ITALIAN OR OTHER languages are listed in the bibliography and cited in the text. Otherwise, all translations from original Italian texts, as well as translations of my interviews with film crew members, are my own.

ITALIAN ECOCINEMA
BEYOND the HUMAN

ON LOCATION: ITALIAN ECOCINEMA

I SPENT A SEMESTER IN ROME CONDUCTING RESEARCH for this book about Italian ecocinema and doing a lot of walking, especially to libraries, cinemas, and interviews. It seemed appropriate to work on a project about Italy, film, and the environment while walking, and not only because less petroleum was burned in the process. Italy, after all, is the land where renowned scriptwriter Cesare Zavattini theorized cinema as "pedinamento," or tailing the film's subject on foot with a camera.[1] From our apartment, my partner and I mapped inevitably winding routes on medieval streets, Roman roads, and imperial Fascist boulevards, and we walked until we reached our destination (when we had one), even if it took hours. We wore out our shoes during the rainy winter of 2013, calloused our feet, and experimented with the different cultural etiquette of bodily distance from others on Italian sidewalks. We learned some routes and never learned others, got lost nearly every day, and almost never minded. We made friends, some of them dogs. We came home to Michigan and tried to keep walking Roman distances in the Detroit suburbs, our legs eager to tire, our minds eager to wander. In A Philosophy of Walking, *Frédéric Gros (2014, 7) says that "the freedom in walking lies in not being anyone; for the walking body has no history, it is just an eddy in the stream of immemorial life."[2] Instead of being someone(s) in the dizzying stream of life immemorial that courses through every layer of Rome, we were somewhere, in a city of (among many other things) cinema. We were on location.*

In his lyrical book titled *The Old Ways: A Journey on Foot*, Robert Macfarlane (2012, 161) writes that "there are kinds of knowing that only feet can enable, as there are memories of a place that only feet can recall." I begin by recalling rambles during a semester spent in Rome to acknowledge that this book is grounded in a way of knowing enabled by feet, memories, places: my feet, my memories, but also those of my many interlocutors. Macfarlane elaborates, regarding footsteps on the earth, that "touch is a reciprocal action, a gesture of exchange with the world. To make an impression is also to receive one" (161). This book explores ecocritical case studies of a series of Italian films that were shot on location rather than in studio, and it examines these films *as* and also *by way of* such gestures of exchange. That is to say, I trace some of the impressions Italian film productions have left on the world, while also documenting part of the process of doing this research. Five films feature in this study: *Deserto rosso* (*Red Desert,* dir. Michelangelo Antonioni, 1964), *Gomorra* (*Gomorrah,* dir. Matteo Garrone, 2008), *Il vento fa il suo giro* (*The Wind Blows Round,* dir. Giorgio Diritti, 2005), *Le quattro volte* (dir. Michelangelo Frammartino, 2010), and *Fughe e approdi* (*Return to the Aeolian Islands,* dir. Giovanna Taviani, 2010).[3] These films, which focus on geographically diverse locations across Italy, constitute significant case studies because of the prominent roles different nonhuman actors play in each. In them, I discover dynamic (if not always happy) stories of intersecting lives and matters, on set and onscreen.

Scott Slovic's (2008, 28) influential work on ecocritical "responsibility" advocates that "[e]cocritics should tell stories, should use narrative as a constant or intermittent strategy for literary analysis. [. . .] Encounter the world and literature together, then report about the conjunctions, the intersecting patterns."[4] Endeavoring to recognize and work through my inevitable embedment in the world that I study, each chapter begins with situated stories of the interviews I conducted in Italy with members of the films' production crews, from directors to location managers, from assistant camera operators to sound recordists. The interviews offer insights into aspects of the process of shooting on location, serving to frame the theoretically engaged studies of the films that follow. Guided by material ecocriticism's recognition of the lively agency of the world around us, I read the films in terms of pressing environmental questions: cinema's dependence on hydrocarbons and its significant waste stream, its use of nonhuman animals, the toxic waste crisis in the region of Campania, and more generally human reliance on the more-than-human world.[5] Material ecocriticism, Serenella Iovino (2012b, 453) insightfully argues, shows that "between matter and meaning, there is a substantial reciprocity, co-implication." *Italian Ecocinema Beyond the Human* works to engage both matter and meaning, and theorizes the ways in which filmmaking practice, from sound recording to location scouting to managing a production, can help interpret a film and its relationship to lively places and vibrant nonhuman actors.

In short, this book seeks to uncover cinema's ecological footprint, or the way a film shapes the world, while also seeing the reciprocal ways the world writes itself on film. Its "ecocinema" framework builds on a growing number of environmentally engaged film and media studies. Although the term "ecocinema" can be used to describe the aesthetic style or narrative content of films, in the way I intend it here, it is an interpretive approach, not a genre.[6] Filming on location, as my interviewees told me on multiple occasions, requires listening to and collaborating with the world. Writing about ecocinema entails a critical project of unraveling the agentic networks on set and onscreen, rethinking and reframing the nonhuman actors who have often only had a marginal role in film scholarship. So I propose asking new questions about how and what films signify, and wonder whether different kinds of actors—not just human actors—can provide some answers.

Going Slow: Cinema/Scholarship

The Roman excursions I embarked upon during the early phases of my research shaped this project in material and philosophical terms, molding and helping to make sense of the entangled theory, analyses, and writing practice that appear on these pages. Rebecca Solnit (2000, 9) writes that "on foot everything stays connected, for while walking one occupies the spaces between [. . .] interiors in the same way one occupies those interiors. One lives in the whole world rather than in interiors built up against it." A lot of the connections linking different elements of my research—locations, actors, material substances, cinematic narratives—made sense on foot, or seemed to. Then came the moment to translate ideas to the page: this, unsurprisingly, was a slow process. Like many academic projects, this book took a long time to mature (or so it seems to me). Though it might sound like an exercise in rationalization, I gradually realized that I aspire to slowness in my approach to analysis. In *The Slow Professor: Challenging the Culture of Speed in the Academy* (2016, 57), Maggie Berg and Barbara K. Seeber outline a kind of manifesto for a slow academic practice that "is about asserting the importance of contemplation, connectedness, fruition, and complexity." Connectedness: like many works in the environmental humanities, my research reaches across disciplinary boundaries to draw on insights from fields as diverse as Italian screen studies, volcanology, animal studies, philosophical ethology, and acoustic ecology; it encompasses sundry actors including goats, volcanoes, and dirt. In the process, I attempt an ethical path, as Berg and Seeber suggest slow scholarship should, or specifically an opening of Italian screen studies to "otherness," and nonhuman others in particular. *Italian Ecocinema Beyond the Human*'s eclectic reach also stretches my disciplinary comfort zone, but I believe this risk might be worth taking.

To an Italianist, it seems like more than a coincidence that Frédéric Gros, a French philosopher of walking, learned an important lesson regarding the value of slowness while ambling in the Italian Alps. On the mountain slopes at the borders of Italy, Gros (2014, 37) writes that he realized that: "[s]lowness means cleaving perfectly to time, so closely that the seconds fall one by one, drop by drop like the steady dripping of a tap on stone." Rather than encountering a landscape that approaches us quickly, as happens when we rely on the speed of petroleum-fired transit, he notes that when we walk, our bodies and minds intersect with the landscape: "it isn't so much that we are drawing nearer, more that the things out there become more and more insistent in our body. The landscape is a set of tastes, colours, scents which the body absorbs" (38).

That the Italian Alps might have been absorbed into Gros' body along with an epiphany about the value of unhurried transit seems compelling because in Italy—the land of icons of speed like Ducati, Ferrari, and Lamborghini—philosophers, sociologists, epicures, activists, and scholars have frequently meditated on questions of slowness. There is the Slow Food movement, perhaps the best-known of these philosophies, with its position against the "tyranny of urgency" and its firm opposition to industrialized fast food.[7] Going slow, for Slow Food founder Carlo Petrini (2007, 180), means "to 'waste' time—not in the sense of discarding it, like everything that is of no use to the disciples of speed—but by taking the time to think, to 'lose yourself' in thoughts that do not follow utilitarian lines: to cultivate the ecology of the mind, the regeneration of your existence." Sociologist Franco Cassano's (2012, 10) influential *Southern Thought* begins with a chapter titled "Going Slow," and in the first subsection, "Thinking on Foot," he insists that "the slow thought is the only thought; the other is the thought that allows us to run a machine; the thought that increases its speed and flatters itself into believing it can do it in perpetuity." Cassano calls on a Mediterranean history of slow thought to oppose the assumption, proper to many currents of modernity (and in particular to what he calls "turbocapitalism," with its fast-paced rhythms of extraction, production, and consumption), that progress equals acceleration. Most recently, in the chapter titled "Slow" in her landmark work *Ecocriticism and Italy: Ecology, Resistance, and Liberation*, Serenella Iovino (2016) invokes the tenets of Slow Food alongside environmental historian Rob Nixon's notion of "slow violence" to consider struggles for environmental justice and preservation of naturalcultural beauty in Piedmont, her home.[8] In Iovino's nuanced analysis, slowness is simultaneously "the pace of suffering creative people and their democratic battles, the pace of the ground, of wine aging in oak barrels, of the asbestos in workers' lung cells" (154).

Going slow, whether in theory or in practice, is radical, a fact I remark each time I drive to work on the rowdy freeways of the Motor City. As Petrini, Cassano, and Iovino explain, slowness can be practiced for ideological (and specifically anti-capitalist) reasons. Going slow can mean to refuse to participate, effectively becoming a strategy of walking away from sources of profit, speed, and strife. Gros (2014, 7), for example, proposes "walking to express rejection of a rotten, polluted, alienating, shabby civilization." But going slow can also be a walking *toward*, a politics of affirmation, a decision to approach problems by way of physical proximity or cognitive and creative engagement. Iovino demonstrates such an affirmative ethics when she links Slow Food's origins to the peasant world of Piedmont, showing how Petrini was inspired by the work of partisan and author Nuto Revelli. Revelli's patient efforts to document the stories of peasants in the Cuneo region effectively gave voice to its population of forgotten inhabitants. Here, by becoming what Iovino (2016, 148) calls a "cognitive reserve of biocultural practices accumulated over time, in spite of all hierarchies of power, ethnicity, age, or gender," slowness becomes an "emancipatory strategy," an ecology of knowledge.

In all of these studies, slowness is evoked as an ideology that can respond to shifts in environmental processes. By identifying the dangers of turbocapitalism, fast food, or industrial pollution, the philosophers of slowness suggest how practices driven by humans are quickly, and often perniciously, altering the planet and its nonhuman occupants. Cassano, Iovino, Petrini, and Slow Food disclose the importance of thinking slowness in the age of the Great Acceleration, at the latter end of what environmentalists and others are calling the Anthropocene.[9] The faster we go, scientists argue, the more our fates are entangled with that of the planet. Advocating for the notion that we have entered a discernably different geological era, Steffen et al. (2015, 94) explain:

> Hitherto human activities were insignificant compared with the biophysical Earth System, and the two could operate independently. However, it is now impossible to view one as separate from the other. The Great Acceleration trends provide a dynamic view of the emergent, planetary-scale coupling, via globalisation, between the socio-economic system and the biophysical Earth System. We have reached a point where many biophysical indicators have clearly moved beyond the bounds of Holocene variability. We are now living in a no-analogue world.

Going slow, however, is to recognize that anthropocentric time is not the time that governs the pace of all life on the planet, even if it is urging along a crisis that exceeds the space of the human. Speed may have coupled socio-economics and biophysical systems in geologically significant ways, but when we slow down, we can be mindful of the fact that we—and our socio-economics—have been part of the world from our origins as humans, not just since the Great Acceleration. We can also perceive the different ways that the world is part of us. Petrini (2007, 184) urges us to reconsider "slow knowledge" because it "is the knowledge which can restore balance to the world, which produces the good, which does not pollute, which saves cultures and identities." Iovino slows down to taste the sedimented layers of sometimes-violent Piedmontese struggles and rocky, earthly bodies in a glass of Nebbiolo, one of the region's prized red wines. Cassano (2012, 9) goes slow to allow thoughts to form, not from goals or the strength of individual will, but "from an agreement between mind and world." Rooted conceptually and materially in an Italian landscape that has long betrayed the entanglement of the human in a more-than-human world, each of these philosophies thus helps cause our anthropocentric perspective to "wobble," as Jeffery Jerome Cohen (2015) suggests narratives can. We "wobble" when we admit the instability of our anthropocentrism, when we "apprehend that the world is not centered around the human—not indifferent, not misanthropic, but *disanthropocentric*" (25). Such an admission helps us read fictional and material narratives differently. Or it can lead us to write entirely new stories.

Locating Italian Ecocinema

Here, going slow means stopping to interrogate the premises underlying this book, starting with the idea of Italian cinema itself. Studying cinema through a material ecocritical lens requires me to question the wisdom of writing about "Italian" cinema, given that ecocriticism frequently concerns itself with geological formations and material agents (mountains, oceans, winds, mutable riverbeds, dirt, to name a few) that crisscross and complicate national boundaries. Environmental crises, of course—from climate change to ozone holes to toxic waste spills and fallout from nuclear meltdowns—disregard the limits of the nation-state. Cinema also often spans international borders, drawing on a globalized marketplace that connects networks of technologies (cameras and recording equipment, editing software, cranes and helicopters), actors, producers, distributors, and audiences across the globe. Calling on a few examples from the films in this book, we might note that the Irish actor Richard Harris stars in *Red Desert*; that *Gomorrah* received financing from the European Union; that postproduction sound for *Le quattro volte* was done in Berlin; or that *Return to the Aeolian Islands* cites a history of Aeolian cinema including *Il Postino* (1994), directed by the English Michael Radford and starring French actor Philippe Noiret as the Chilean poet Pablo Neruda. Or we could observe that *Gomorrah* was shot using an Arricam LT, made by the Munich-based multinational ARRI Group, on 35-mm Kodak film probably manufactured in Rochester, NY. Our thought experiment could also follow the paths of resource extraction needed to create electronics, the disposal of digital waste, or the distribution of films to sundry locations across the globe.

Yet between the global concerns of environmentalism and the global interests of the marketplace (in which cinema generated an estimated $40.6 billion worldwide in 2017), there emerges a critical tension, a tension that ultimately makes places—however arbitrary their borders—all the more important.[10] Environmental historians and ecocritics point out how a neoliberal global marketplace strategically places greater environmental burdens and fewer economic benefits in places already poor in global capital. Iovino (2006, 47–48) emphasizes that capital thus "globalizes" while poverty is localized, and nature (of course) becomes nothing more than a resource used to accumulate profit. She cites the multinational reach of organizations like the World Bank, the United Nations, and international nongovernmental organizations (NGOs) at the head of global environmental efforts, arguing that many decisions about our shared planet are made outside of the context of democratic debate:

> Even when referring to environmental politics, the adjective 'global' indicates not so much protecting the entirety of the planet, but rather 'the political space where a particular, dominant local power attempts to obtain global control, freeing itself from local, national, and international restrictions.' On an environmental level, thus, globalization reveals itself to be a form of colonization.[11]

In this undemocratic globalized landscape, place becomes an important tool for resisting and refiguring the never-truly-free flows of resources, contaminants, and stories. Here, participation matters, and my project recognizes this by calling upon some of the voices of otherwise unseen (or unheard) human and nonhuman participants in film production crews and cinematic narratives: a sneezing baby goat in Calabria, for example, or a screenplay writer who lives in the valley adjacent to the one where *The Wind Blows Round* was filmed. Relationship to one's material surroundings matters, too, and the locatedness of global subjects can provide key alliances and knowledges to work against the homogenizing powers of the global. As Iovino (2010a, 45) elaborates: "in its uniqueness, place is the bearer of a value in itself and of a value shared universally, with every other place."[12] Regarding film specifically, Elena Gorfinkel and John David Rhodes (2011, xvi) argue in *Taking Place: Location and the Moving Image* that cinema and the mobile images it relies upon may offer a key means to challenge the vast, colonizing, unimagineable power of the global.[13]

If place does indeed matter, however arbitrary or porous the borders of the nation in a globalized society, the historic-geographic aggregation that is Italy offers some particularly useful tools for thinking ecologically. In Italy, closely interwoven human and nonhuman spaces have created a legacy of cohabitation, both constructive and destructive, that resonates with particular force today. The overlapping of anthropic and nonhuman spaces has also long shaped human perception of the peninsula. Environmental historians Marco Armiero and Stefania Barca (2004, 51n49) contend, for example, that:

> Italian environmental history did not begin from the assumption that nature works without humans, and thus it never lost itself in the search for truly natural spaces (without humans), or the naturalness of space (before the arrival of man). It accepted, more or less entirely, the challenge of keeping economies, nature, society, and ecosystems together.

In the United States, it took the "Great Acceleration" to convince many (and not yet nearly all) that socio-economics and biophysics were connected; Armiero and Barca suggest that in Italy, these systems were never viewed as independent. Walking slowly in Italy, you can find many reasons to scoff at the idea of a world where human and more-than-human matters are decoupled. Hiking in the wildest areas of Abruzzo, as Patrick Barron (2003, xxvi–xxv) notes, you still might stumble upon traces of ancient terraced hillsides, or the foundations of a hermit's hut. Strolling down the densest thoroughfares in Naples, you are still aware of the active volcano on the skyline. Or taking your feet off the *terra firma* to sail or swim in open, crystalline Mediterranean waters, you are still likely to find a boat overburdened with refugees just over the horizon, or toxic waste seeping from a ship sunk by the ecomafia. To the attentive, slow-gazing eye, Italy's posthuman landscape insistently reveals itself, reminding us, as Donna Haraway

(2015, 159) observes, that "no species, not even our own arrogant one pretending to be good individuals in so-called Western scripts, acts alone; assemblages of organic species and of abiotic actors make history, the evolutionary kind and the other kinds too." Intermingled natureculture appears around every bend in the road, and although a slow, more-than-human gaze might be attuned to the beauty and pleasure of entanglement in Italian ecologies, such a perspective can perceive injustice, too, and environmental degradation, toxicity, overbuilding, or waste. Going slow offers our human sensorium the time to discern the world around and within us, as well as to take stock of the effect of our posthuman footprint on the planet.[14]

Such mutually constituted human and nonhuman landscapes have even been framed in legal terms, making Italy an unusual geopolitical landscape. Article 9 of the Italian Constitution states that "The Republic promotes the advancement of culture and scientific and technical research. It safeguards the landscape and the historic and artistic patrimony of the Nation."[15] Italy is one of a very small number of nations, and was among the first, to expressly call for the protection of landscape in its constitution. In Italian, the words that are used, often interchangeably, to contextualize environmental questions—*ambiente, paesaggio, territorio*, or, roughly, environment, landscape, territory—are indicative of the close ties between the natural and human worlds, between ethical and aesthetic imperatives. As Salvatore Settis (2012) shows, however, this terminology has also fractured and confused the protection of Italy's naturalcultural patrimony: landscape is protected by the State; territory by regional governments; environment by a convoluted combination of legislation. The resulting tangle of laws has led to significant and repeated abuses of the very environment such legislation was designed to protect.[16]

And as a matter of fact, as I have already indicated, the story of contemporary environmental crisis in Italy is also, tragically, a prolific one. The litany of abuses includes illegal building, deforestation and subsequent hydrogeological instability, urban blight, urban sprawl, poorly maintained historic centers, dependence on the roadways for all kinds of transportation, chronic inefficiencies in public administration, and entire sectors of the economy, including disposal of waste and excavation, controlled by organized crime (Della Seta 2000, 61). The Legambiente, Italy's largest environmental NGO, has coined a growing list of neologisms to condemn the prevalence of such problems. The first of these, "ecomafia," which refers to organized crime's dark legacy of harming the environment, is now an umbrella term that encompasses "agromafia," "archeomafia," "zoomafia," and "ecomostri," words meant to underline how a criminal underworld, often in collusion with developers and local governments, threatens agriculture, archaeological heritage, nonhuman creatures, and the integrity of built landscapes, respectively.[17] In his extensive study of the changing face of the Italian landscape, Settis (2012, 3, 9) has shown how, between 1990 and 2015, growing urban sprawl, or "cementification," swallowed up 3,663,000 hectares of land formerly available for agriculture, in the process eliminating green spaces and increasing the probability and the gravity of landslides and floods. In this worrisome, particularly Italian, naturalcultural crossing, Settis suggests that "the invasion of asphalt and cement appears to be a sort of inescapable natural calamity, which like an earthquake is beyond human control" (12). In the Italian context, scholars and artists have always known that the human and the nonhuman are co-constituted, and that their relationship is not always—or ever—perfectly harmonious. Here, though, Settis suggests that the narrative itself is out of whack: if cement is seen as a "natural" calamity, Italians cast themselves as helpless to stop its advance. And so new Italian stories are needed to reshape a sense of agency, to identify a posthuman collaborative force that can reimagine human responsibility in the face of ecological distress.

In this socio-eco-cultural landscape, cinema, with its powerful ability to figure places, offers a particularly promising means to shift the narrative, and the embeddedness of these Italian films on location offers a rich site for inquiry. But another doubt remains: not everyone agrees that watching screens is an effective way to slow down, or to understand the entangled nature of humans and the environment. Ecophenomenologist David Abram, for instance, advocates strongly that we need to retune our senses and reawaken awareness of our participation in the nonhuman world. His proposal for how to activate such mindfulness includes, logically, walking. In *Becoming Animal: An Earthly Cosmology,* Abram (2011) contends that we must materially reconnect our flesh to the dirt beneath us, so that the bodily sensation restores our cognition of co-constituted lives. Walking barefoot one morning, he writes: "My legs inadvertently slow their pace as the sensitive presence of the land seems to gather beneath my feet, the ground no longer a passive support but now the surface of a living depth; and so my feet abruptly feel themselves being touched, being *felt*, by the ground" (59). Later in the book, Abram expresses concern that as dwellers of the contemporary world, we spend too much time staring at screens and pages (my apologies, reader, and thank you for bearing with me). Encouraging us to sense the effects we have on the world and that the world has on us, to notice the "reciprocity" in earthly relationships that have coevolved over millennia, Abram worries that the flatness of computer, television, and cinema screens and the smooth surfaces of a book's pages desensitize the depth perception that allows us to observe our rootedness in the world: "It matters little that the things written of on those pages may be filled with creative nuance, or that the glowing screen carries an image rich with perspectival programming and simulated depth—for it is first the flat surface that intercedes between us and that depth. Our animal senses are no longer in direct relation with the sensuous terrain; our muscled body sits immobilized before the smooth and scintillating surface upon which we gaze, enthralled" (90). This flattened perspective, he argues, citing as an example a television documentary about female lions, causes our "organism" to learn "that nature is something you look *at*, not something you are *in* and *of*" (91). It thus bolsters the belief that an objective, disembodied understanding of the world is possible (93).[18]

Can glowing screens, or the productions that create them, intercede meaningfully in the quest to understand the more-than-human world? A growing body of scholarship is devoted to "slow cinema," which Ira Jaffe (2014, 3) defines as films that are "slow by virtue of their visual style, narrative structure and thematic content and the demeanour of their characters." According to one of its theorists, slow cinema can help environmental thought "communicate and represent timescales that are outside human perception" (Lam 2016, 207). My book does not argue that the five Italian films I analyze constitute a slow cinema, though they have some qualities of these slow films. *Le quattro volte* in particular is cited by Song Hwee Lim (2014, 1) as exemplary of a cinema of slowness, and the films of Antonioni are frequently named as precursors of a contemporary "slow cinema" (Jaffe 2014, 3; De Luca and Barradas Jorge 2016, 9). As I indicated above, *Italian Ecocinema Beyond the Human* does not seek to define a cinematic genre, a particular visual style, or a contemporary film movement, but rather to challenge the notion that cinema necessarily flattens our perspective on the world. I postulate that as students, scholars, or spectators, we can approach films and screens more actively, asking new questions of them: "slow" thus provides a path through the dense, deep layers of cinematic creation.

Italian Ecocinema Beyond the Human speculates that to understand the complexity of a film's engagement with the world, we should examine what happens *before* the film makes it to the screen. Prior to bringing us enthralling narratives, cinematic productions—and, in particular, productions filmed on location—mesh with the world's matter in a multitude of ways that are often collaborative. Films are cyborg forms: they are hybrids, places where naturecultures are formed, composed of light particles and technologies and interactions between human and nonhuman bodies. The process of their birth influences their life afterwards. As Anat Pick and Guinevere Narraway (2013, 2–3) indicate in their introduction to *Screening Nature: Cinema Beyond the Human,* film has a complicated (and, in their view, "ambivalent") "relationship to its own materiality: its locations, onscreen lives, mise-en-scène, narrative structures, spectators, exhibition spaces, its carbon footprint and chemical building blocks, from celluloid to silicon." But regardless of the "nature" of this relationship, they argue for a reciprocity in filmmaking that means that the world imprints itself on film, just as film imprints itself on the world.[19] In other words, as Stephen Rust and Salma Monani (2013, 1) posit in their introduction to the pathbreaking collection *Ecocinema Theory and Practice,* "cinema is a form of negotiation, a mediation that is itself ecologically placed as it consumes the entangled world around it, and in turn, is itself consumed."[20]

Although all films participate in this negotiation with the world, the five films at the heart of my study have something in common in aesthetic terms—specifically, a shared commitment to what Luca Caminati (2011, 123) has identified as a "hybrid narrative" style that works "at the edge of the fiction/ nonfiction divide." Like the works Caminati discusses (*The Wind Blows Round* is one of these), they tend to deal with "peripheral groups who exist at the margins of the mainstream discourse manufactured in the great centres of imperial power" (124). In aesthetic terms, they often use non-professional actors, long takes, handheld cameras, and long shots to figure these groups onscreen. The commitment to the periphery, and the blurred boundaries between fiction and documentary, result in part from the films' intense relationships to the places where they were made. As productions and narratives, they get "under the skin" of the film, living the material relationship with places and things profoundly, and passing on part of the experience of this contact to viewers.[21] Making a film on location, whether celluloid or digital, draws countless "materials" into the conversation, and all of these "matters" are actors in the naturalcultural life on set. In the process of recording something to look *at,* the members of these film crews were *in* and *of* the spaces of location shooting, although their cohabitation with place could not be carbon-neutral or politically neutral. As the film crews I interviewed considered how various objects and creatures and people might resonate onscreen, they lived the realization that Iovino (2012b, 451) suggests should guide our material-ethical relationship to the world: the fact that we "share this horizon [of distributed agency] with countless other actors, whose agency—regardless of being endowed with degrees of intentionality—forms the fabric of events and causal chains." Along that chain, in other words, the production process inflected the world onscreen.

My goal is not to argue that these films are "sustainable" or "environmentally friendly" products, or that the process of making them led the human actors behind the scenes to participate in environmental activism or embrace specific, "green" relationships to the filmmaking process. Time after time, though, I heard stories from production managers, set designers, sound recordists, make-up artists, and directors recounting how the process of filming on location transformed their human awareness of the nonhuman world. Director Michelangelo Frammartino, for example, articulately characterizes his filmmaking as a way to build a relationship with the world, and says that in the process "the barrier between myself and the fabric of things gives way."[22] Production designer Paolo Bonfini muses in similar fashion that in film production, there is a "synergy between human and matter."[23] Production secretary Katia Goldoni observes that, when working on set, "you learn to respect a particular environment. Respecting the environment means understanding that you cannot live the same way in one place as you do in another."[24]

Arguably as a result of the intensity of the collaboration with a physical location, cinematic narratives—some cinematic narratives—can teach us to better apprehend the depth of our coevolution with the world. Acoustic ecologists advocate for a process they rather inelegantly call "ear cleaning"— a way to train ears to distinguish sounds with greater attention to their frequency and their complexity (Schafer 1977, 208–9).[25] In what follows, I attempt some "sensory cleaning" of my own, seeking to pay attention to these Italian films in creative ways. I focus on a diverse array of nonhuman cinematic subjects to see how they—like a canted camera angle, an unusual framing, an especially intricate sound design, or a thoughtful montage— can shift our understanding of what, or how, the world signifies. I aim to show that that these films, and the stories of their genesis, contain threads that can lead us to understand Italy, cinema, and our entanglement in the world in more nuanced ways.

Peripheral Details and Nonhuman Cinematic Agency

This book takes a new approach to Italian film studies, weaving together first-hand interviews with members of film crews, theoretical insights from the environmental humanities, and readings of specific scenes in cinematic narratives. The five case studies in the chapters ahead propose ecologically engaged ways to talk about cinematic sound, nonhuman actors, cinematic waste, energy use, the toxic elements of filmmaking, and cinematic and volcanic "recycling" of archival material. In line with theories of material ecocriticism and posthumanism, I widen the understanding of "agency" to propose that films are composed of actors of all kinds, from goats to airborne dioxins, from film cameras to cinematic extras, and from hydrocarbons to volcanoes. In the process, I uncover possibilities that are opened by considering the more-than-human horizon of cinema. The chapter structure intends to allow nonhuman actors and material texts to have a voice. Each begins with a story about an interview that shaped the chapter, marked in italics. Since formal concerns are important "material," too, the chapters are then punctuated with descriptions of key scenes in the films that focus my analysis, and that follow and nuance the theoretical framework. From the particular framing of a "deleted scene" depicting piles of burning waste in *Gomorrah*, to the thundering rumble of Stromboli as lava flies from its crater in *Return to the Aeolian Islands*, soundtracks, camera angles, and montages are important elements of the analysis, too. As De Luca and Barradas Jorge (2016, 13) argue regarding slow cinema, aesthetics are political, and aesthetic choices can destabilize "the 'consensual' social order through unexpected reframings that accordingly reconfigure modes of sensory experience by overturning the idea that only certain subjects, bodies and themes belong to the domain of the aesthetic and the sensible."[26] Considerations of specific narrative "locations" in each film where such reconfigurations are particularly evident thus guide the structure of each chapter.

As is probably already evident, some of the actors—like the playful goats in Chapters Three and Four, or the pervasive dirt in Chapter Two— might seem a bit quirky. In a celebrated 1986 article, Roger Cardinal makes a case for the radical possibilities inherent in "pausing over peripheral detail" when analyzing films. In the case he discusses, the "peripheral detail" (which happens to be, fittingly for my argument, a runaway chicken) "does not fit in with the intended meaning of a work," and paying close attention to it means to "adopt a posture of refusal—a refusal of the unitary message of the work, and more importantly a refusal of the dominant rhetorical codes which structure that message" (113). In the case of the goats, dirt, volcanoes, nonhuman sounds, or hydrocarbons, I am not considering things that "do not fit" within the cinematic narratives, but rather calling on actors that are peripheral to dominant, anthropocentric film cultures (though admittedly goats are more than a sideline in YouTube culture, and volcanic eruptions have also had their cinematic moments).

Calling on human and nonhuman actors who are often relegated to the margins of film studies in the humanities, including the location managers, sound recordists, and production secretaries who are too frequently overlooked in still-prevalent auteurist studies, I seek to prioritize stories of more-than-human conflicts, collaborations, and crises. In the process, my position is not one of refusal, but rather inclusive affirmation. Cardinal (1986, 114) maintains that: "there can be creative energies released by virtue of a studied dislocation of the gaze from the center of the frame to its quirky circumference." By nudging along a disanthropocentric gaze, my project hopes to stimulate the kind of creative energy needed to confront contemporary environmental problems, whether in the classroom or far beyond its walls. Such attention to the vast nonhuman "periphery" of human experience can help us to reconsider human responsibility—and perhaps even rewrite our human narrative—in the Anthropocene world that we are precipitously reshaping.

Before outlining what I do, I will specify a few things that I do not. This is not a study of reception, so I cannot say definitively what the intellectual or material experience of a given spectator might be. Nor is it a study calculating the environmental impact of the film productions I discuss. Although I think through some of the environmental costs of making films, my work does not specifically figure the carbon footprint of heavy film equipment, the miles travelled to and from location shoots, the waste associated with used batteries, discarded celluloid, or outmoded equipment, the plastic bottles used and jettisoned by film crews. The material impacts of filmmaking and media technologies are critical horizons for ecomedia studies, and are being innovatively considered by scholars including Nadia Bozak, Jennifer Gabrys, Stephanie LeMenager, Richard Maxwell and Toby Miller, and Nicole Starosielski and Janet Walker.[27] In Italian cinema, to my knowledge, they are wide open for scholarly inquiry. Finally, while this study maps a horizon of posthuman Italian cinema, it is only a partial map. Dozens of other recent Italian films might also have been excellent candidates for investigation, and countless nonhuman actors could have taken the stage. Here, too, the book's inevitable incompleteness is an invitation to continue engaging Italian cinema beyond the human.

This is, however, a study that involves me in the first person. Although I have already mentioned that narrative scholarship plays an important role in ecocriticism, I want to acknowledge my sense of ethical responsibility, and also my awareness that this first-person participation comprises a risk: a position outside of the inquiry is of course impossible, but am I too close? (Do I love baby goats too much?) Cardinal's (1986, 119) essay locates the spectator's experience of the peripheral in a self-reflexive moment in which the "witnessing subject" plays a critical part. In his stirring conclusion, which affirms the deep material promise of the "flat and fixed" cinema screen, he writes: "I stretch towards it [the screen] in a concentrated act of participation which involves my whole being and transcends intellectual reserve" (128). The gesture of "stretching towards" was fundamental to my research, and is reciprocated by many of the book's subjects. My project has only been possible because of the generous hospitality of people willing to talk about their work. This fact causes me to think of the transformative effects of hospitality outlined by philosophical ethologist Roberto Marchesini in his posthumanist philosophies: hospitality hybridizes all parties to the encounter. "Would you like a thick ceramic cup or a fine one?" asks Carlo Di Carlo during an interview about Antonioni's *Red Desert*, offering a selection of espresso cups as he prepares coffee for us both. I chose the fine blue china, and today as I listen to the recorded interview, I can hear the whistle of the pot and recall one of many instances of physical and affective nourishment encountered on this intellectual path. From the interviews I conducted and the time spent on location in Italy, I became acutely aware of my own entanglement in this project, and of how it shaped me in countless ways. My scholarship is "contaminated" by these encounters, but in my posthuman framework, I am happy for the notion of "purity" to hold no purchase. Instead, I hope that the mesh of disciplines, protagonists, and theories might open the way to new alliances and unanticipated crossings.

Chapter One begins with a case study of Antonioni's *Red Desert*, the film in this project most extensively studied in existing scholarly literature. I call on its expressive representation of the encounters of film, industry, and environmental awareness in the Italy of the economic boom to illustrate how profoundly film is enmeshed in global petroleum cultures. Drawing on Flavio Nicolini's production diary, and recounting the story of my interview with director and Antonioni scholar Carlo Di Carlo, the chapter investigates the hydrocarbon culture evident in 1963–64 Ravenna. The organic chemical compounds known as "hydrocarbons" help build and power many of the products of industrial modernity, such as rubber, plastic, explosives, and the film industry. Two island sequences in *Red Desert*—the mystical Budelli Island fantasy scene and a visit to a steel docking island for large ships—show us how the protagonist Giuliana's body is enmeshed in industrial Ravenna's hydrocarbon landscape. The contrasting scenes also lead us to see, in broader terms, how the production of *Red Desert* vibrates between its fascination with industrial, hydrocarbon-powered "progress" and its documentation of toxic industrial traces that will long outlive the film. *Red Desert* offers a perceptive tool with which to begin to unveil cinema's posthuman hybridities (Rosi Braidotti) and its trans-corporeal flows (Stacy Alaimo).

Chapter Two argues that *Gomorrah*'s production crew and their composed acceptance of cinematic dirt mirror the film's audio-visual portrayal of a dirty Naples, and demonstrate a willingness to interact with substances (including dioxins) and topics (like ecomafia) that many would prefer to ignore. My interviews with the film's location manager, production designer, and assistant camera operator confirm that the crew of *Gomorrah* rolled up their sleeves and worked willingly in conditions that were at times hazardous but also often hospitable. Calling on Heather Sullivan's material ecocritical "dirt theory," I argue that dirt does not just help show how *Gomorrah* engages issues of criminality (and especially eco-criminality, rampant in Campania), but also unearths its relationship to questions of social and environmental justice. In *Gomorrah*'s locations across Campania, but especially in the cement apartment blocks known as "Le Vele," or "The Sails," the cinematic crew collaborated daily with the locals in a gray zone that was both exclusionary and democratic. As this chapter proposes, the notion of "dirty" cinema helps blur distinctions between production and narrative, reality and fiction, and criminal and victim.

Chapter Three draws on posthumanism and animal studies to examine the relationship between film and nonhuman animal actors. As a cinematic production, *The Wind Blows Round* enabled what Marchesini calls "performative shifts" that "de-anthropocentered" cast, crew, and inhabitants of the Valle Maira, where the film was made. Interviews with a number of members of the urban crew, who were mostly from Bologna, revealed how time spent on location required them to live with and care for goats, pigs, and sheep. Marchesini's posthuman theories offer a key to see how filmmaking, a technopoietic dance coordinating technologies, landscapes, and human and nonhuman actors, can constitute a hybridization with the world. However, *The Wind* also tells a more tragic story of the death of two goats, and reveals in the process how filmmaking relies on a logic of sacrifice. Animal life and death provide the material underpinnings for the technologies creating *The Wind* (celluloid, for starters, is made of animal byproducts), and permeate the film's stories of conflict and cohabitation. Both as narrative and as production, *The Wind Blows Round* is potentially transformative but also deeply implicated in a biopolitical world that too often disregards the nonhuman.

Chapter Four, which also features goats in a leading role, engages with sound studies and acoustic ecology to argue that *Le quattro volte,* a film with almost no discernable human dialogue, challenges conventions of cinematic sound in order to strategically collaborate with its locations of filming and cast of characters. *Le quattro volte* tells four interlocking stories about a goatherd, a kid goat, a tree, and charcoal, creatively screening the Pythagorean notion of metempsychosis, or the passage of the soul through human, animal, vegetable, and mineral phases. Filmed over the course of three years in three different Calabrian locales, which are the material landscapes of Magna Graecia where Pythagoras lived and the Pythagoreans were based, *Le quattro volte* speaks through a soundtrack that sound recordists Paolo Benvenuti and Simone Paolo Olivero captured on location. Both in visual and acoustic terms, the film upends the anthropocentric focus of conventional cinema, choosing to amplify the sounds of "silence," or a broad soundscape that the human ear tends to filter out. Like in the case of *The Wind Blows Round,* crewmembers involved in making *Le quattro volte* opened themselves to the nonhuman world beyond the narrative. They worked in partnership with goats, dogs, snails, goatherds, charcoal burners, and charcoal, creating what I suggest is a new, material cinematic history for Italy: a history proper to interactions between human and nonhuman actors of all kinds, and a history audible in the film's lively soundscapes.

The concluding chapter focuses on a narrative documentary film, *Return to the Aeolian Islands,* that stitches together a long history of films made on the Sicilian volcanic island chain of the title. As a cinematic archive, *Return* cites decades of Italian film history, and also tells the story of the dynamic geological past, or ultimately how cinematic, human, and lithic history are co-constituted. Active volcanoes like Stromboli and Vulcano can inspire an apocalyptic form of imagination prevalent in many conversations about the contemporary state of the environment. Some climate scientists, for example, advocate for the "Pinatubo Option," or geoengineering a volcanic eruption to cool our climate-changed planet. Yet volcanoes also have more nuanced stories to tell, as the film's multiple narratives show, and these stories warn against the dangerous hubris of geoengineering volcanic eruptions. Chapter Five draws on theories of memory and on feminist ecocriticism, hypothesizing that a particularly porous, transgenerational memory emerges in *Return* as a consequence of living with the volcanic landscapes. I advocate for a volcanic pedagogy supported by Taviani's imaginative film. Learning volcanic lessons—which in this case are stored in a warehouse of cinematic memory—honors a cinematic past and helps safeguard a shared more-than-human future.

I began this introduction with a story of walking: a story of embodied intellect in contact with place, but also a story of movement. Traversing this text, you will find tiny particulate matter, toxic and benign, blown by Mediterranean winds. You will encounter blasting lava and eroding beaches. You will cross paths with cavorting kid goats, strategically creeping snails, and silent, padding dogs. You will hear the voices of soundtracks, sound recordists, and silence. Your eyes will scan the pages, drift away from them—or perhaps your fingers will move across the raised surfaces of the words—or your ears and brains will process the undulating waves of sound as your e-reader pronounces the text. Moving with words through time and space is a good way to encounter a book about film, and to overthink such an encounter. As they stream by our field of vision, moving pictures document mobile bodies, matter, and meaning. Films are part of the assemblages of culture, particles, and forces that compose places we love (like Italy), but that also relentlessly disassemble and decompose those places. These five particular films keep moving, obstinately. New scholarship emerges about them, and they age, get reissued, re-envisioned as television series, are re-mediated. Their locations, crews, and actors shift, age, erode, and change, too. This book, which will never be complete, can consider only slivers of their significance, offering its own series of moving pictures as it tells a story about nonhuman matter in Italian cinema. Onward, then, slowly.

Notes

1. Zavattini (1952, 8) defined the concept of "pedinamento," one of the underlying theories of neorealism, by describing how he would approach a woman he would like to film: "You need patience, you have to follow her [*pedinarla*], and when possible surprise her: it seems so clear to me that to make this kind of film you need a new technique, I think. It is a question of patience." In another evocative metaphor, he explained that cinema must work to "trace man's footsteps" (Zavattini 1954, 24).

2. Thank you to Dominic Nanni for gifting me a copy of *A Philosophy of Walking*.

3. A note on titles and their translation: *Il vento fa il suo giro* also circulated with the Occitan title *E l'aura fai son vir*. *Le quattro volte* was released in the United States with its Italian title, which means "the four times." I use the Italian title throughout this project. *Fughe e approdi* could be translated as "escapes and landings," but I use the title with which it was released in English-language markets.

4. Slovic (2008, 28) continues, urging: "Analyze and explain literature through storytelling—or tell your own stories and then, subsequently, show how contact with the world shapes your responses to texts."

5. In this book, I use both "more-than-human" and "nonhuman" to refer to matter, creatures, and experiences that surround, inhabit, and exceed the human. "More-than-human" is used by ecophenomenologist David Abram in *The Spell of the Sensuous: Perception and Language in a More-Than-Human World* (1997); "nonhuman animal" is frequently used in animal studies, and "nonhuman world" is a frequent designation in ecocriticism. All of these formulations intend to decenter the human, signaling that humans, too, are animals, and that humans, too, are in and of the world.

6. Scott MacDonald's (2004, 109) seminal essay, "Toward an Eco-Cinema," outlines a broad concern with the materiality (and inherent fragility) of the cinematic medium, but he primarily focuses on an eco-cinematic genre of films that provide "something like a *garden—* an 'Edenic' respite from conventional consumerism—within the *machine* of modern life." A wide range of approaches to ecocinema has emerged since, including the helpful overview collected in *Ecocinema Theory and Practice* edited by Stephen Rust, Salma Monani, and Sean Cubitt (2013, 2), which specifies that "ecocinema studies is not simply limited to films with explicit messages of environmental consciousness." Various approaches are also outlined in Kiu-wai Chu's (2017) excellent bibliographic overview of anthologies and monographs addressing "Ecocinema."

7. Carlo Petrini (2007, 18) uses the expression "the tyranny of urgency" quoting Jérôme Bindé of UNESCO. Regarding the problems of "fast life," he directly cites Bindé's argument that "'Our societies live in a kind of instantaneanism which prevents them from controlling the future.'"

8. Donna Haraway (2003, 16) adopts the term "natureculture" to signal the "implosion of nature and culture," rewriting the binary to demonstrate the necessary entanglement of the two.

9. In a 2015 article, Steffen et al. update the original, influential graphs that charted this "Great Acceleration," images designed to help synthesize the results of the International Geosphere-Biosphere Programme. The project was inspired by a proposal by Paul Crutzen, who is credited with one of the most authoritative definitions of the Anthropocene as the age (starting near the end of the eighteenth century) when human impacts on the earth led to a new geological era. The Great Acceleration, on the other hand, refers to the period starting

in the 1950s when the magnitude and rate of the "human imprint" increased dramatically. The graphs chart changes in major features of the earth's structure and functioning: "atmospheric composition, stratospheric ozone, the climate system, the water and nitrogen cycles, marine ecosystems, land systems, tropical forests and terrestrial biosphere degradation" (83).

10. For current information about global box office earnings, see the annual publication of Theatrical Market Statistics released by the Motion Picture Association of America. In 2017, Italy was number 13 in the top 20 international box office markets, according to the report.

11. All translations from *Ecologia letteraria* are mine. Throughout this book, when I cite from articles, interviews, and books in Italian, I have used my own translations unless otherwise indicated.

12. In the face of the colonizing power of global capital, Iovino (2010a) advocates for an "ecological citizenship," a form of citizenship that recognizes the importance of a shared global space and more-than-human concerns, and also valorizes participatory democracy, responsible use of resources, and an understanding of the consequences of socioeconomic behaviors on a global scale.

13. To cite Gorfinkel and Rhodes (2011, xvi): "The images that we are so used to trafficking in and sifting through play a crucial role in the derealization of our experience of the local. At the same time, the ability of an image of a place to be circulated globally suggests that such an image may be one of the most powerful means at our disposal to pose challenges to the unimageable, unrepresentable totality of our globalized contemporary condition."

14. By "posthuman" here and elsewhere in the introduction, I intend to indicate the human as an assemblage who exists in a relational network with technology and the more-than-human world, a notion particularly indebted to the thinking of Rosi Braidotti, Donna Haraway, and Roberto Marchesini.

15. Because of the legal weight of the words, I include the original Italian here: "La Repubblica promuove lo sviluppo della cultura e la ricerca scientifica e tecnica. Tutela il paesaggio e il patrimonio storico e artistico della Nazione" (Settis 2012, 128). Settis points out that most constitutions focus on individual rights rather than on responsibilities of the State.

16. Settis (2012, 251) specifies that in the: "jungle of regulations, [. . .] there does not seem to be any limit to the cannibalization of territory, the sacking of the landscape and the environment." As Giorgio Bertellini (2012, 44) explains, reading Settis, "the legal confusion that has ensued over time has affected both the Italian actual landscape and our understanding of its civic and ethical cogency."

17. "Ecomostri," or "ecomonsters," are defined by Legambiente as buildings that are extremely incompatible with their physical surroundings.

18. Catriona Mortimer-Sandilands (2008, 268) reports on a debate between Abram and Ted Toadvine discussing this point, or whether Abram is "castigating the advent of literacy and 'alphabetical thinking' as the source of human alienation from the richness of our perceptual experiences." She suggests that the "necessary move for environmental ethics, as Abram sees it, is more about redeploying than rejecting reflection" (269). Although my own work does not constitute a return to ecopoetics such as Abram calls for, a redeployment of reflection is consistent with what this book proposes.

19. As Pick and Narraway (2013, 5) argue, "Cinema (like other arts) is ecologically oriented and zoomorphic: it expresses the interconnectedness of human and other life forms, our implication in and filtering through material networks that enable and bind us."

20. Pick and Narraway (2013, 4) underline that: "each and every film, whatever else it may be, is first and foremost a record of a relationship to the material world and the forging of a cinematic habitat."

21. The notion of the "skin of the film" is adopted from Laura U. Marks' work on intercultural cinema. Marks (2000, xi–xii) specifies that the "skin of the film" "offers a metaphor to emphasize the way film signifies through its materiality, through a contact between perceiver and object represented," and she also argues that film, like skin, can be actively transformed in the process: it is "impressionable and conductive."

22. Michelangelo Frammartino, interview by author, Milan, June 29, 2011.

23. Paolo Bonfini, interview by author, Rome, May 21, 2013.

24. Katia Goldoni, interview by author, Bologna, March 8, 2013.

25. Pioneering acoustic ecologist R. Murray Schafer (1977, 208) argues that "ear cleaning" is "especially important in a busy, nervous society"; he offers specific exercises in the book *Ear Cleaning* (1967).

26. Here, the authors follow Jacques Rancière's notion that aesthetics is a mode that offers "'configurations of experience that create new modes of sense perception'" (Rancière qtd. in De Luca and Barradas Jorge 2016, 13).

27. See, for example, Bozak's *The Cinematic Footprint: Lights, Camera, Natural Resources* (2011), Gabrys' *Digital Rubbish: A Natural History of Electronics* (2011); LeMenager's *Living Oil: Petroleum Culture in the American Century* (2014); Maxwell and Miller's *Greening the Media* (2012); or *Sustainable Media: Critical Approaches to Media and Environment*, a collection edited by Nicole Starosielski and Janet Walker (2016). Some eco-reception studies have been done on James Cameron's film *Avatar*, including several essays in the collection *Avatar and Nature Spirituality* edited by Bron Taylor (2013).

1

HYDROCARBONS, MOVING PICTURES, TIME: *RED DESERT*

*I*N THE AUDIO RECORDING OF MY 2013 INTERVIEW *with Carlo Di Carlo in his apartment in Rome, our voices approach the microphone and then recede into the distance, and frequent silences are punctuated by the crisp sound of turning pages.*[1] *As I took copious notes and flipped through volumes large and small, Di Carlo made trip after trip from the living room to his extensive library on the cinema of Michelangelo Antonioni to identify useful references for my bibliography. He spoke of an important interview Antonioni gave on the* Maurizio Costanzo Show, *an interview that would have been lost along with six years of misplaced footage of the popular television talk show had Di Carlo not recorded it on VHS. Clips from the interview were part of his project-in-progress. Di Carlo, a director and scholar, spent much of his life preserving Antonioni's cinematic legacy, and his numerous books and documentary films comprise archives of interviews, essays, articles, project plans, and production diaries. Di Carlo met Antonioni in 1961 and published a book on* Il deserto rosso (Red Desert) *in 1964, the same year the film came out, initiating a long intellectual relationship with the director and his work.*

Red Desert, a film that bears witness to the expanding industrial landscape of 1960s Italy, was filmed on location in Ravenna from November 1963 through March 1964. Like the places it captures on celluloid, the film is the product of an energy-intensive industry. Di Carlo's trip to the set to study the film, and my visit to Di Carlo to learn from him, add further layers to the film's hydrocarbon legacy. Along with the screenplay (attributed to Antonioni and Tonino Guerra), the print publication contains Antonioni's famous essay on "The White Forest," an essay by Di Carlo on color, a page written by producer Antonio Cervi, a series of photos from the set, and an extensive production diary written by Flavio Nicolini, one of the assistant directors. The book, a valuable account of a groundbreaking experience in cinematic history, is it-self a material document produced with the help of plant, petroleum, and human resources, and is subject to the forces of time. The edges of the pages of my copy from the library (the original 1964 edition) are yellowed but not frag-ile. Di Carlo's life work documents the collaborative networks that produced, promoted, and interrogated the films directed by Antonioni, but it also re-veals the evanescence of the media, and the nonhuman and human energy— as all those trips to the bookshelf attest—required to create and preserve it.

Di Carlo died in 2016, while this manuscript was in progress. Listening to his voice now, while thinking about preservation, hospitality, fragility, and time, is both poignant and haunting.

This is a story of cinema, energy, and the passage of time, and it starts during Italy's industrial boom.

Red Desert is a signal moment in Italian cinematic history because it illustrates an intense exchange between industry, cinema, and environmental awareness in Italy. Location shooting embedded the film deeply in the environment around Ravenna: the film production and cinematic narrative traverse and permeate the place in significant ways. Given the substantial transformations occurring in Italy at the time of filming, and in part because of the enduring artistic legacy of *Red Desert,* the 1964 film speaks eloquently for the convergence and mutual transformation of media and matter.

As scholars have often observed, *Red Desert* captures the advent of a culture of neocapitalist consumption that changed the landscape into something "that would have been unrecognizable only a decade or so before" (Restivo 2002, 140). The "boom" or "economic miracle," which historian Paul Ginsborg (1989, 286–90) locates in the years spanning from 1958 to 1963, saw industrial production double, Italian exports increase dramatically, and both urban and rural landscapes change radically. Per capita income more than doubled between 1952 and 1970, and alongside newly acquired televisions, refrigerators, and other durable goods, a culture of mass mobility began to take shape (325–30). The wealthy protagonists of *Red Desert* are at the apex of the boom. Corrado (Richard Harris) and Ugo (Carlo Chionetti) are part of what P. Adams Sitney (1995, 211) identifies as "a new class of neocapitalist managers" who populate the coastal areas near Ravenna, where expansive petrochemical refineries amidst the Dantean pine forests provide a dramatic backdrop for many scenes in the film.

Environmental degradation accompanied this rapid industrial expansion and mass motorization. Near Ravenna, large fields of methane were discovered offshore in 1955, and ENI (*Ente Nazionale Idrocarburi*, or the Italian National Hydrocarbon Authority) constructed a petrochemical district that went active in 1958. Some of the main products manufactured near Ravenna, one of Italy's primary port cities, were vinyl chloride and PVC, which were used to create the stuff of modernity: plastic and vinyl products, wires and cable coatings, packaging, and automotive parts. Methylmercury and other toxic, carcinogenic byproducts of the production process were dumped in a tributary channel through the mid-1970s. Recent studies have found that high concentrations of the contaminants persist in the area in the new millennium (Trombini et al. 2003, 1821–22). *Red Desert* demonstrates concern for this noxious element of boom-era prosperity through its focus on yellow smoke and other airborne vapors pouring from factory chimneys, and by following the liquid tributary channels via which these contaminants move and mingle with the surrounding environment and its human and nonhuman inhabitants.

In part in response to the swiftly changing industrial landscape of the boom, the environmental movement that was taking off around the globe began to take root in Italy around this same time. At first, Italian environmentalist concerns were primarily conservationist and aesthetic: *Italia Nostra*, a non-profit organization dedicated to protecting Italy's artistic and environmental heritage, was founded in Rome in 1955 by seven prominent intellectuals, who contested the "sacking" of Italy's cities by unchecked development (Della Seta 2000, 13).[2] Then, in 1963 (the year *Red Desert* began filming), Rachel Carson's *Silent Spring* was translated into Italian, and according to Roberto Della Seta's (2000, 19–20) history of the environmental movement in Italy, attention shifted from conservation to the fight against pollution. In spite of their increasing visibility, though, in many ways ecological concerns remained marginal on a national-cultural level, and rather than becoming a central part of the social movements in the 1960s, they "were depicted largely as hobbies for the well-to-do" (Armiero and Hall 2010, 4). In 1963–64, during the filming of *Red Desert*, Italy's first antismog legislation had not yet taken effect (it was instated in 1966), and national concerns about environmental crisis had not yet been honed by the dioxin disaster at Seveso or the arsenic poisoning at Manfredonia, both of which happened in 1976 (Adorno 2010, 182–83).[3] At the end of *Red Desert*, Giuliana (Monica Vitti) explains to her son, who asks why the factory smoke is yellow, that it is poisonous. Her comments indicate a burgeoning awareness of the dangers of industrial pollution for human and nonhuman inhabitants of the region. Yet when her son worries that the birds flying through the smoke will die, she reassures him that they have learned to fly around it: a simple act of adaptability, she says, will keep them safe from harm.

According to the director, the question of adaptation to change was the guiding problem in creating the film. Antonioni ardently disavowed that his film was motivated by anti-modernist nostalgia, insisting, in an interview with Jean-Luc Godard, that he did not intend in *Red Desert* to "accuse this inhuman, industrialized world" but rather "to translate the beauty of this world, in which even the factories can be very beautiful [. . .]. It's a rich world—living, useful" (Sarris 1972, 4). Yet Antonioni acknowledged in the same interview that he does not believe that "the beauty of the modern world in itself can resolve our dramas," and asserts that Giuliana's adaptive difficulty was simultaneously moral, perceptive, and *"epidermic"* (4–6, my emphasis). Although the bodily, "epidermic" crisis was listed by the director as the most obvious of the crises in *Red Desert*, a return to the material pathways navigated by the film exposes a subcutaneous—and subterranean—world of interpretation. *Red Desert* helps reveal that, as films represent experience, they also pass into human and nonhuman bodies to become *part* of experience in all kinds of material ways. The film is an apt starting point to see how, as Giorgio Bertellini (2012, 43) has argued, Italian film quite literally *"has absorbed* lessons and discourses that have recently risen to national consciousness about the defacement of the national territory" (my emphasis).

Showing the radical openness of the human in these toxic landscapes, in *Red Desert,* Giuliana is traversed by the things with which she comes into contact, things that can literally pass right through her skin. Stacy Alaimo (2010, 2) describes this experience of bodily porosity as "trans-corporeal," and uses the word to describe the "interconnections, interchanges, and transits between human bodies and nonhuman natures." Our bodies host toxins carried in air and by water; the film acknowledges these contaminations through the poisonous yellow smoke emitting from factory chimneys. Our bodies are sites of disease, as *Red Desert* reminds us when a ship docks and raises a flag to indicate that its passengers are infected by some kind of illness. Our bodies—and not just our human bodies, but nonhuman bodies, too—are subject to the flux and flow of global capital and to the technologies that modify landscapes; a conversation with fishermen along one of the shipping canals reveals that the eels swimming in the canal's waters now taste like petroleum.[4] It would perhaps not be too much of a stretch to suggest that some of the symptoms that Giuliana manifests—her convulsive lovemaking to Corrado, her fatigue, the apparent "brain fog" that causes her to see strange colors or nearly drive off of a pier—could be signs of multiple chemical sensitivity (MCS) or environmental illness (EI). As Alaimo explains, this controversial condition, for which no standard medical test or definition exists, is nevertheless a recognizable disease that may constitute a "somatic indictment of modernity" (Steve Kroll-Smith and H. Hugh Floyd qtd. in Alaimo 2010, 115).[5] In any case, from Giuliana's house, where enormous ships pass as if just outside the window, to the color stains that cloud her field of vision, to her disappearance into a foggy mist, the protagonist's "domestic enclosure" is broken open, and as in Alaimo's concept of trans-corporeal space, "human corporeality and textuality effortlessly extend into the more-than-human world. Word, flesh, and dirt are no longer discrete" (14).

The concept of trans-corporeality does not just help explain Giuliana's environmental-existential crisis, though. It also urges us to contemplate a new, broadened interpretive frame for cinema—all cinema. First, this materialist philosophy of lived experience "necessitates more capacious epistemologies" and "allows us to forge ethical and political positions that can contend with numerous late twentieth- and early twenty-first century realities in which 'human' and 'environment' can by no means be considered as separate" (Alaimo 2010, 2). If we take seriously the movement of substances through human flesh and the openness of the human body to the world, we are bound to a corresponding opening of our ethical framework, compelled to consider the more-than-human world within and beyond our borders, including when we watch films. Second, although the notion of trans-corporeality proposes to read human experience with a heightened attention to the fabric of the human body, it "denies the human subject the sovereign, central position" and requires attention to "a more uncomfortable and perplexing place where the 'human' is always already part of an active, often unpredictable, material world" (16–17). If we recognize trans-corporeal movements of bodies when examining cinema, we can witness time and again how the human takes its place in a cosmography of beings that includes all manner of nonhuman actors.[6] And at the same time, the world of the film passes in ways literal and figurative into our bodies.

Theories of trans-corporeality, which resonate strongly with Giuliana's precarious experience as human protagonist in *Red Desert,* thus lead us into the posthuman domain, a space for questioning "the very structures of our shared identity—as humans—amidst the complexity of contemporary science, politics and international relations" (Braidotti 2013, 2). Because theories of the posthuman focus on our entanglement with nonhuman animals and technologies, they open myriad interpretative pathways for film, beginning with a film's formal composition. Onscreen, Giuliana's presence is frequently marginal, out of focus, off-center, and at times she wanders out of the frame entirely, leaving the camera to examine a more-than-human landscape without anthropic distractions. But once again, posthuman concerns should not only impact our understanding of the actors onscreen. Such a framework dissolves the surface of the screen, showing how film narrative intermingles in time and space with shooting locations, production timelines, film technologies, distribution networks, and human and nonhuman spectators and actors. This kind of theoretical stance urges us to see that, beyond its visual evocation of a posthuman terrain, *Red Desert* also leaves traces of its passage through a long chain of material interactions.[7] The film's position as a historical document of the Italian economic boom in 1963–64, its material-discursive presence today, and its ties to a political and ecological landscape that long preceded it in the world, reveal a network of what Rosi Braidotti (2013, 193) characterizes as "embodied subject[s] [. . .] shot through with relational linkages of the contaminating/viral kind which inter-connect it to a variety of others, starting from the environmental or eco-others and include the technological apparatus." Regardless of any authorial forswearing of the risks or consequences of industrial modernity, *Red Desert* was thoroughly entangled in the petrochemical landscape in which it was filmed, and was a byproduct of those very industries. *Red Desert*, in other words, is not just an image that moves on the flat screen monitors in twenty-first century classrooms (or on laptops, iPhones, and tablets), nor is it just that play of light through celluloid that illuminated the screens in movie theaters in the 1960s. It is not just the story of Giuliana, Corrado, and Ugo, nor is it exclusively the product of one brilliant auteur's imagination. *Red Desert* is the encounter of industry, location, local human laborers, professional and nonprofessional actors, human and nonhuman actors, and energy regimes, among other things, and the story, still in progress, of the mutual transformation and interpenetration of these actors.

This is not the first study to underscore the magnitude of the nonhuman presence in films directed by Antonioni. A long history of Antonioni scholarship has emphasized the importance of the material object for the director, or the role of landscape as protagonist.[8] Some recent work has taken a more specifically posthuman or ecocritical approach to Antonioni's films. In her innovative book *Italian Locations*, Noa Steimatsky (2008, 39) argues that from the start, Antonioni's cinema was "based in a fracturing of the figure so as to test the ground and see how ground emerges *as* figure, capturing the movement by which one evolves into the other." This movement between the human and the nonhuman is a critical tool in all of the essays in the section "Ecologies" in the edited volume *Antonioni: Centenary Essays* (Rascaroli and Rhodes 2011), where different kinds of matter become lively makers of meaning. For Karl Schoonover (2011, 238), the presence of waste (and specifically of discarded paper) is part of a declaration of the "abandonment of narrative authority, an invocation of the randomness of life and a reflection on modernity's inherent relation to and production of excess." Karen Pinkus (2011, 256) identifies a play on the concept of "ambiente," which in Italian "refers simultaneously to both interior/set design and the *Umwelt*—what is 'out there' beyond the human." Her essay suggests the ways in which Antonioni's cinema awakens us to concerns about climate change. John David Rhodes (2011, 293) sees how "Antonioni's style—as autonomous formal articulation—produces itself through an exaggerated attention to the material features of global development," and how *Red Desert* in particular uses visual abstraction to show us the "abstraction of economic and social life." Yet given the complexity of all of the actors in the cinematic game, from the image onscreen to the fuels driving the film industry, from film crews to film stock, many avenues of investigation remain open. To consider *Red Desert* through a material ecocritical lens (trans-corporeality and posthumanist notions dialogue, too, with this capacious "disanthropocentric" framework) means to ask what happens when intertextuality begins to take into account the idea that matter "acts as a text composed by multiple agencies, at once material, semiotic, and discursive" (Iovino 2012b, 451). Such a line of questioning can spiral down infinitely many pathways.

In what follows, I consider the hydrocarbon culture evident in *Red Desert*'s 1963–64 Ravenna, in particular when Giuliana and Corrado visit the SAROM steel docking island in the Adriatic Sea where large ships stopped to refuel. As I noted before, hydrocarbons, a category of chemical compounds that includes petroleum and natural gas, fueled the creation of many of the products that made Italy's economic "boom" (and its cinematic boom) possible: rubber, plastic, solvents, explosives, and industrial chemicals, for example. The SAROM island and its hydrocarbon flows connect, via unexpected conduits, to the other island sequence, a lyrical fable filmed on a private island in the Sardinian Maddalena Archipelago, the Budelli Island. Via some of the material-discursive intertextual pathways that lead to, from, and through these onscreen events, *Red Desert* offers a point of departure for doing some of the work of material ecocriticism: that of "redrawing the maps of knowledge and practice, [. . .] rethinking object and subject, nature and culture not as juxtaposed terms but as a circulating system" (Iovino 2012b, 454). From its settings, to its immersion as production in the material landscape of the economic boom, to its afterlife as a Criterion Collection film, *Red Desert* circulates through the complex hydrocarbon networks of Italian modernity and into our present, all the while inviting questions about our own permeability. The film stands for a sort of mystical epiphany, the realization of the radical connectedness of all matter, while admitting the ontological and environmental crises that can result from such entanglement.

Ravenna, Cinema, and Petrochemical Modernity: The Steel Island

Long, foggy shot of a large ship at sea, flanked by a small platform: the Isola d'Acciaio or steel docking island off the coast of Ravenna where large ships fill up with fuel. The frame (which rocks with the movement of the boat from which it was shot) cuts to Giuliana on the platform, looking out at seagulls on the water. From a variety of angles and distances of framing, the camera interacts with the machinery on the platform. Cables, chains, tubes, steel beams, valves, wenches, cisterns, ladders, staircases. The camera follows the curvatures of a long black tube attached, like an umbilical cord, to the ship. In soft focus behind Giuliana, on the ship in the background, a sailor dumps a bucket of black liquid or powder into the sea. Giuliana and Corrado discuss his departure for Patagonia, and Giuliana tells Corrado that if she were to leave, "I would take you with me, yes, because now you are part of me—part of what is around me, that is."

In his essay "The White Forest," Antonioni (1964, 17) observes that the forest in question was replaced by "continual cars trucks scooters, even a train,

Figure 1.1. Steel Island. Screen capture, *Red Desert* (1964), directed by Michelangelo Antonioni.

against the constant background drone of machinery mixed with the hiss of steam, and as for smells, the smell of a yellow smoke full of acids that infected the whole area." Studies of films directed by Antonioni frequently refer to his intense practices of observation, including time he liked to spend alone on set before the rest of the cast and crew joined him for the day's shoot. Part of the mythology of the auteur, the story of this moment of *being present* with the landscape of filming casts the director as a kind of cinematic naturalist, who as an attentive eyewitness translates his vision to film. Yet the documents assembled in the book by Di Carlo make clear that *Red Desert*'s view of industrial Ravenna emerged from a choral, multisensory perspective that resonated throughout the entire cast and crew. When the production crew for *Red Desert* looked around Ravenna, they all marveled at the metamorphosis in progress. In his diary, Nicolini (1964) chronicles the crew's focus on the industrial zone around Ravenna where, a decade before, swamps and pine forests dominated. The "miracle's" magic, though, swiftly replaced these with the material objects proper to industry:

> *Industrial zone. Where, ten years ago, there were still swamps and pine forests, today there rise ANIC, SAROM, SADE, AGIP, SOJA, and a whole series of other small and medium industries. Towers and tanks, tubes, iron, and ships. In the sky, AGIP's mining helicopter. In the sea, six kilometers from the coast, SAROM's steel island, and the Paguro, the navigating platform for oceanic drilling.* (39–40)

Di Carlo (1964, 27) also took note of the "other face of Ravenna," where iron tubing, cranes, and puddles of petroleum waste dominated the landscape, and nauseating smells filled the air. "It was unbearable," he recalled in our discussion, while noting that the crew was not exposed to the stench for too long. The production photos included in the diary show cameramen on top of tall towers, painters on enormous ladders, and lights and tripods taking their place among the pipes, cables, tubes, and steel buildings. All of the accounts—from the director, assistant director, film scholar, set photographer—cast this landscape in vivid terms, evoking strong horizontal and vertical lines of land, sea, and sky and suggesting the contaminations and crossings inherent in these "interstitial spaces" (Seger 2015).[9] They follow the petroleum-fueled vehicles that transport people and goods, as well as the liquid and gaseous byproducts left in their wake.

More than just a collection of perceptive observations, the information assembled in the book by Di Carlo documents the production crew's and cast's immersion in the same forces that feature in the film's narrative. Nicolini charts the movement of the production through the offices and spaces operated by major industrial players in Ravenna: SAROM (*Società Azionaria Raffinazione Olii Minerali*, or Mineral Oil Refining Corporation), ANIC (*Azienda Nazionale Idrogenazione Combustibili*, or National Combustible Hydrogenation Company), SADE (*Società Adriatica di Elettricità*, or Adriatic Electric Company), ENEL (*Ente Nazionale per l'Energia Elettrica*, or National Electric Company), and Carbon Black. SAROM provided spaces for filming factory interiors and exteriors, and the aforementioned steel docking island; ANIC allowed them to shoot in an office from which a phone call was made; ENEL and SADE (the latter incorporated into the former when electric energy was nationalized in Italy in 1962) gave the production access to a control room and a machine room where Ugo works, as well as locations for exterior shots and a house on a canal that would be the home of Giuliana's family; Carbon Black provided the exteriors for shots of striking workers, and a dumping ground for factory waste (Nicolini 1964, 43–71).

David Forgács (1996, 51–55) argues that in Italy, the years of the economic boom represent an industrial *and* cultural watershed even more decisive than World War II. Forgács focuses on road-building, mass motorization, the boom in consumer spending, and also the increased circulation of print and non-print media as critical to the major changes taking place in Italy. Of interest here is the notion that the transit of people and goods, the movement that the booming hydrocarbon industry made possible, flowed through ideas and the media, too. Cinema and petroleum are not just two products of the boom, in other words, but part of the same, circulating system. In her remarkable study of the material residues left by the film industry, Nadia Bozak (2012, 11) argues that "cinema has always demonstrated an awareness of its industrial self and therefore a connection to the environment, the realm from which it derives its power, raw materials, and, often enough, subject matter. But because this biophysical layer is so inextricably embedded within film's basic means of production, distribution, and reception, its effects remain as overlooked as they are complex." As the observations collected in the book by Di Carlo illustrate, the case of *Red Desert* raises the curtain on this entanglement of cinema and industry, and reveals a captivating network of nonhuman forces at work behind (and underneath, and beyond) the "scenes" that would normally be the focus of cinematic scholarship. The film—as event and as production—can be read as an exceptional example of what Bozak calls the "hydrocarbon imagination" at work (11).

That so many petrochemical companies, large private and public corporations doing business around the harbor of Ravenna, opened their doors to a film production is not surprising considering that, in the 1950s and '60s, energy producers were themselves heavily involved in the media industry. In his study *L'energia e lo sguardo* (*Energy and the Gaze*), Giulio Latini (2011, x) notes that, in the mid-1950s, ENI, headed by the charismatic and controversial Enrico Mattei (1906–1962), realized the importance of locating "scientific-industrial culture, political culture, and humanistic culture on the same strategic horizon." As mentioned before, ENI was in large part responsible for the development of the petrochemical industry in Ravenna. The company opened a film office in 1958 and began producing motion pictures, which Paola Bonifazio (2014, 331) argues worked to make "Italian citizens fit in the modern world."[10] Over the course of twenty or so years, some of the most prominent Italian filmmakers and artists collaborated with ENI's film office. Vittorio De Seta, Bernardo Bertolucci, Valentino Orsini, Gillo Pontecorvo, and Folco Quilici directed films for the company; Alberto Moravia, Leonardo Sciascia, and Tonino Guerra collaborated on writing screenplays; Egisto Macchi and Lucio Dalla worked on musical scores and composed songs (Latini 2011, xv–xvi). The borders between publicity, industrial documentary, and commercial cinema were often blurred, and industrial cinematic technologies, as for example the one used to capture

2,700 frames per second, were transferrable back into the world of commercial cinema (xiii–xiv). Hydrocarbons, too, were "making" films during the boom.[11]

When the production crew of *Red Desert* traveled six kilometers offshore into the Adriatic Sea to film Monica Vitti and Richard Harris discussing business, travel, and the composition of their worlds on the SAROM steel island, they were traveling in Mediterranean waters continually traversed by a cinematic apparatus directly tied to energy production.[12] In 1965, the year after *Red Desert* finished filming, director Gilbert Bovay worked with cinematographer Massimo Dallamano to create an award-winning documentary, *Gli uomini del petrolio* (*The Oil Men*) for ENI. Although the film would transition quickly to locations in the Persian Gulf, Iran, Egypt, and then Libya, Bovay chose to begin the 30-minute documentary in the port of Ravenna. An early establishing shot depicts the Paguro platform, a floating deep-sea drilling rig operated by AGIP (*Azienda Generale Italiana Petroli*, or General Italian Oil Company), rising from the fog. In a transcendent (if inverted) origin story, the voiceover announces that, from the time that the decision was made to perforate the earth to extract energy, the industrial apparatus visible onscreen is the "necessary and perfect structure" for searching for oil. Numerous aerial shots from a helicopter are interspersed with low angle shots of the helicopter circling the platform's helipad. The documentary articulates connections via invisible and visible channels: air, water, and subterranean flows; visual and verbal metaphors. The voiceover emphasizes how the drilling platform is connected to the mainland: via helicopter to Ravenna; by radio to Ravenna and "Metanopoli," or "Methane City," an industrial center in Lombardy built by ENI in 1952; by analogy to Gela, San Salvo, Ferrandina, Gagliano, Pisticci—other places hydrocarbons were discovered in Italy. Images conjure some of these liquid, airborne, and industrial connections: a radio operator, who smokes and reports on his work; the helicopter; gray, sludgy clay spitting from a pipe; men being lifted in a cage onto the platform; the sea. Immediately following the segment in Ravenna comes an overhead shot of undulating white sand dunes in the desert near Iran's Zagros Mountains, which recall the Adriatic swells. The voiceover explains that AGIP does not only work in Italy, but also in Iran, Egypt, Libya, Morocco, Sudan, and Nigeria: via its petroculture, Ravenna takes its place in a web of geophysical forces far beyond its borders. That we can envision these connections by way of a medium that thoroughly depends on that same petroculture reveals the degree to which our imagination is indeed a "hydrocarbon imagination."

In an establishing shot that parallels the one of the Paguro in *The Oil Men*, *Red Desert* shows SAROM's steel island, essentially an Adriatic gas station for ships too large to come into Ravenna's harbor.[13] Corrado travels there to visit a vessel bound for Argentina, making it a material waypoint on the path of transnational capital, of which the film was also a part.[14] The scene's focus on the black tube connecting ship to fuel source initially seems to be a part of the abstract landscape, the "stylish surface" of an Antonioni film that, as Laura Rascaroli and John David Rhodes point out, has been object of both critical abuse and praise (2011, 5–6). This, according to critics of European art cinema in general and Antonioni in particular, constitutes a pretentious cinematic style that is self-reflexive and excludes the world beyond the image. Yet Millicent Marcus (1986, 206–7) indicates perceptively that, although "Antonioni's highly abstract, aestheticizing vision may seem worlds away from the concrete, documentary approach of postwar Rossellini or De Sica, [. . .] whatever happens within his autonomous aesthetic framework has a bearing on the extracinematic world." Similarly, Rascaroli and Rhodes' collection offers convincing evidence that the "severity of his forms" reflects "a keen interest in the visual and spatial relations among bodies, objects, surfaces, and monuments," an interest that translates into an "openness to the world and the world's influence" (6). In the SAROM island sequence, formal abstraction, non-anthropocentric image-making, anthropic action, and material forces are continuous, all part of that conduit joining ship, Adriatic Sea, petroleum, film, and existence. They divulge the profound conflict at the heart of the film, a movement between appreciation for the surfaces of modernity and a concern for what the mingling of surfaces and interiors—of inside and outside— means for modernity's human and nonhuman protagonists. That this conflict is in motion, however, means that it does not crystallize into the binaries of nature vs. culture, inside vs. outside. On the SAROM island, we see what Nancy Tuana (2008, 191) calls material "interactionism" at work, the force that acknowledges the "agency of materiality and the porosity of entities."

In shooting the black tubing, the camera moves smoothly along its curvatures: up, then left, up again, then left, and then down, down, precipitously, to where Corrado hangs in a chair lift over the water. This mobile camera traveling along the pathways of liquid fuel offers a moment of reflexive petrocinema, where the technology of the film industry investigates the petrochemical industry upon which it is based.[15] The camera's fluid movement also underlines the fact that oil and gas are liquid—if not always by nature, then upon compression for easier storage and transport. In his study of oil in contemporary American capitalism, Matthew Huber (2013) emphasizes that the formal structure of our energy sources has a significant impact on the roles they occupy in our lives. In the case of oil, he underlines that: "Oil is the *liquid* fossil fuel. Unlike bulky coal or indiscernible gas, crude oil is an incredibly cooperative substance fueling the 'time-space compression' of global transportation and commodity circulation [. . .]. Its propensity to *flow* cannot be underestimated" (133). Petrochemical modernity is built in the image of the liquid hydrocarbons that drive nearly every aspect of contemporary life. Both in form and subject, *Red Desert* traces the shape of this dynamic landscape.

Following the hydrocarbon chain to a platform in the middle of the Adriatic Sea, the SAROM island scene connects subterranean liquid fuel to the film's many other liquid landscapes. A scene shot in dense fog along a pier, for example, allows an array of characters to disappear and re-materialize in space in front of us. There are innumerable chimneys and pipes that spew clouds of steam in the industrial zone surrounding Ravenna, and in several scenes, pressurized vapors are released from a factory violently and dramatically, rendering human voices inaudible and human bodies insignificant. Giuliana and Ugo's house is so close to a shipping channel that freighters seem to pass just outside of their windows. The shack where a group of friends gathers for lunch and sexually suggestive play is on another such channel, and the sound of waves pulses hypnotically on the soundtrack.

The narrative role of fluids in *Red Desert* corresponds to a liquid presence that also flows across the film as production. Ravenna, it seems, was chosen not so much for its concrete industrial landscape, but for the low clouds of water droplets that envelop the area, changing the way light is absorbed and reflected. The week before filming was scheduled to begin, Nicolini (1964, 39) frets at the bright sunshine and explains: "According to the Ravennans, in the next month we should be drowning in a sea of fog." Liquid challenges surrounded the filming of the SAROM sequence, too. Arriving at the SAROM platform in the first place meant traveling out into the Adriatic, a voyage that the crew and some of the cast completed four different times according to Nicolini's report. On the third attempt, the sea was rough and they had to leave; on the fourth, Richard Harris had already departed to work on another film, and was replaced by a body double where necessary (72–73). If choppy seas, fog (or lack thereof), and fluid acting schedules created aesthetic and productive challenges, so did petroleum itself, even if these may have been less obvious. LeMenager (2014, 13) makes the important point that petrochemical modernity changes the aesthetic of landscapes in ways more totalizing than we might think: "oil is a form of capital that bulks out and inhabits place, changing the quality of air, water, noise, views, and light." Air and water pollution, and not just the architecture of factory smokestacks, change the "nature" of what gets recorded on a celluloid strip; Ravenna's boom-era economy and its industrial-environmental profile were imprinted on the film at an elemental level.

Of course the SAROM island scene, like many in *Red Desert*, has a deeply existential dimension, but this element too ties into the circulation between the fluid bodies of the film production, petroleum, and Giuliana's body. Throughout the film, Giuliana's illness is explained in liquid terms that specifically relate to the hydrocarbon-enabled mass mobility of the economic boom. She is riveted by the sea, contending, while looking out a window, that: "It's never still—never, never. I can't look at the sea for long; otherwise, I lose interest in what happens on land." The "loss of interest" in her terrestrial life is a cipher for two nearly fatal accidents that happen while Giuliana is driving alone, and both involve water. Wet roads apparently caused a pre-diegetic car accident, and another near-auto accident within the film involves her almost driving off the edge of a pier, in the fog, into the sea. In this latter scene, the camera frames Giuliana alone in the driver's seat and the small vehicle stopped on a narrow strip of pier in the bottom right, with a tall, slender beacon rising beside it. The rest of the spare shot is filled with gray fog and water, which mingle into one another indistinguishably. Her isolation from the group makes the automobile the place from which to wonder, with Huber (2013, xi): "What if the most problematic relation to oil is the way it powers forms of social life that allow individuals to imagine themselves as severed from society and public life?" In the cab of the small car, Giuliana's petroleum-fueled escape brings her to the brink of self-destruction, a near-death-by-drowning in the industrial shipping channel that in any case traverses her life.

Given the film's fluid focus, and given Giuliana's concern with the liquid composition of her body, it seems particularly significant that, on the SAROM steel island, in the middle of the Adriatic Sea, Giuliana enunciates an alternative to this view of the discrete nature of things in the contemporary world. She says to Corrado: "now you are part of me—part of what is around me, that is." As she pronounces these words, Corrado looks at her intensely, and then the scene cuts to a medium long shot of the gas tube, curving up to the top of the frame. A large ship sits anchored in the fog behind it, separated by the waves of the Adriatic Sea. When it cuts back to Corrado and Giuliana, she expresses gratitude to Corrado for "looking" at her in a way that her husband has not. On the soundtrack, a mechanical rumble, the sound of waves, seagulls squawking. Giuliana's affirmation constitutes a declaration of trans-corporeal solidarity, punctuated visually and acoustically by the energy of industry and the more-than-human world. What is around her at that moment, in large quantities, is salt water and petroleum.

If Giuliana were to leave, she would indeed take these two things with her. In a much-cited quote from the scene in the shack, Giuliana asks what she should look at: "Cosa devo guardare?" Yet another part of this dialogue leads us to see that her comment involves her sense of her material self, not just as holder of the gaze, but as biophysical being. Giuliana says, perplexed, "I feel like my eyes are all wet. What do they expect me to do with my eyes? What am I supposed to look at?" Giuliana's observation about wet eyes underscores the formal constitution of every cinematic viewer, not just her own troubled vision. Alaimo (2012, 477) recalls the salty composition of our organs of sight: "We see the ocean through the ocean—since our eyes are surrounded by saltwater." Our bodies, too, are part sea. Rachel Carson recalled that, in our blood, there runs a "salty stream in which the elements sodium, potassium, and calcium are combined in almost the same proportions as in sea water . . . In the same way, our lime-hardened skeletons are a heritage from the calcium-rich ocean of Cambrian time" (qtd. in Alaimo 2012, 482). Contemplating the Adriatic through her wet eyes, Giuliana suggests that the borderlands of "materia" or matter are indeed characterized by what Iovino (2012b, 453) calls an "all-encompassing generativity [that] justifies the etymological bond between the Latin words *mater* ('mother') and *materia* ('matter')."

We might even posit that the petroleum landscape facilitates, rather than hampers, Giuliana's declaration of connectedness on the SAROM island. Although it isolates drivers in their vehicles, in some ways, oil also connects us to a more-than-human world. Discussing the gas stations scattered across the United States, Huber (2013, 133) observes that "gasoline consumption is one of the most banal ways in which nature-society relations interface with the geographies of everyday practice." He quotes geographer Gavin Bridge, who argues that, "refueling the car is one of the relatively few moments when one becomes conscious of the material resource flows that undergird both personal and corporate economic activity. Pump in hand, connected fleetingly by a streaming umbilical cord of gasoline directly to the material substances of the earth, the familiar boundaries between self and other, human and nature begin to look a little less certain" (qtd. in Huber 2013, 133). As Giuliana runs her hands along various platform surfaces, both she and the camera seem to contemplate the curious mechanisms that move them. Her momentary sense of connection, however, is not necessarily comforting. At the scene's conclusion, Giuliana offers a less-than-reassuring "fine" in response to Corrado's question "how are you?" after confessing an earlier suicide attempt. She descends the stairs of the SAROM platform to the water level, where a restless, green-brown sea rocks the small boat moored nearby, its motor puttering noisily. As the camera frames them from the top of the platform, an actor who might be Harris' body double follows her down (in this cut, we do not see his face). The frame cuts to a large map of Argentina, as Corrado enters the frame, explaining the location of Patagonia. The corporeal and existential risks of a petroleum society, the crossings and departures, the uncertainties (who am I? Is that Harris?) and the affirmations (I am fine; you are part of me) play out on and beyond the SAROM island.

Color, Time, Life: The Pink Sand Beach

Giuliana narrates a fable to her son, who is bedridden, claiming to have lost the use of his legs. Cut to a Mediterranean island in soft focus, and the camera pans down to capture first sand, then sand and water, then just water, then a smiling girl swimming, in close-up, in focus. Giuliana's voice in voiceover recounts the story of a young girl who liked being alone. Yet her solitude is immediately contested visually by the presence of cormorants, seagulls, and wild hares, who appear, one by one, in a series of rhythmic frames as the voice evokes them. Then, as her voice trails off in an apparent ellipsis, the film cuts to the pink rocks of the beach, making these, too, island inhabitants. "Nothing made noise," she says, and the soundtrack is alive with sounds of waves, wind, and birdcalls. An apparently unmanned sailing ship appears, then disappears, leaving in its wake a strange, disembodied singing voice. As the girl swims, a series of close-ups of the pink rocks flows by. In a voice that begins to fade, Giuliana says that the girl suddenly realizes that rocks were like flesh, and that the sweet voice belonged to "tutti . . . tutti." The subtitles on the Criterion disk aptly translate "tutti," or "everyone," as "everything."

Figure 1.2. Fleshy Rocks. Screen capture, *Red Desert* (1964), directed by Michelangelo Antonioni.

In discussions of the film, the Budelli Island sequence is called upon to explain, by contrast and by opposition, or to counterbalance, or problematize, the industrial world. It is called "phantasmatic" (Restivo 2002, 129), a "fantasy sequence" (131), something from a "mythical past" (Dalle Vacche 1996, 54), and is characterized as "marked off from the rest of the film in many important ways" (Restivo 2002, 131). Peter Brunette (1998, 106) writes that it shows Giuliana's desire for stability, and that the female singing voice that we hear is "an apparent fantasy signifier for the simple purity of 'nature.'" Victoria Kirkham (2004, 121) shows that the island is "obviously an Eden, its features like those of the Earthly Paradise in medieval imagination." Yet while, in some ways, this sequence is clearly differentiated, the Isola di Budelli connects to the rest of the film, and specifically to the SAROM island scene, where Giuliana extends her subjectivity to encompass the "things around her." The fable envisions a nonhuman gaze capable of seeing matter—organic, industrial, or otherwise—as generative in both narrative and material terms, and shows some of the film's Mediterranean circulating systems. Although this island is sun-drenched and rosy and the SAROM island is gray, similarities are evident in the maritime settings: as in Ravenna, the frame often captures landscape and seascape together, hovering at the border between the two. The arrival of a number of sailboats, and then a mysterious, apparently unmanned sailing ship, visually echo the port of Ravenna, where the oil tankers also float by with no apparent sailors. Sutured in the midst of the film's industrial landscapes, the Budelli Island demonstrates how entangled islands, and naturalistic fantasies, and organic matter, and industrial societies, and ideas of progress, always already were in the rest of the film, and continue to be here.

Arguably the most important feature of the Budelli Island sequence is the agency imparted to nonhuman actors. These include water, rocks, nonhuman animals, inhuman and nonhuman sounds, and the sailing ship. All are things we see and hear in other parts of the film, but now they are focalized by Giuliana's voiceover, and by the gaze of a young girl, often squinting, who is perplexed by them. On the island, the preoccupations Giuliana has voiced elsewhere come into focus, confronting us with their material and ontological weight. The voiceover casts these concerns as "mysteries," numbering two: the mystery of the unmanned sailing ship (who sails it?), and the mystery of the bodiless voice (who sings?). How, the question seems to run, can things move and speak without anthropic power? As the scene unfolds, the film creates more mysteries through audio/visual dialogues: the island is a space of solitude, the voiceover pronounces, but full of beings, the camera responds; it is a space of silence, says the voice, but alive with noise, answers the diegetic soundtrack. Between camera and voice, a rift seems to exist, and yet, as critical reactions suggest, the sequence is received as prelapsarian: Edenic, pure, a quest for stability. What if, in the case of each apparent opposition, both terms were true?

In a provocative essay that considers "Feminist Ontology and the Question of Essence" (the essay's subtitle), philosopher Timothy Morton (2013, 62) proposes that we humans need to rethink our commitment to Aristotle's law of noncontradiction, "which has never formally been proved." Morton evokes an apparent paradox in quantum physics, a tiny paddle that, isolated from other things (and thus seemingly not entangled with or intra-acting with other objects), seems to "breathe," vibrating and not vibrating concurrently. While received wisdom would suggest that a paddle cannot move all by itself, nor do two opposite things at the same time, the miniscule object observed by physicist Aaron O'Connell in a quantum laboratory performed otherwise (61). This phenomenon provides the basis for Morton's reconsideration of the ontology of the object and proposes an interesting ecological logic suggestive in *Red Desert*. Morton wonders: "What would be the advantage of *changing our logic*, rather than disavowing the 'breathing' paddle? If we could formulate logics that tolerated things such as vibrating and not vibrating simultaneously, we would no longer see single objects as static and dead. These logics would be *dialetheic*—capable of holding two truths simultaneously" (61–62). Ecology, he argues, is full of such uncanny apparent contradictions.[16] What if, on the Budelli Island, Giuliana articulates a changing logic, a logic that reflects her—and the film's—growing uncertainty in the face of purported anthropocentric privilege, a logic willing to admit more than one concurrent truth about the world?

The pink rocks of the Budelli Island embody a kind of dialetheic logic. In a montage near the end of the sequence, both voice and camera awaken the island's rocks, objects we might think of as static and inanimate. The Budelli Island rocks are sedimentary, which is to say rocks formed by the depositing and compression of mineral and rock particles over many years ("sedimentary" 2013); they are composite, material histories of the region's past. They have an inorganic component, formed of heavy minerals including zircon and monazite, and also mica, quartz, alkaline feldspar, and plagioclase. But they are particularly notable for their organic component, the bioclasts, or shells, that come from bryozoa, tiny marine organisms. The fossilized fragments of these bryozoa give the rocks and the beach their pink color (Biondi and Bagella 2005, 6).[17] Thus the pink color of the beach leads us to another important mystery unveiled on Budelli Island but also evident elsewhere in the film. In these pink rocks, like in petroleum, there exists evidence of what LeMenager (2014) calls a "category confusion" stemming from the fact that they were once, in part, living matter (as alive as the film's protagonists, the film crew, the inhabitants of Ravenna, the viewer of *Red Desert*, and the reader of this chapter). Deposits of petroleum and natural gas, similar to sedimentary rocks, are formed over millennia, and embody the compression of huge amounts of plant and animal matter.[18] Living and dead, organic and inorganic, the island's vibrant color, then, is kin—not in color, but in material composition—to the makeup of crude oil, also derived from ancient organic material. Its living form is built from dead organic fragments of the past, making it precious, finite, and irreproducible. Citing its "deep geologic history as life-through-time," LeMenager suggests that petroleum "forces questions of how biology, geology, and culture come together to define what counts as living matter" (6–7). This is a biogeological mystery that can weigh heavily on the human, especially that human caught in the flow of petrochemical modernity. In the sedimentary rock, or in deposits of petroleum, the slowness of geological time clashes with the speed of human consumption. Such a clash of timescales leads us, at least in our imaginations, toward the feared moment of peak oil. It is a clash vividly envisioned by Italo Calvino (1996) in the short story "*La pompa di benzina*"

("The Petrol Pump"). As a nervous driver speeds around town in search of a place to buy gas for his near-empty tank, he muses about disappearing oil supplies, imagining that in a single moment, he lives "the rise the peak the decline of the supposedly opulent societies, just as a rotating probe passes in an instant across millennia, perforating the sedimentary rocks of the Pliocene, the Cretaceous Period, the Triassic" (160). Like Calvino's driver, Giuliana's voice in the fable finds an uncanny ontology in the geological past.[19]

Firmly rooted in the landscape of the Anthropocene, when "the effects of humans on the global environment" have led to a "new geological era" (Crutzen 2002, 23), *Red Desert* captures the accelerated time frame of modernity, an acceleration mirrored in the flashing by of celluloid frames on a screen.[20] Antonioni (1964, 17) asked the head of a factory whose chimneys marred the shot he wanted of the white forest whether he could interrupt the smoke billowing out of them for a few minutes. "Do you know how much one minute would cost me? A hundred and fifty million," answered the industrialist. Yet in contrast with the neocapitalist timeframe of petrochemical industry, *Red Desert* features geology—rocks—and a dilated time that challenges an anthropocentric perspective. Further, it shows how non-anthropocentric time, the time of dinosaurs and sedimentation, ironically fuels petrochemical modernity and its speed. In Giuliana's formulation, the rocks are "*come carne*," flesh-like, or literally, like meat. As she recognizes their uncanny power, her voice, which at the beginning of the episode is cheery and confident, becomes fragile and tenuous. The moving camera, meanwhile, captures rocks with anthropomorphic qualities, most notably large noses and strong chins. These framings give them a "thing-power" (as Jeffrey Jerome Cohen formulates it) that questions the notion that only humans can speak. In *Stone*, Cohen (2015) argues powerfully that we think of stones as immobile only because we are bounded by our short, human timeframe. If we observe more carefully we can see, with Giuliana and Cohen, that "differences between the human and the lithic, the inorganic and the biological, the material and the creaturely seem firm but prove porous" (216–17).[21]

Contemplating stone may challenge human patience, just as Antonioni's films sometimes try students' attention spans in the age of YouTube. Critics evoke the notion of "dead time" in films directed by Antonioni to explain those "empty moments, directionless passages in which the seconds and minutes crawl by" (Rascaroli and Rhodes 2011, 9).[22] Taking a cue from the concept of "still life," known in Italian as "natura morta," or "dead nature," Rascaroli and Rhodes recall "dead time," suggesting that the subjects of still life paintings "are either inorganic, or doomed to become thus—to be consumed and excreted, or else to rot, decay, become mere matter, formless, dead" (10). But although *Red Desert* may push us to confront, protractedly, the "inorganic nature of the aesthetic itself" (10), for Giuliana, for the rocks on the Budelli Island, and for the unmanned sailing ship, matter is very much alive, even when it is composed of dead fragments of a past distant on a human timescale. Looking at the rock's human-like shapes, suddenly we might imagine the human's rock-like shape, and envision, with Calvino (1996, 160), a day when we will become rock, become petroleum: "The day when the earth's crust reabsorbs the city, the plankton sediment that was the human race will be covered by geological layers of asphalt and cement, and in millions of years will condense into oily deposits. For whose benefit, we do not know."

If we are patient enough to linger over them, as the camera is, the Budelli Island rocks, vibrant matter animated by Giuliana's imagination and the cinematic apparatus, compress time and expose the contradictions of consumption (of energy), in a way that extends beyond the film. Such sustained attention can reveal to us that, far from an isolated island paradise, the Budelli Island and the Maddalena Archipelago of which it is a part also recount stories about encounters of public and private, sea and capital, cinema industry and history: important contextual motifs of the 1960s boom in Italy, and encounters that take us far from Eden and closer to the neocapitalist landscape of Ravenna. In the history of *Red Desert*, this story, like Giuliana's, begins with a mystery. In Nicolini's (1964, 72–73) production diary, the filming of the island is an absence. One line, on March 7, 1964, records that the crew is leaving Ravenna, and that they must wait for summer to "film the fable in Yugoslavia." The reason for the change to the Sardinian island is unarticulated in the diary. But the island does appear in name in the opening credits, where Antonioni thanks Piero Tizzoni for allowing him to use "his" island as a location. Tizzoni, a Lombard developer, was responsible for parceling out land in Sardinia to create the Costa Paradiso, a stretch of coast that was to rival the famed Costa Smeralda (Pinna 1999, 22). Although it is part of a park system and largely subject to Italian laws protecting the "demanio," or public domain, the Isola di Budelli was privately owned for many years. As recently as October of 2013, it was offered for sale and purchased by a wealthy New Zealander for three million euros, spurring a court battle and incensed public debates about its future.[23]

The beautiful Maddalena island chain was not only privately coveted, however, but also adopted strategically as part of the military-industrial complex: a sister island in the chain, Santo Stefano, was for many years site of a US Navy base for submarines (from 1973 to 2008). In *Facing the Anthropocene,* Ian Angus (2016, 160) writes that "today the US military is the world's largest user of petroleum, *and* the largest polluter, producing more hazardous waste than the five largest chemical companies combined, *and* the largest producer of greenhouse gases." Although the submarine base post-dates the filming of *Red Desert,* in the wake of World War II the hydrocarbon flows that would locate it there already lurked beneath the surface of the sea.[24] Finally, thinking by way of these global flows, it takes little imagination to see that seas and their undulating waters carry modernity's hydrocarbon objects to every shore. With an even more prolific capacity to travel than ships, PVCs and other petrochemical products made in Ravenna (and Gela, and other seaside industrial sites) populate our seas, too. *Red Desert*'s Ravenna helped fuel a trend that today finds, as Patricia Yaeger (2010, 52) has observed, oceanic plastic all over the globe: "In the vasty deeps, in fishes' bellies, in the craws of dead albatrosses, plastic keeps cropping up. It is impossible to find a seabird without a little product inside or a square foot of ocean without debris." If on the Adriatic side of Italy, the film was already cognizant of petroleum in the bellies of Ravennan eels, the Budelli Island shows that our constructions of a "pristine nature" have always mistakenly been, as Morton (2010, 5) suggests, "the mirror image of private property: Keep off the Grass, Do Not Touch, Not for Sale." Viewed through the lens of a changing eco-logic, the Budelli Island holds various truths simultaneously. The "pristine," "natural" beauty of the Isola di Budelli and the Maddalena Archipelago is subject to the interconnected flows of global capital, hosts to petroleum-burning and nuclear-powered instruments of war, and not so far removed from the steel island on which Giuliana recognizes her connection with everything that surrounds her.

Rust, Decay, Cinema: Giuliana and the Rusted Ship

Nighttime. Once again, the camera moves from high to low, down the length of a silver pole in front of a red metal background, apparently part of a large ship. Strange metallic sounds emit from the soundtrack. Giuliana enters the frame on the left and wanders through a cluttered landscape, a dock full of protruding tubes and bars. The camera focuses on oily sludge on the surface of the water, then moves with Giuliana along the hull of a rusty ship. She walks partway up a gangplank and a sailor walks down to meet her. Speaking Italian to the man who responds in Turkish, Giuliana observes that while she is inquiring about sailing away with the ship, she cannot decide to do so on her own because she is not a "donna sola," not alone in the world. But then she explains that she has come to understand that bodies in the world are separate: "Bodies are separate. If you prick me, you don't suffer." As the two speak on the cold night, warm breath emerges from their mouths in vapor clouds, which almost touch before diffusing invisibly into the atmosphere.

As on the Budelli Island, Giuliana's voice makes an assertion that the image in front of us belies. Her affirmation in some ways represents the status quo of 1960s Italy, the logic of capitalist individualism, an assurance of the separate nature of bodies and, by extension, their separate fates. Yet condensation from Giuliana's speaking mouth almost intersects with the cloud of condensation coming from the mouth of the sailor. These visible exhalations remind us that breath is one of the ways in which inside and outside meet, where we, like factory smokestacks, emit substances toxic to us in exchange for others vital to our functioning, and where other bodies pass into our own. As she speaks, many of the surfaces around her are dirty or decaying: an oil spill on the greenish water, a rusty ship, corroded by years of exposure to salt water and salty air. On the celluloid, transposed into the digital language of the DVD, a spot appears fleetingly, marring the upper left-hand side of the dark frame.[25] The surface of the film, too, is subject to corrosion and decay; the digital image to obsolescence.[26] Inside and outside of the narrative, this is a space of what Caroline Schaumann and Heather I. Sullivan (2011, 105) term "dirty nature" (to which I return in Chapter 2) or that nature "without the artificial dichotomies that falsely divide the cultural from the natural as if human beings were independent from the physical world and used it only as a 'resource' at their convenience." In the Anthropocene, argue Schaumann and Sullivan, "all surface matter and all bodies in the biosphere contain some particulates from anthropogenic industrial processes" (105).

In this late scene, the conviction lacking at the end of the earlier voiceover on the Budelli Island returns to Giuliana's voice, even as she enunciates a contradiction. Bodies are separate, *and* her body intersects with that of the sailor, of the rusty ship, of the world at large. This incongruity recognizes both the integrity of the human actor and her entanglement in a nonhuman universe of things. In positing his "object-oriented feminist ontology," shaped by the dialetheic logic outlined earlier, Morton (2013, 67) proposes that recognizing objects as "themselves and not-themselves" *simultaneously* offers an ethical position from which to view the world, one that is "deeply non-violent." If, he suggests, we allow entities to be self-contradictory, we allow for a "universe of unique beings" somewhat like the one posited by *Red Desert* in these frames: "An ethics of deep concern for the inviolable reality of entities, no matter whether we interact with them or not, could develop from this. Sooner or later, politics would have to include nonhumans and nonsentient beings, since humans are surrounded and permeated by them, yet are irreducible to them" (67). Irreducible to her surroundings, Giuliana is yet *of* these surroundings. Both of her "epidermic" epiphanies are true: "Now you are part of me—part of what is around me, that is"; and "bodies are separate."

Accepting Morton's invitation to change our thinking—and by extension our critical, artistic, and philosophical practice—to admit a dialetheic logic, capable of holding two truths simultaneously; accepting Alaimo's call for "more capacious epistemologies" to take into account the complexity of the material world; we can tentatively accept the contradictory truths that make up *Red Desert*. Both polluting and apt in pointing out the dangers of pollution, both industrial by-product and critical of the industrial world, both embedded in the petrochemical landscape of its on-location shoot and irretrievably other, the film walks the threshold at the encounter of art and industry. There is no doubt that *Red Desert* left a "cinematic footprint," a physical impression, on the industrial landscape it captured, that it consumed resources and emitted toxins, that it polluted and wasted. It also left behind a string of relationships, new aesthetic perspectives, ideas.

Nicolini (1964, 41) uses an intriguing metaphor to describe the work of the production crew on location, writing that: "The study of the underlying conditions is commensurate with the events that happen to the characters in the film, just as the gelatin of a culture is to the bacillus immersed in it." Those "underlying conditions," which at least in part lie beneath Ravenna, include the energy fueling the economic boom. The background conditions, in this formulation, nourish the protagonists in the film, who are thoroughly immersed therein—but the occupying guests, presumably, also consume that background.[27] The choice of the concept of the "bacillus" as the "characters" in the film is curious, since "bacillus" is generally pathogenic, or disease-causing. Thus Nicolini offers us a vision of a relationship of immersion, dependence, and also potential harm, linking film crew and location. These complicated relationships are suggestive of the material interactions between *Red Desert* and Ravenna. Antonioni and Nicolini both described, for example, a "cloud" of paint released when a crew of painters, perched precariously on tall ladders, worked through the night to paint trees white for a shot the director wanted.[28] This cloud, a volatilized, likely petroleum-based, and probably toxic airborne mass of color, marks color itself as another horizon of petrochemical, liquid connectivity. For the same scene, workers used handheld pumps that launched flaming gasoline to burn the grass, which was to contrast with the white forest (Nicolini 1964, 16). Yet, as is well known, the white forest never appeared in the film, because after a strenuous night of work, a bright sun rose in notoriously foggy Ravenna, backlighting the trees and rendering Antonioni's desired shot impossible. Thus the white forest, aside from being toxic, is also *absent*, and stands as an invisible monument to cinema as consumption, pollution, and waste. And these are but minor examples of what is evident in the photographs included with the production diary: between burning bushes, burning lights, rolling cameras, and the energy required to transport cinematic machines and actors from place to place, the film's carbon footprint is not inconsequential. Through the white forest, though, that place we do *not* see, we know with all the more certainty that, as Schoonover (2011, 248) observed, "Antonioni's cinematic images are by-products of waste," *and* that "the film is itself a glorious by-product of the petrochemical industry."

We also know, however, that in *Red Desert*, as Pinkus (2011, 270) has argued, "there is no question of facing the environment since we are in it, of it." Antonioni (1964, 19) was aware that the world around him was toxic: he wrote about black and yellow factory waste water that was "no longer water," dying trees, fish with their bellies full of petroleum. Di Carlo (1964, 27) observed the "nauseating smells," burned trees, and dying birds. And together in this landscape, production crew, actors, director, and scholar-friend ate and drank, breathed, sneezed, and laughed. The production crew drank champagne with SAROM, and we can imagine effervescent bubbles escaping the glasses in the corporate offices, mingling with noises and fumes and machinic exhalations from the factory floor. Carbon Black was less festive in receiving the crew, fretting that the film would show the company's "dirty laundry." During filming, one of the company's engineers disapproved of the workers' dirty uniforms, sending them to wash their hands and faces before the scene was shot (Nicolini 1964, 43–44). But the production crew really did film the waste canals, and Giuliana and her son really did walk along them. In an early scene, Giuliana eats a sandwich along a corridor where carbon black, a byproduct of burning petroleum, is smoldering, sending up a cloud of ominous black smoke. Actor and protagonist are thus both ingesting carbon black, which can irritate the respiratory system and lodge in the lungs, and may cause cancer.[29] "Dirty laundry" indeed: in "dirty nature," these are not the kinds of stains that wash off hands and faces easily. Analogous to the volatile cloud of white paint, these stains carry across bodies and surfaces; they are airborne or applied to skin; they wash into nearby ditches and canals and take their place in the circulation of substances that traverses landscape, film, filmmaker, eels, actors, and viewer.

Earlier in this chapter, I cited the industrial disasters at Seveso and Manfredonia as petrochemical events, both in 1976, that honed public awareness of trans-corporeal fragility in Italy. However, closer to the filming of *Red Desert*, there loom two disasters that haunt the production and its hydrocarbon pathways. The first happened on October 9, 1963, just six days before the first entry in Nicolini's production diary. In an Alpine valley north of Venice, part of Mount Toc crumbled, creating a massive landslide that crushed into the Vajont Dam. Under the leadership of SADE, one of *Red Desert*'s principal hosts in Ravenna, a massive hydroelectric project had precipitously raised the height of the dam (and thus the amount of water held in the reservoir) to fuel postwar Italy's electric needs. In spite of resistance from area residents and a number of experts, and in spite of concrete evidence of geological instability, the project went ahead. When the landslide occurred, disaster struck, predictably and tragically, with a force twice that of the bomb at Hiroshima. A thundering mass of rocks and waves hit nine villages below the dam, killing 2000 people (Armiero 2011, 173–94). Today, environmental historian Marco Armiero calls the calamity a "massacre" and a "metaphor of Italian modernization" (155, 174).

The second disaster happened in 1965, the year after *Red Desert*'s release: the Paguro drilling platform, manufactured island sister to the SA-ROM docking island that featured in the film (and that appeared in *The Oil Men* that same year), unexpectedly struck a reserve of natural gas and exploded. Three men died in the explosion, and a plume of gas up to fifty meters high continued to burn until AGIP was at last able to cement over the perforation, almost three months later. Photographs of the disaster show the platform's helipad leaning at a dramatic angle above the waterline. Today, the submerged skeleton of the drilling platform sits under the sea, the highest part about ten meters below the water line. As an artificial reef, it has become a haven for aquatic creatures and for divers, and is now a protected site for marine life.[30]

Neither of these catastrophes, as far as I am aware, are mentioned by production crew members, by Antonioni, or by scholars working on *Red Desert*. Yet through the film's association with SADE and ENI, the petrochemical industry, and the economic boom, and by chronological proximity, these stories trouble its borders. In sharp contrast with the confidence of *The Oil Men* or the booming success of Ravenna, where Corrado and Ugo struggle to find workers willing to leave for Patagonia because they are all jealously guarded by Italian employers, these stories show the rent in the fabric of the economic "miracle." They demonstrate the dangers of working in a petrochemical landscape, including hazards (like carbon black) most acute for those exposed over long periods of time, but perilous nonetheless for film crews working on location. They show the complicated relationship of human and more-than-human life with petrochemical modernity, and the breakdown of distinctions between "nature" and "culture" so powerfully articulated when disaster strikes. The Paguro platform accident and its subsequent transformation into artificial reef also, tentatively, suggest the ways that disaster can be creatively reenvisioned, without necessarily erasing or forgetting the past.

If *Red Desert*'s "dead time" stretches cinematic form onscreen to acknowledge the temporality of matter, its entanglement in Italy's industrial modernity shows how swift and destructive that modernity can be. Bozak (2012, 31) argues that "the cinematic and photographic image correspond as an amazingly succinct visualization of the geological component of industrial culture." Flowing by on our screens, frame after frame, relying on energy to do so, and featuring hydrocarbon landscapes, *Red Desert*'s compression of geology into creative cinematic energy vibrates with significance.[31] On the one hand, the film does not explicitly condemn industrial practices that led, in the days immediately preceding the beginning of filming, to the death of 2000 people. Its collaboration with SADE, its spray painting and discarding of the scene in the forest, its burning bushes and meandering strolls through waste canals of carbon black make the film complicit on some level with dubious industrial practices. Yet on celluloid and in the production diary, *Red Desert* also candidly records this complicity for the historical record. Thus through a compelling dialetheic logic, it merges its complicity with a deep, creative concern for the fates of the beings, human and more-than-human, entangled in the petrochemical web. Barthes (1989, 211) eloquently renders this tension, and its ethical consequence, when he says that in Antonioni's cinema, "[t]he object represented vibrates, to the detriment of dogma."

Figure 1.3. Final Factory Scene. Screen capture, *Red Desert* (1964), directed by Michelangelo Antonioni.

In the film's final scene, Giuliana returns with her son to the factory where the story began. Valerio plays in the steam rising from metal pipes and hissing on the soundtrack; the camera captures a waste canal beside him, then cuts to the poisonous yellow smoke coming from refinery chimneys. Giuliana reassures her son that there's nothing to worry about—bodies are separate, birds have learned not to fly through the yellow smoke. The camera's subsequent tack, though, is to blur the colors of the factory, moving Giuliana to the far side, and then to focus on piles of colorful barrels likely containing toxic industrial waste. The bodies of petroleum and water, of airborne toxins and vapors, of family and capital, of self and cinema and world, are shown in their mutual transformation. Cinema can offer an ethical alternative to the celebratory or unilateral logic of petrochemical progress, although it must also admit its entanglement with industry. As we watch *Red Desert* decades after its production, we, too, can see with Giuliana that our bodies are separate, even as we say, with the film, the factories and their toxic emissions, the pine forests, and the eels with petroleum in their bellies, "You are part of me."

Notes

1. Carlo Di Carlo, interview by author, Rome, May 16, 2013. Except where otherwise indicated, all information from Di Carlo was collected during this interview.

2. Italia Nostra's first president was writer Giorgio Bassani. The organization's founding members were Bassani, Umberto Zanotti Bianco, Pietro Paolo Trompeo, Desideria Pasolini dall'Onda, Elena Croce, Luigi Magnani, and Hubert Howard. For more on the history of the organization, see www.italianostra.org.

3. On July 10, 1976, an accident at the ICMESA chemical plant in Seveso, Lombardy, released a toxic cloud of dioxin and other pollutants into the air. Evacuation of the area did not begin until July 24, following the death of many domestic animals and a widespread outbreak of the skin disease chloracne. On September 26 of the same year, in Manfredonia, Puglia, tons of arsenic spilled from the ANIC chemical factory, killing many animals and resulting in the hospitalization of many residents. For more on the Seveso disaster, see Laura Centemeri (2010), "The Seveso Disaster Legacy," and Serenella Iovino (2013b), "Toxic Epiphanies: Dioxin, Power, and Gendered Bodies in Laura Conti's Narratives on Seveso." The disaster in Manfredonia is discussed in Stefania Barca (2011), "Bread and Poison: Stories of Labor Environmentalism in Italy, 1968–1998."

4. Barca (2011, 127) notes that, during the economic boom, epidemiological shifts in fact mirrored industrial ones, and that there was a transition "from infectious to degenerative diseases, especially those correlated with environmental poisoning from mercury and benzene hydrocarbons."

5. Alaimo (2010, 114) explains that the condition "causes a range of reactions, including rashes, tremors, convulsions, breathing difficulties, headaches, dizziness, nausea, joint pain, 'brain fog,' and extreme fatigue."

6. Iovino (2010a, 35) formulates this move away from anthropocentric humanism as an act of "widening the scope of the objects of moral responsibility from a singular 'centre' (humankind) to a multiplicity of 'peripheral', ethically as well as ontologically marginalized subjects."

7. The notion of "interactionism" has been widely theorized in material ecocriticism and material feminism. Nancy Tuana (2008, 191) explains that interactionism "removes any hard-and-fast divide between nature and culture" positing instead a "world of complex phenomena in dynamic relationality." This notion is closely tied to theories of trans-corporeality (Stacy Alaimo), vital materialism (Jane Bennett), "intra-action" (Karen Barad), or posthumanist performativity, among others. As Iovino (2012b, 451) explains, in these formulations, humans share a horizon of immanence "with countless other actors, whose agency—regardless of being endowed with degrees of intentionality—forms the fabric of events and causal chains."

8. On this latter topic in particular, see, for example, Bernardi (2002), Chatman (1985), and Kirkham (2004).

9. Monica Seger's (2015, 4) work suggests that "interstitial spaces" are a key for approaching Italian naturecultures, since these in-between places (half-built oceanfront landscapes, for example, or polluted watersheds) "teach us to observe closely before forming judgment, and remind us of the continued transition of the lived world."

10. Bonifazio (2014) explains (in an article that also briefly treats *Red Desert*) that these ENI films offered "instructions on how to 'adapt' to the changing life-style and landscapes affected by industrialization. Rather than indoctrinating viewers, ENI films excited and mobilized the emotions of audiences with lures of prosperity and happiness" (331).

11. For more on ENI's support of petrocultural productions, see Enrico Cesaretti's enlightening work on both ENI films and *Il gatto selvatico*, an ENI publication (forthcoming in the chapter "Oil. Slick Territories: Petroculture Italian Style," in his book *Telling Matters: Narratives of Environmental Entanglements in Modern Italy*).

12. One of the most intriguing projects to come from the ENI film office was Dutch communist film director Joris Ivens' *L'Italia non è un paese povero* (*Italy Is Not a Poor Country*, 1960), on which Paolo and Vittorio Taviani, Tinto Brass, and Valentino Orsini collaborated. The film was made for Radiotelevisione Italiana (RAI) but was ultimately released in a fragmentary format; it began in Gela and concluded in Porto Marghera. For more on the film, see Elena Past, "Mediterranean Ecocriticism" (2016b). In Ravenna, Fernando Cerchio's *Il gigante di Ravenna* (*The Giant of Ravenna*, 1960) detailed the construction of the ANIC factory. Gillo Pontecorvo's *Una storia per l'energia* (*A History for Energy*, 1984) also features hydrocarbon discoveries in the waters around Ravenna. The ENI video channel on YouTube offers a sampling of the company's cinematic productions.

13. SAROM, which provided prominent filming locations for *Red Desert*, was owned by Ravennan entrepreneur Attilio Monti (1906–94), and primarily dedicated to refining crude oil. Ravaged by the oil crisis in the 1970s, it would eventually be acquired by ENI in 1981.

14. The intertextual impact of Antonioni's films demonstrates the transnational flows of the cinematic image: Gianni Celati (1989, 219–20) traced a generative line between Antonioni's vision and the cinema of Wim Wenders and Jim Jarmusch; Karl Schoonover (2011, 240) notes the influence of Antonioni's films on Todd Haynes' *Safe* (1995), Samira Makhmalbaf's *The Apple* (*Sib*, 1998), and Jia Zhangke's *Still Life* (*Sanxia haoren*, 2006). Antonioni's films, which were filmed in Algeria, Spain, England, Germany, and the United States, among other places, also reflect a boom-era mobility as global capital extended its borders. William Arrowsmith (1995, 92) argues that, embedded in the films themselves, we find a sort of transnational "nomadism," or the "sense and degree, the universality, of modern mobility," as, for example, the Italian workers being recruited to labor in Argentina in *Red Desert*.

15. Pointing out that we experience, for example, "only 'miked' voices as natural in the theater," LeMenager (2014, 6) argues that media relies heavily on oil: "Oil itself is a medium that fundamentally supports all modern media forms concerned with what counts as culture— from film to recorded music, novels, magazines, photographs, sports, and the wikis, blogs, and videography of the Internet."

16. As an example, Morton (2013) proposes that we think of Darwin's theory of evolution, which concludes that *"there are no species."* Considering a cat, we might note that at no point along a genome's mutation can we find a "cat essence." Yet cats exist, and continue to evolve, and are different from their ancestors. From this, he suggests, we see that *"there are real objects* that exist apart from their relations, such that objects are uncanny and contradictory" (63, emphasis in original).

17. Through this play around the organic/inorganic border, the film thus gets at a sort of "material vitality" or "vital materialism" that resonates with Jane Bennett's innovative theory of matter. In discussing the structure of metal, Bennett (2010, 57) writes: "The aim here is to rattle the adamantine chain that has bound materiality to inert substance and that has placed the organic across a chasm from the inorganic. The aim is to articulate the elusive idea of a materiality that is itself heterogeneous, itself a differential of intensities, itself a life."

18. Bozak (2012, 31) elaborates: "Buried beneath the weight of oceans and ice, sand, and rock, time reduces this raw compost so thoroughly that its energy yields are such that a gallon of gasoline represents about ninety tons of plant matter, or forty acres of wheat. The immensity of such figures translates into enormous social, cultural, political, economic, and environmental effects."

19. Italo Calvino and his non-anthropocentric imagination appear in *Red Desert*: when Giuliana visits Corrado's hotel room, the camera focuses on the distinctive cover of his 1963 novella, *Giornata d'uno scrutatore* (The Watcher) on the nightstand. Iovino (2011, 71) proposes an absorbing ecocritical reading of this work, suggesting that in the context of the Cottolengo hospital for the mentally and physically disabled, the protagonist sees "the human being exposed to unpredictable metamorphoses, due to the force of 'the random element,' be it uranium, viruses, or generation." Questioning the boundaries of the human, the threshold "between reason and non-reason, light and shadow, and universal and individual" (73), the novel on the nightstand echoes Giuliana's material and existential concerns in the film. Thank you to Robert Rushing for pointing out the presence of Calvino in this scene.

20. Braidotti (2013, 66) argues: "The fact that our geological era is known as the 'anthropocene' stresses both the technologically mediated power acquired by anthropos and its potentially lethal consequences for everyone else."

21. In Manuel De Landa's (1997, 27) terms: "The human endoskeleton was one of the many products of [. . .] ancient mineralization," a process he calls the "geological infiltration" of the human species.

22. Discussing *L'avventura*, Celati (1989, 219) describes "temps mort" as "pauses within the landscape, as tarries." For Barthes (1989, 212), the "temps mort of an adventure" is "what you were asked not to look at by [. . .] narrative convention."

23. On one website (Vladi Private Islands) offering the island for sale, Antonioni's film was cited as a selling point ("Isola" 2014). At auction, it was bought by New Zealander Michael Harte, but the Italian Parliament voted shortly thereafter to exercise its right of preemption to make the island public again. For current information on the island, see the website for the National Park: http://www.lamaddalenapark.it/argomenti/isola-di-budelli.

24. Angus (2010, 145, 147) also charts the ways in which World War II and the Marshall Plan helped "convert Europe to Oil," and shows that oil "accounted for 10 percent of all Marshall Plan spending—20 percent in 1949—far more than was allocated to any other commodity."

25. This stain is visible at 1:51:45 on my copy of *Red Desert*.

26. Pinkus (2011, 265–66) discusses the fragility of celluloid and the impermanence of media. Regarding Antonioni's enthusiasm at the supplanting of film stock with videotape, she points out that in the case of the latter, "the backing is usually acetate, polyester, Mylar, or polyvinal chloride—petrochemical products!" Bozak (2012, 26) warns that: "If rates of innovation and obsolescence are not curbed, in only a generation we could find that the twentieth century's analog film records are still extant, while the digital record of the twenty-first has disappeared into unreadable formats."

27. The choice of "gelatin" as the nourishing substance is suggestive, too, in the context of cinema, where lights and celluloid have relied on gelatin to function.

28. The painted forest was only one of the chromatic modifications of *Red Desert*; there was also a fruit cart painted gray along with the human fruit-seller; a bush painted purple; a pond dyed yellow-green. Schoonover (2011, 240) connects color specifically to "modern plastics that are created from petroleum refuse," arguing that the "flexibility, vibrancy and abstraction of form result from the indelible imbrication of image and content at a molecular level."

29. The Centers for Disease Control lists carbon black as a "potential human carcinogen," and emphasizes that exposure can happen via inhalation, ingestion, or dermal contact

(recalling the "epidermic" theme of the film); it has been known to cause decreased pulmonary function in workers and myocardial dystrophy. Exposure guidelines and more information about the effects of carbon black are available on the CDC website: http://www .cdc.gov/niosh/docs/81-123/pdfs/0102.pdf.

30. For more information on the Paguro explosion and on the site as a protected marine area, see http://www.associazionepaguro.org/index.html.

31. I borrow this notion of "vibration" from Barthes' (1989, 211) celebrated letter to Antonioni, in which he writes to the director: "you strive to render subtle the meaning of what man says, tells, sees, or feels, and this subtlety of meaning, this conviction that meaning does not crudely limit itself to the thing said, but goes on, ever further, fascinated by what is beyond meaning, is the very conviction, I feel, of all artists, whose object is not one or another technique, but this strange phenomenon of vibration."

2

LOCATION, DIRTY CINEMA, TOXIC WASTE, STORYTELLING: *GOMORRAH*

*I*MET GENNARO AQUINO, THE LOCATION MANAGER FOR *the film* Gomorra *(Gomorrah, 2008), in Piazza Vittorio in Rome on a Sunday morning, and we sat for several hours talking about his work preparing the Neapolitan "stage" for the film.*[1] *This was an unofficial interview, as we made plans to meet again in Naples, where he would show me around some of the filming locations that he had helped to arrange. At the time we spoke, Aquino was organizing the production of the television series "Gomorra: La serie," and thus retreading much of the ground previously scouted for the film. The day I arrived in Naples, though, the production, which had been plagued with difficulties, ran into another snag and our tour had to be cancelled. I also spoke with assistant camera operator Greta De Lazzaris, and later with production designer Paolo Bonfini, in the Pigneto neighborhood in Rome—De Lazzaris in the café of an independent cinema, and Bonfini in his modern interior design studio.*[2] *De Lazzaris, who is also a documentary filmmaker, spoke tranquilly of on-set experiences that involved getting muddy, dirty, not always having places to wash her hands, and wearing dust masks when filming in dumps. Bonfini recalled touring the countryside with officers from the* Corpo forestale dello Stato *(the State Forestry Corps), and learning about green hillsides that disguised mounds of highly toxic manufacturing waste.*

All three interviewees were deeply entangled in the film as material production: Aquino seeking out its locations, Bonfini selecting and shaping objects for the sets, De Lazzaris carrying the heavy equipment with which the images were created. All three spoke passionately about the spirit of collaboration and the sincere bonds of friendship formed in the process of filming Gomorrah, *bonds that were nurtured by director Matteo Garrone. They also underlined their sense that cinema is a privileged, temporary presence that passes across a landscape, something that makes everyone, as Bonfini said, "fall in love."*

Figure 2.1. Gomorrah. Screen capture, *Gomorrah* (2008), directed by Matteo Garrone. DVD extra materials, The Criterion Collection.

They reminded themselves and me that they, secure in their privileged position as creators of spectacle, leave most of the problems—and the dirt, and lots of empty plastic water bottles—behind them at the end of filming.

This is a story of dirty cinema, a cinema that embraces the margins and openly inhabits a space trafficked by organized crime, drugs, and toxic waste, leaving its own trail of refuse in the process. It is also the story of a cinema that does not shy away from narrating its complicity in waste and resource use, or from letting dirty matter narrate its own story. In the process, Gomorrah, which according to its creators is not primarily a "cinema di denuncia" or cinema that aims at political condemnation (unlike the investigative book by journalist Roberto Saviano on which it is based), nevertheless opens itself to a relationship with place and with matter, unleashing a creative force that offers ethical possibilities for envisioning an alternative, collaborative future. [3]

Making films creates waste. Gennaro Aquino, a native of Naples who specializes in finding locations for films and television series in the city, notes that in a single day, a film crew uses huge quantities of plastic water bottles and plastic plates; sorting and recycling trash is not often a priority. Then there are the props, the fuel needed to run vehicles and generators, the lights, cameras, and batteries. The art, construction, set design, and paint departments leave "tangible waste streams," and large amounts of paper are often used for scripts and other photocopies, as Charles J. Corbett and Richard

P. Turco (2006, 45, 47) show in their report, "Sustainability in the Motion Picture Industry." Waste and the footprint of the cinematic industry have increasingly been the subject of scholarly and industrial attention. Filmmakers for Conservation, the Center for Environmental Filmmaking, and the Center for Media & Social Impact collaborated in 2009 on the creation of a "Code of Best Practices in Sustainable Filmmaking," a report that makes recommendations for calculating energy use, reducing consumption, limiting travel, and offsetting carbon usage.[4] The Code provides checklists for productions seeking to reduce their impact, and urges pragmatically: "do as much as you can, and try to do more on your next production" (Engel and Buchanan 2009, 7). While the Code's introduction celebrates cinema's ability to raise environmental questions, it also admits that "[c]urrently most producers, broadcasters, and distributors do not acknowledge the true costs of environmental impact that arise from producing and distributing film" (1). In 2014, the Italian production company Tempesta Film created Eco-Muvi, a European environmental film certification that provides practical advice for more sustainable productions. The award-winning 2018 *Lazzaro felice* (*Happy as Lazzaro*, dir. Alice Rohrwacher) used EcoMuvi protocols in pre-production and production to save 10 tons of Co_2, according to publicity for the film. EcoMuvi ultimately hopes to lead efforts to re-envision the entire filmmaking process, conceiving of a production as a "mobile village" whose functions can be more efficiently integrated into locations of filming (Marino 2014). So far, however, only a few films have sought and been awarded the certification.[5] Aquino confirms that matters of consumption, and willingness to consider these matters, are important future horizons for the Italian film industry, although he adds: "It's a bit taboo to talk about it," all the while speaking frankly with me.[6]

In their 2006 report, Corbett and Turco analyze the significant environmental impact of the film industry in Southern California, noting "the apparent paradox between the industry's often admirable efforts to protect resources and locations and the industry's pervasive throwaway mentality" (3).[7] Part of the problem, they suggest, is the structure of the industry: "highly decentralized, with its focus on short-term ever-changing production teams rather than long-term physical supply chains" (3). Filming on location means that cinema is nomadic, an industry that lacks the stability (at least in the moment of filming) and the infrastructure of a brick-and-mortar studio home. While this kind of industrial nomadism might suggest a rather ephemeral lightness, it actually represents one of the biggest challenges to environmentally conscious filmmaking. As productions move from place to place, they leave behind a stream of waste that must somehow be absorbed into the location, or carted off with further expenditure of energy. Further, the ever-changing aggregates of human and nonhuman actors and technologies who come together to create any given film make it more difficult to establish and maintain the collaborative practices necessary to confront issues of waste and recycling. Although making a film constitutes an experience of intensely shared work, many film sets, as impermanent microcosms, operate according to a logic of immediacy, where time pressures and tight budgets take precedence over more sustainable long-term practices.

Filming on location is not just a wasteful business, it is also a grubby business, and to participate in creating a film is to get dirty. Greta De Lazzaris says that she has often accompanied productions through mud and dirt, or into abandoned buildings and lots. In the housing project "Le Vele" in Scampia, the neighborhood in Naples where the crew for *Gomorrah* spent several weeks filming (longer than they spent at any other location), they had to knock on doors and ask to use people's bathrooms. In a scene where *camorristi*, or members of the organized crime syndicate in Campania, hide weapons in a stable, the crew filmed from among a small herd of *bufale*, the buffalos from whose milk the region's celebrated *mozzarella di bufala* is made. "There, we really descended into the shit," laughed De Lazzaris. The experience was not unique to the filming of *Gomorrah*. Describing scenes filmed in the goats' stables in *Le quattro volte*, Marco Serrecchia remembered, laughing, that the crew had to accompany their filming equipment "into a sea of shit and pee."[8]

Speaking of dirt does not necessarily mean to speak of something distasteful or harmful. An idiomatic expression, "getting your hands dirty," can mean pitching in, taking part, allowing an experience to get under your fingernails and become a material part of you. From an ecocritical perspective, dirt as matter and dirt theory as philosophy help further complicate the conceptual binaries that divide humans from the natural world, and that have kept ecocritics from turning their gaze to urban landscapes and problems. Anthony Lioi (2007, 17) has argued that much ecocriticism has been "dirt-rejecting": "In our quest to promote wildness and nonanthropocentric cosmologies, ecocritics have shunned texts and places compromised by matter-out-of-place, the ritual uncleanliness of cities, suburbs, and other defiled ecosystems." Lioi's resulting call for a "symbolic place in ecocriticism for dirt and pollution" (17) is in turn amended and broadened by Heather I. Sullivan (2012, 517), who urges that "we want to include not just a symbolic place but also a conscious and concrete embrace of dirt, which cannot be avoided since we live and breathe it daily." Dirt is soil, that sustaining matter composed of living microorganisms, fragments of rocks and minerals, industrial and other toxins, and decomposing organic matter that geomorphologist David Montgomery (2007, 1) vividly evokes as "a whole world of life eating life, a biological orgy recycling the dead back into new life." Dirt is dust, that fine particulate matter that is equally complex but light enough to be airborne, so that we breathe it and it accumulates in the crevices and crannies of our houses and film equipment. Like films made on location, dirt too is nomadic, moved by wind, water, feet, paws, hooves, and vehicles. Dirt sustains life on our planet, and Montgomery credits soil quality with determining the rise and fall of empires.[9]

Thinking with dirt is not difficult in Italian ecocriticism, where a long history of entangled human and nonhuman cultures means that ideas of natural "purity" are seldom evoked as notions upon which ecology should be based. As Fulco Pratesi (2010, 9) maintains in his *Storia della natura d'Italia* (*History of Nature in Italy*), the Italian landscape has been "totally modified, transformed, degraded by the work of nearly 300 generations [of people]."[10] Thinking with dirt is not irrelevant in Naples and its surrounding countryside, either. "Campania felix," or the "fertile country," was a felicitous place in no small part because of the volcanic soils that supported, and continue to support, a rich and diverse agriculture and various harvests each year. Soil quality has long been a matter of interest in the region, since civilizations ancient and modern relied heavily on Campania for nourishment. Montgomery (2007, 60–61) cites a number of treatises written during the Roman Empire concerned with practices of maintaining the soil. One such document, *De Re Rustica*, by Marcus Terentius Varro (116–27 BCE), recognized almost one hundred different types of soil, and was based in part on studies of Campania's earthly foundations. Varro, who owned an estate on Vesuvius' slopes, made recommendations for rendering soil more productive, including multiple annual plowings and fertilizing with cow dung and bird droppings. However, in spite of an awareness of the importance of stewardship of the soil, eventually erosion, a growing Roman population, and an increasing reliance on large plantations worked by slaves led to compromises and, finally, to compromised soil (64). While he underlines that "soil erosion alone did not destroy Rome," Montgomery suggests that it certainly played an important part in its decline (68).

In contemporary Italy, apprehensions about Campania's soil are crucial because of the activities of what the *Legambiente* (Environmental League), the leading Italian environmental nongovernmental organization (NGO), calls the *ecomafia*. The term "ecomafia," coined by the Legambiente and now used widely in the media, refers to organized crime where it is involved in activities that harm the environment, including trafficking in toxic and other industrial waste.[11] Around Naples, camorristi are also active ecomafiosi (or *ecocamorristi*, as they have recently been called).[12] In what has become a hugely profitable business, companies run by Camorra clans bid to collect, transport, and dispose of industrial, municipal, and other waste. Frequently following a north to south trajectory, such waste is illegally or inadequately disposed of in Campania more than in any other region; it leaches carcinogenic substances into water and dirt, contaminates food supplies, or becomes airborne, especially when burned.[13] Thinking specifically in dirty terms, ecocamorristi threaten the integrity of the soil when they dump and bury toxic and other waste in fields dedicated to growing food and raising animals, or when they disguise toxins as fertilizer that they sell to farmers to "replenish" their soil.[14] Dirt is important everywhere; as Montgomery (2007, 2) expresses in limpid terms, "everything comes from it, and everything returns to it." In Campania, though, both because of the exceptional quality of the volcanic soil and the criminal undermining of its integrity, the stakes are particularly high.

The tension between "dirty" and "clean" is explicitly expressed in *Gomorrah* when a wealthy executive in Venice says, as he negotiates with a businessman from Naples to get a rock-bottom price for the removal of industrial byproducts, that he just wants to make sure the waste disposal process is "clean." His insistent use of the English word in the midst of an Italian conversation ("a me interessa che sia 'clean,' come dicono in America" [I just want it to be clean, like they say in America]) shows the sanitizing tendency of the global elite, anxious to distance dirt and waste from their sight as well as from their linguistic and material surroundings. Such sterilizing of the immediate surroundings at the cost of other, distant communities corresponds to what Rob Nixon (2011, 47) calls "geographies of concealment in a neoliberal age." In Camorra territory, the logic is somewhat different, however, and doesn't inevitably require this practice of distancing. Saviano (2007, 284) elaborates: "The life of a boss is short; the power of a clan, between vendettas, arrests, killings, and life sentences, cannot last for long. To flood an area with toxic waste and circle one's city with poisonous mountain ranges is a problem only for someone with a sense of social responsibility and a long-term concept of power. In the here and now of business, there are no negatives, only a high profit margin." Undermining the very foundations on which everyone's life depends (food, air, water, dirt), including their own lives and those of their families, the criminals who contaminate the region's dirt raise the curtain on the ecological and political fragility of life in Campania. Because of the criminal activities of the ecomafia in and around Naples, Serenella Iovino (2009, 339) insists that individuals are "forcibly separated from both their social and territorial identities."

The production crew's willingness to engage with cinematic dirt goes hand-in-hand with *Gomorrah*'s audio-visual portrayal of a dirty Naples, and demonstrates a disposition to interact with a substance and a topic that many would like to sweep under the rug. In this sense, dirt becomes a means to understand *Gomorrah*'s engagement both with criminality and with questions of social and environmental justice. Dirt can be exclusionary, or democratic, or a combination of the two. Sullivan (2012, 529) cites dirt's potential associations with the notion of "mother earth" as well as its condemnation by "anti-dirt campaigns of cleaning-products industries," and the fact that it can be "laden with gendered, racial, and class connotations." Arguing that theory should inhabit terrain that incorporates the cultural and the scientific, or the symbolic and the material, she insists that dirt "demands our ecological and cultural attention" (518, 529). In cinema, and specifically in *Gomorrah*, dirt helps blur distinctions between production and narrative, reality and fiction, and criminal and victim. As this chapter proposes, "dirty" cinema does not need to constitute a moral judgment but rather can be a means to embrace process over static acceptance or unconditional disapproval. "Dirty" Naples is a place where multiple symbolic and material senses of dirt are pertinent, whether the substance is reviled or revered, life-giving matter or carrier of toxicity. And "dirty" cinema enters the field (a space that can be understood literally here) to engage its complexity.

Location, Location, Location: Le Vele and Dirty Landscapes

The adolescent Totò emerges from his mother's shop, arms weighed down with plastic grocery bags filled for delivery. He stops to greet a friend, one of a number of men guarding the entrance to a large building. A shaky handheld camera pans 180 degrees, capturing graffiti-marked walls covered in stained white plaster, streets lined with rubbish, rusty iron railings, all in soft focus. As the camera follows Totò inside, it reveals concrete floors missing large sections of tile, flaking red paint, moldy walls, dimly lit, open stairwells, and more graffiti. Totò rests his

Figure 2.2. Location, Location, Location. Screen capture, *Gomorrah* (2008), directed by Matteo Garrone.

chin on a scaly red railing and watches as, one floor below him, men distribute drugs through a rusted iron guardrail to anxious men one floor beneath them.

Totò plays with friends in a small wading pool on an expanse of green artificial grass. Now the camera pans up, revealing that the pool is on the rooftop terrace of a large concrete building, and that above it, a Camorra sentinel circulates on another expanse of roof, and another above him, and then others still. An extreme long shot from above captures the ill-kept, multi-storied Vele housing projects, where, over the pool terrace, dirty expanses of rooftop become lookouts for camorristi watching for police.

In its five, interlocking episodes about the Camorra, *Gomorrah* travels across a wide swath of the Neapolitan metropolitan area, its suburban periphery, and the neighboring countryside. The film recounts events surrounding a war of secession within a Camorra clan and exposes how the crime syndicate's priorities dictate the way life unfolds in and around the city. It focuses on a series of different human actors: the foolhardy and ambitious Marco and Ciro, who aspire to Scarface-like greatness; Don Ciro, a money carrier for the Camorra; Pasquale, a frustrated tailor who agrees to give sewing classes in a Chinese garment workshop; Totò, a young Camorra initiate; and Franco and Roberto, who traffic waste of all kinds. Location is also decidedly a protagonist in *Gomorrah*, and a number of the film's locations, framed in dramatic long and extreme long shots by Garrone's painterly eye, recall the industrial aesthetic in *Red Desert*. Some of these shots include the above-described housing complex, but the Antonioniesque style is most evident in episodes starring Franco and Roberto, the former a middleman (or in Camorra language, a "stakeholder"), who navigates between organized crime bosses and industries looking to dispose cheaply of toxic and other waste, and the latter, his young protégé. Long shots and extreme long shots of Franco and Roberto at the port of Naples, or emerging from underground gas tanks at an abandoned gas station, tend to de-center the human protagonists, showing how the scale of industrial operations—and the magnitude of industrial waste—dwarf anthropic action. Strong architectural lines cut across the frame, showing an attention to stark, structural beauty that recalls many frames in the 1964 film.

Dirty discourse and dirty images are prevalent in the segments featuring Franco and Roberto, too. Aside from the Venice trip and the assurances that their dirty business is "tutto clean," other episodes feature Roberto dusting himself off after climbing out of an underground gas tank; trucks circling around a dusty quarry where a bulldozer is moving dirt into terraces; an elderly woman who calls Roberto to "clean up the countryside"; and a frame of Franco gesturing expressively at rows of terraced earth. In these episodes, the instability between dirty and clean plays out in complex ways: the not-yet-criminalized hazards in *Red Desert,* including toxic smoke and petroleum-laced waters, in *Gomorrah* take their place in a globalized circulation of goods and capital that embraces legality, semi-legality, and, implicitly or not, illegality.[15] The enterprising Franco, equally comfortable speaking Neapolitan with a Camorra boss, French with a captain at the port, or standard Italian punctuated by English words with a businessman in Venice, represents a new class of neoliberal manager, a generation or two beyond Corrado and Ugo in the earlier film. *Gomorrah*'s Naples is continuous with *Red Desert*'s Ravenna, connected by the flows of the Mediterranean Sea and by the persistence of industrial toxins in a post-industrial landscape.[16] Yet rather than nod to the exploitation of laborers and the (perhaps) inadvertently toxic byproducts of industry, as *Red Desert* does, *Gomorrah* shows global capitalism's reliance on black market labor and its ruthless contamination of the environments of those who are too poor or too marginal to protest. Its episodic structure weaves a fabric of continuity between the exploitation of landscapes and the disregard for human and more-than-human life, as well as complicity between interwoven black, white, and gray economies.[17]

The scene at the port of Naples has particular symbolic and socio-political significance, showing a city at the crossroads of international crime, global capital, and global environmental crisis; in material terms, it is the place where the "dirty" earth meets the fluid sea. Franco and Roberto emerge from a container at the port in hazmat suits, material and symbolic skins shielding them from the substances they traffic. Franco, impeccably dressed in a tan linen ensemble under his fluorescent green protective suit, speaks with the captain of a ship, shaking hands and signing a confirmation that the container carries "humanitarian aid." Franco's job disposing of toxic waste consists not only of burying it in the Neapolitan countryside, but also shipping it overseas, possibly to Africa. In this practice, his business strategy reflects standard global practice in waste management.[18] Rob Nixon's (2011, 1) landmark study, *Slow Violence and the Environmentalism of the Poor*, opens with the shocking disclosure of a confidential memo written in 1991 by Lawrence Summers, at the time president of the World Bank: "I think the economic logic behind dumping a load of toxic waste in the lowest-wage country is impeccable and we should face up to that. . . . I've always thought that countries in Africa are vastly under polluted [. . .]. Just between you and me, shouldn't the World Bank be encouraging more migration of the dirty industries to the Least Developed Countries?" This affirmation, writes Nixon, is articulated "in the calm voice of global managerial reasoning" (1), and reflects a deeply troubling dirt binary. Cleaning up rich nations involves dumping unsightly and unhealthy waste "onto the world's poorest continent," creating a "direct link between aesthetically unsightly waste and Africa as an out-of-sight continent" (2).[19]

The fact that bogus "humanitarian aid" is being sent abroad from Naples signals another form of myopia dominating the port city, however, where the socio-political gaze fails to see, or address, human and more-than-human need within the city's borders and along its outskirts. While Franco's "aid" sets sail from the port, an earthly sort of harbor also exists in the city's interior and features in the film. Two of the five episodes are set in the housing project in the neighborhood of Scampia known as *Le Vele*, or "The Sails," and the large multi-family structures occupy significant narrative and visual space. Don Ciro, a money carrier for the Camorra, and Totò, a young boy moving to take an active role in the criminal world, appear in segments that rotate around a bloody war of secession between factions, a war largely played out on the concrete walkways of the housing complex. Nicknamed for their sail-like shapes, the Vele are located about 10 kilometers north of the port of Naples, and thus are peripheral with regard to the city center and its maritime edge. As the story of this housing project reveals, though, Le Vele and the challenges it faces are closely tied to both the liquid flows of global capital and the telluric makeup of the Italian interior.

The Scampia episodes of the film are somewhat grimy in terms of aesthetic quality, reflecting the "earthly" foundations of the neighborhood's difficulties.[20] In the scenes featuring Totò cited at the beginning of this section, but also in numerous others, the housing complex is framed to capture broken, leaking pipes and tubing, rusty railings, dirty puddles of water, and formerly white walls darkened by air pollution and wear. The "dirtiness" of this suburban cityscape is both historic and metaphorical, rooted in dirty politics and disregard for real dirt. In the recent past, Scampia was primarily dirt: prior to 1960, what is now a populous suburb was a rural area on the edge of Naples. Singer-songwriter Enzo Avitabile vividly captures the transition from farmland to a well-armed drug market when he sings of his neighborhood in dialect: "Ave Maria, ie veng acopp' Scampia / addo 'na vota era canapa / mo spade e neve pe' a via" (Ave Maria, I come from Scampia, where once there was hemp, and now there are 'swords' and 'snow' on the street).[21] The Vele complex, a government-sponsored INA-Casa housing project, was designed by architect Franz Di Salvo and built between 1962 and 1975 (Ghirardo 2013, 163).[22] Celebrated as a work of Italian avantgarde architecture in the style of Le Corbusier and Kenzo Tange, the buildings that comprise Le Vele are simultaneously lauded for their "technical and aesthetic qualities" and decried as being "uninhabitable" (Benedetto Gravagnuolo qtd. in Ghirardo 2013, 164). Ghirardo explains, regarding low-cost housing in Italy, that many innovative works of architecture failed spectacularly because they disregarded histories of Italian urban spaces and the way Italians actually lived (164).[23] In the case of Le Vele, what was supposed to be an intelligent part of the city's Master Plan quickly succumbed to significant failings. First of all, although the planned public housing was at least partially completed, it was intended to be part of a neighborhood with integrated social services, including infrastructure and office districts. When funding fell short, all but the housing part of the plan fell through, leaving a neighborhood with a dearth of municipal services and poorly connected to the city center. Now, De Muro, Di Martino, and Cavola (2007, 227) describe Le Vele (evoking an apt maritime metaphor) as a "series of concrete islands" that lack "collective areas for relaxing, such as parks, gardens, piazzas," and have scant public facilities.[24] The crumbling concrete, evidence of "premature urban and social decay" (225) marks a material disintegration, or what Iovino (2009, 340) calls "the underground destiny of civilization and of the city itself." The housing project is on an accelerated timeline for returning to dirt once more.

Dirt, or earth, figured in the history of Le Vele in another significant moment, specifically, when an earthquake struck a mountainous area in the regions of Campania and Basilicata on November 23, 1980. The seismic shock (magnitude 6.8 on the Richter scale) rocked the ground in Naples, too; aside from nearly 2800 fatalities, it left 280,000 people homeless, 50,000 of these in the city of Naples (Chubb 2002, 214).[25] In the ensuing months and years, Naples became a center for the homeless and displaced, groups in which, as too often happens in "natural" disasters, the poor were overrepresented.[26] With thousands of homes reduced to rubble, the not-quite-completed Vele housing projects were occupied—in many cases, illegally—by those who had nowhere else to go (De Muro, Di Martino, and Cavola 2007, 224–25). The seven apartment blocks housed between 40,000 and 70,000 people, with authoritative counts uncertain as officials have historically been reluctant to enter to verify the numbers (Ghirardo 2013, 163). The dense population is varied and complex. In a study sponsored by the European Union, Giovanni Laino and Daniela De Leo (2002) categorized the residents of the Vele projects thus: those assigned public housing, homeowners, illegal occupants of unfinished public housing, *scantinatisti* or squatters living in the partially underground first floors, and Roma from the nomadic camps.[27] Although its human population is not monolithic, in many ways, the Vele housing complex is a landscape of the dispossessed. The population is younger than the city's average, and disproportionately unemployed (6–7). Rates of criminality and drug use are also higher than elsewhere in Naples (7). In part because it is disconnected but not distant from the city center, Scampia is an ideal location for what is one of the largest open-air drug markets in the world. For Corona and Sciarrone (2012, 14), the resulting landscape (which includes the "immense metropolitan area around the capital city," and not just Le Vele) is lonely, dysfunctional, and perilously dirty: it is "the image of a landscape dotted with improvised constructions, disconnected from public services and infrastructure, fragments of city without piazzas or sidewalks, scraps of rural land that are no longer cultivated, open sewers, mountains of abandoned trash, stinky waste dumps." As of 2018, three of the original seven housing blocks had been demolished. Although there are plans in the works to bulldoze three more of the buildings, the process is a "chess game," reports local media, because hundreds of families still occupy the buildings and lack the means to go elsewhere. Vibrant, crowded, and decaying, Le Vele and its inhabitants reflect multiple understandings of waste: "something to which no future is bestowed," and also "something thrown out, excluded, discarded" (Iovino 2009, 341).

Gomorrah's opening scene garishly stages the myopia of Camorra-style short-term thinking. Shot in bright fluorescent colors in a beauty and tanning salon, one camorrista is getting a manicure, and a close-up shows a nail tech cleaning his fingernails. Garrone repeatedly exposes the Camorra's obsession with appearance, from manicures to collective shopping sprees, and scenes such as this one suggest the sanitized, "clean" image that gangsters attempt to project. Yet much like the bloodbath that ends this homosocial grooming appointment, Le Vele expose the fact that while "clean" may be a personal aesthetic choice, grit is the order of the day when the Camorra is in charge. In the *mala-architettura*, or infernal architecture of Le Vele, Totò and Don Ciro move through the long open-air walkways and multi-storied structures exposing the Camorra's panop-tical hold on the territory and the fragility or aggressive danger inherent in its public spaces.[28] Don Ciro circulates around the extended gangways, delivering money to Camorra families whose members have been incar-cerated. Following his meanderings, Millicent Marcus (2016, 310) argues that the architectural structure serves "as the objective correlative for the Camorra's sovereign power over its subjects." The above-described shot of Totò in the wading pool, even more nefariously, shows how the most promising public spaces can be "swallowed up by the vast and malignant reach of the architecture that has come to embody Camorra rule" (312). In fact most all of the spaces in the film are tainted by criminality and blood. The spare open area where Totò plays on a motor scooter with a friend, and where residents of Le Vele gather to flirt and dance, is the site of a drive-by Camorra execution; parking garages and walkways are plat-forms from which doses of drugs are handed out; one apartment has been bombed or burned to its concrete bones; Don Ciro knocks on the door of another, which falls in; the walkways between apartments are stained by the blood of Totò's friend's mother Maria and other camorristi killed by secessionists. Against the backdrop of the broken, decaying housing pro-ject, public failings stain public space and make it dangerous to use.

The landscape of fear and mistrust that feature in Le Vele is endemic in the globalized world, argues Zygmunt Bauman (2004), and key to its untamed expansion and deregulation. "Without trust," warns Bauman, "the web of human commitments falls apart, making the world a yet more dangerous and fearsome place" (92). Le Vele's haphazard construction and occupation, which built in a future of neglect, isolation, and dirty common spaces, contributed to the collapse of the web of human commitment, as *Gomorrah* amply illustrates. The dystopian dirty politics offends the more-than-human landscape as well, entangling humans, nonhumans, and dust in a crisis that threatens the integrity of each and the vital relationships of interdependence that link them.

Wasted Scenes: Ecomafia, Toxic Waste, and Toxic Media

Ominous red and yellow mud bubbles and gasses at the base of a looming, unfinished concrete skeleton of a building. As the camera wanders around the construction site, Franco reassures a man in a business suit that they will drain the water and disguise the toxic stench by planting an orange grove.

Dense black smoke emanates from a pile of rubbish and old tires as the camera shoots from overhead, filming in the path of the smoke. In a tighter frame, children play in the trash heap, picking out plush toys and discarded wallets. The camera cuts back to the shot from above, as an elegant black Volkswagen SUV drives up and all the kids get in.

The two episodes described above do not appear in the film *Gomorrah*, but on the Criterion Edition second disk, they are available for viewing as "deleted scenes." The first of these two locations, chosen for the scene where Franco strategizes about how to mask smells and runoff at a housing project being constructed on toxic mud, was the most—perhaps the only—scary one for the production to film, according to Aquino. Whereas the crew felt largely welcome in the Camorra-run Vele projects, this less populous, less obviously notorious site felt somewhat touchy. Since the crew needed to use a real construction site, and since many such sites around Campania are run by Camorra bosses, Aquino felt that it was among the most risky to capture on camera. Someone powerful, in short, could have been offended.[29]

These scenes bring us to the fact that the earthquake—that continental movement of dirt—had another significant effect on the area around Campania: it was in the wake of the 1980 seismic disaster that massive amounts of reconstruction funds and contracts for huge recovery projects landed in the hands of the Camorra (Ghirardo 2013, 163).[30] The earthquake itself had already brought some questionable construction practices to light: various multistory buildings collapsed in the quake, which Chubb (2002, 214) cites as "testimony to widespread corruption in the construction industry and

Figure 2.3. Wasted Scenes. Screen capture, *Gomorrah* (2008), directed by Matteo Garrone. DVD extra materials, The Criterion Collection.

violation of anti-seismic building codes." Yet after the earthquake, money and concrete began flowing more freely. The impact of such movement of finances and materials should not be underestimated. Calling cement "Southern Italy's crude oil," Saviano (2007, 214) argues that "[c]ement gives birth to everything. Every economic empire that arises in the south passes through the construction business: bids, contracts, quarries, cement, components, bricks, scaffolding, workers." Most of the INA-Casa projects, and certainly Le Vele, were constructed by "a building industry newly enamoured of reinforced concrete and precast concrete" (Ghirardo 2013, 152). But cement and construction empires are built on subtraction, the removal of earth and building materials from one place to raise up another. The Camorra, taking into account each business opportunity along the construction chain, saw that void as an opening. It is no coincidence that the 1980 earthquake is also cited as the moment when the ecomafias emerged as a force, a logical extension of organized crime's work in concrete, earth moving, and urban waste removal.[31] Where construction emptied rural areas of their raw materials, managers like Franco filled them back in with industrial waste from elsewhere in Italy and Europe. Franco tellingly reassures the shady cement magnate in a quarry, "Don't worry. You emptied it, and I'll fill it for you." The rising expanse of concrete that comprises the housing project exists in an inverse but complicit relationship to the empty quarries that Franco and Roberto scout for toxic waste dumping. Moving earth out of the countryside, making cement, building housing projects, leaving them to decay, filling the empty spaces with toxic waste: a catastrophic, dirty thread links criminality in Le Vele and the contamination of the country-side around Naples. When there is no room in the quarries, dumps, and fields, the resourceful criminal bosses can mix toxic waste into cement and asphalt to construct roads and buildings, completing the toxic cycle (*Ecomafia* 2014, 136–37).[32] Campania's ecomafia "destroyed [. . .] the natural base from which, historically, the main sources of well-being spring: the fertile earth, natural beauty, alimentary and artisanal traditions, historic identities, cultural and artistic excellence" (Corona and Sciarrone 2012, 21). The Legambiente provocatively refers to the criminal dumping of toxic waste as "ecocide" (*Ecomafia* 2014, 131). In 2014, the organization declared that more than 220 hectares of earth in the *Terra dei fuochi*, the Land of Fires in the provinces of Naples and Caserta where the practices of dumping and burning waste have been rampant, are now *terra morta*: dead earth (131).[33]

Dead human bodies proliferate throughout *Gomorrah*, legacy of the Camorra's war of secession, but human deaths in the film were fictional; frames of the dead earth were not. As part of their location scouting, the production crew toured the Land of Fires and other toxic areas of Campania with outspoken activist Raffaele Del Giudice, former director of Legambiente Campania and an impassioned presence in documentaries about the ecomafia including *Biùtiful cauntri* (2008). They also were escorted to sites of toxic dumping by the State Forestry Corps, who have been responsible for some of the most significant investigations of waste dumping. In the dumps, De Lazzaris reports that the crew put on dust masks, which are prevalent in the documentary films about the ecomafia where they are worn by Del Giudice and others, even though they are insufficient to shield human bodies from tiny toxic particulate matter. Aquino says that the crew was aware of the risks of filming in areas where asbestos had been dumped, but De Lazzaris said she was not concerned about spending time in the toxic landscape. "We are not risking anything," agreed Bonfini, arguing that the film crew inhabits these spaces for a short period of time and thus limits their exposure to the hazards.

No matter the length of the exposure, *Gomorrah*'s narrative content and its engagement with contaminated territories embed all kinds of cinematic actors in a landscape where invisible trans-corporeal flows endanger human and more-than-human lives. While at least some of the film crew felt exposed when filming on a construction site in the suburbs of Naples—exposed, that is, to the powerful panoptical gaze of the Camorra—the periods spent filming in scarcely populated rural areas were perhaps more hazardous to their health. In locations like the burning dump described at the beginning of this section, "exposing" the celluloid to capture the image paralleled bodily exposure to invisible toxins. When the crew visited and filmed in the waste dump described at the beginning of this section, where the dark black smoke of burning tires provides visual evidence of unhealthy airborne substances (including dioxins), the toxic particulate would not have been captured only on film but also, inevitably, in the air passages and lungs and eventually cells of anyone on hand to act in the scenes or help film them. As Stacy Alaimo (2010, 18) recalls regarding hazardous waste, "all that scary stuff, supposedly out there, is already within." "Exposure," that moment when celluloid captures the imprint of the world on film, here becomes a sign of the film industry's passage through the bodies of actors, crew, and earth. And in rural Campania the earth, according to Legambiente, has been laced with poison (*Ecomafia* 2014, 136).

Studies focused on Campania have identified arsenic, dioxin, cadmium, mercury, and lead in bodies of water and human and nonhuman bodies in the region. Cancerous tumors, precocious puberty, endometriosis, sterility, and thyroid problems are some of the conditions on the rise in areas where significant illegal dumping has occurred. Yet it is important to note that most of the dangerous substances that contaminate food, water, air, and dirt in Campania are invisible to the human eye. This means that Campania's ecological and socio-political crises are also crises of representation, or in the case of *Gomorrah*, cinematic crises. Alaimo (2010, 71, 72) argues that, "our most basic sense of the material world is that it is self-evident, apparent, substantial, and visible," but underlines that "many EJ [environmental justice] problems cannot be visually discerned nor photographically documented."[34] *Gomorrah* plays at the edges of visibility, strategically disclosing the distorted gaze of those who traffic toxic waste and the lengths to which they go to hide the poisonous traces of their work. The segments starring Franco and Roberto, as I have discussed elsewhere, challenge us both visually and narratively to see what is not in the frame. The pair are audible but not visible when they explore underground gas tanks; they are suspicious of toxic traces on what seem to be beautiful peaches; they examine digital photographs of seemingly vast landscapes and conclude that they are "too small" for the quantities of waste they need to dump. On these occasions and others, *Gomorrah* deliberately unmasks the limits of vision in a toxic landscape. By the same token, my interviews with the crew reinforce how hard it is to keep toxic emergencies cognitively present, even when your job involves bringing them to light.

The play of waste, invisibility, and toxicity resonates at an even deeper level in the film, however. In Saviano's (2007) version of the scene at the dump in the book *Gomorrah*, the author describes the technique for burning trash in the "Land of Fires," using obsolete VHS tapes as fuses:

> Gypsy boys are the best at it. The clans give them 50 euros for each mound burned. The technique is simple. They circumscribe each hill with videocassette tapes, pour alcohol and gas all over it, twist the tape ends to form an enormous fuse, then move away, putting a cigarette lighter to the fuse. In a few seconds there's a forest of flames, as if they'd launched napalm bombs. They throw foundry remnants, glue, and naphtha dregs into the fire. Dense black smoke and flames contaminate every inch of land with dioxins. (296)

In *Gomorrah*'s final cut, the young boys from the deleted scene at the dump emerge from Franco's SUV in the episode at the quarry, when they are recruited to drive trucks of toxic waste from the top ridge down to the bottom. Thus the children still take their places in the landscape of toxic waste, volunteers called to literally drive their own future into the ground. Yet deleting the scene at the dump, and choosing not to film the children's use of VHS tapes-as-fuses, creates an intriguing subterranean dialogue with film's own complicity with toxic waste.

In the scenes at the dump in Saviano's book and Garrone's film, disposable children, chosen to perform toxic tasks too dangerous for adults, encounter the problems of the digital age in metaphorical and material ways. First, there is the analogous problem of the toxicity, disposability, and obsolescence of technology, a problem endemic to *Gomorrah* and to all films. While Garrone chose to film on 35-mm celluloid film stock, his film circulates beyond theaters via streaming, clips on YouTube, DVD, etc. It thus straddles analog and digital technologies and exists as part of a contemporary debate on the longevity and environmental impact of each. In its analog format, *Gomorrah* relies on celluloid film, the creation of which requires large volumes of clean water and a whole range of chemicals. As Maxwell and Miller (2012a, 278) demonstrate, Kodak Park in Rochester, New York, which supplied 80 percent of the global supply of film stock at the end of the twentieth century, was a primary source of pathogens in New York state, especially dioxins. Workers making film stock were exposed to acids and acid vapors and developed respiratory problems (279).

The digital formats in which *Gomorrah* the film circulates—for example, streaming on an array of possible devices, from cellphones to tablets to laptops and large screen televisions—might seem ephemeral, created as they are from binary codes of 1s and 0s. Yet digital technologies rely on the material world and impact it in decidedly enduring ways. As Elizabeth Grossman (2006, 5) has illustrated, "digital wizardry relies on a complex array of materials: metals, elements, plastics, and chemical compounds. Each tidy piece of equipment has a story that begins in mines, refineries, factories, rivers, and aquifers and ends on pallets, in dumpsters, and in landfills all around the world."[35] When electronics become obsolete, are physically damaged, or dismantled, the toxic elements within them are released into the world (5). In *Gomorrah*, the VHS tapes that we do not see burning in the garbage pile are remnants of obsolete technologies and the cinematic past. As they are destroyed, however, in the ways described by Saviano, they leave lingering and toxic traces of their passage on the earth. Burning VHS tapes, composed of plastic, metals, and binders, would release hazardous gases and vapors including ammonia, carbon monoxide, and hydrogen cyanide. These substances, evoked memorably in the form of the burning videocassettes in Saviano's book, are a spectral presence in the later cinematic rendering of the Land of Fires. As film crew and celluloid film stock pass through the toxic countryside, the residues of former analog and digital technologies become part of their embodied histories. They also speak to the technologies' future as high-tech trash, circulating in a global marketplace that will dismantle and recycle some of their component parts, even as the earth and our bodies absorb some others.

The fact that the above-described scenes and several others were not included in the final version of the film, that they were in effect "wasted" or converted into "waste" themselves, makes the cinematic garbage discussed at the beginning of this chapter a strangely coherent part of *Gomorrah*. In the editing process, when scenes are eliminated, we say that they end on the "cutting room floor," evoking images of discarded filmstrips cluttering film studios and, later, landfills. Bozak (2012, 159) argues that filmmaking and sculpting are both "premised on elimination, paring away, cutting down, and then discarding the unnecessary waste that envelops the piece of perfection hidden within." Yet the practice of including "extra materials" and in particular "deleted scenes" with commercial DVDs means that waste can be recycled, incorporated both as trash and as visual material with a coherent presence in the film's paratactic narrative universe. The critical play of presence and absence in a toxic landscape resonates strongly with a work filmed on location. Whether exposed for a long time or not, a film crew working in the Land of Fires encounters toxic waste, breathes it in, incorporates traces of it into its collective body. And a film focusing on that same landscape "captures" that waste, and also creates it. This level of entanglement and trans-corporeal exchange, between film, film crew, and filming location, means that even "deleted scenes," the detritus of a cinematic production, are valuable and enduring parts of the final moving picture. In *Gomorrah*, where these deleted scenes play against the evocatively cinematic moments in Saviano's account, the image's toxic waste stream unveils the hazards bubbling beneath Camorra building sites and Camorra-inspired films.

Democracy, Dirt, and Storytelling: Maria and Silvana

Totò enters an apartment through an open door and greets a caged monkey, Silvana, by name. "Si pùo?" [May I come in?] he asks the humans within, repeatedly. Maria does not hear him over her own laughter. She and another woman are preparing food in the small kitchen, where streaks of sunlight illuminate the peachy-tan cabinets, cheery tiles, and collection of magnets. Disarray on the counter and table seems to have accumulated as they prepare food. A pan shot captures the adjoining living room, where women gathered around a table deal cards and chat, children play on the floor, and a television flickers in the background.

Using a stranger's bathroom; accepting an offer from a drug pusher to help you carry heavy camera equipment up seven flights of stairs; inadvertently creating a cover for drug dealers who sell in the middle of your film production because the police leave them alone when you are around. As De Lazzaris explained to me, during the filming of *Gomorrah*, residents of Le Vele extended a generous hospitality to the crew.[36] While other episodes involved more changes of location and briefer intervals spent filming on location (only three or four hours near dawn at the Port of Naples, for example), the crew spent days at a time in and around Le Vele, getting to know spaces and residents and getting dirty.[37] Besides opening their doors, some residents of the housing complex also took advantage of the crew's presence to deal (and at times use) heroin, crack, and cocaine, and even to spin novel tales of Camorra hits.[38] In order to film on location, "you have to really create relationships. If not, it doesn't work," argued De Lazzaris. But relationships are inevitably complicated.

Pauline Small (2011, 122) argues convincingly that Le Vele is the central set in the film *Gomorrah*, a space with a privileged relationship to the narrative, and also asserts that "though ostensibly open to the street, the space of the tower block is effectively wholly controlled, thus legitimizing its definition

Figure 2.4. Democratic Storytelling. Screen capture, *Gomorrah* (2008), directed by Matteo Garrone.

as the circumscribed set." As the interwoven narrative threads unwind, people in the film gradually begin closing their doors to those who knock. Most notably, Maria, whose door had initially been left unlocked, barricades herself behind several layers of iron gates after her secessionist son exposes her to the danger of Camorra retribution. For Small, shots of the caged monkey, Silvana, and frames of drug buyers pushing money through grates "may be read as a visual metaphor that extends to all those on the estate, living as if in enclosed cells (or sub-sets) accessed by means of bolts, bars, and gates" (123). Through the sets, suggests Small, and particularly by way of movement through Le Vele, Garrone shows his "indictment of the Mafia-dominated life from which none of [his] screen characters can escape" (125). That such a closed set represents the claustrophobic gridlock of life in Camorra territory seems convincing, especially when characters like Maria, who begin locking their doors, are betrayed and brutally murdered by people to whom those doors were originally opened. In one sense, it seems that there is indeed "no way out" for inhabitants of Le Vele, as the title of Small's study argues. Yet in this final section, I propose that dirt and dirt theory offer a significant way in.

While I focused above on Le Vele as a significant "place" in Naples, and then on locations of the toxic crisis, returning to dirt theory helps to shift the focus back, as Sullivan (2012, 515) suggests dirt can, from place to process. Traveling with airborne dirt particles across Campania from toxic waste sites to decaying public housing projects, we trace connections between the Irpinia earthquake, life in Le Vele, Camorra violence, and the work of aggressive stakeholders who seek profit at any cost. Such an entangled itinerary locates the dirty building walls at the encounter of political disinterest in the poor suburbs of Naples and the active contamination of living and agricultural spaces by corrupt politicians and Camorra bosses. Yet in these spaces, we also see the potentials for connectedness as resistance, a connectedness equally rooted in dirt. These potentials have been realized in many ways in Campania by environmental justice movements, efforts that Marco Armiero (2014) has powerfully shown are alive and well and that protest the despoiling of the dirt upon which the protestors' food systems, cultural traditions, health, and very lives rely. Armiero argues that such movements articulate and live philosophies of connectedness: "environmental justice activists, in Campania as everywhere, are able to see the connections linking places, bodies, power and science; defending their neighbourhoods, they defend their health, they challenge the 'normal science,' and they criticize the power relationships among groups and territories" (175). Documentaries about the waste crisis, including *La bambina deve prendere aria* (*The Baby Needs Some Fresh Air*, dir. Barbara Rossi Prudente, 2008), *Biùtiful cauntri* (dir. Esmeralda Calabria, Andrea D'Ambrosio, Peppe Ruggiero, 2008), *Una montagna di balle* (*A Mountain of Lies*, dir. nicol* angrisano, 2009), and *Campania infelix* (*Unhappy Country*, dir. Ivana Corsale, 2010), foreground these powerful connections, the voices that articulate them, and the collectives where the courage to contest the ecomafia is born.[39] In *Gomorrah*, the environmental justice movement does not have a specific narrative presence, but the film hints at alternative forms of connectedness, collaborations that are critically dependent on knowing how to tell stories.

Such a potential alternative collective and its link to Campania's dirt is rooted in *Gomorrah*'s radically slow cinematic pace, a pace that contrasts sharply with the career impatience of the camorrista. The impetuous gangsters Marco and Ciro, for example, whose models are cinematic and American (and specifically Al Pacino's Scarface), move through life in a drug-induced frenzy, seeking adventure and their next high. In the final frames of the film, they hurry to their death on a motorcycle, and speed hastens their demise. Reduced at last to human waste, their limp bodies are carried away in the indifferent bucket of a front-loader. The quest for speed and for instant gratification is not unique to the Camorra, of course, but also underlies the logic of profit; it is a familiar target in studies of modernity. Slow Food founder Carlo Petrini (2007, 18) (following Jérôme Bindé of UNESCO) calls such behavior the "tyranny of urgency," explaining that it "creates a new ideology which denies and conceals the complexity of the world and of the relations and interdependences that characterize it."

It is thus all the more significant that, unlike certain canonical action-packed gangster films, and in spite of its fracturing into multiple narrative sequences, the film often lingers over peripheral subjects and narratives. Whether in long tracking shots following Ciro the money carrier down the passageways of Le Vele, lengthy scenes of camorristi meticulously filling tiny capsules with white powdery drugs for later sale, or banal conversations between adolescent friends as they serve as lookouts, *Gomorrah* captures organized crime as an unromantic quotidian affair that intersperses violent shootouts with tedious work, and that exists in the midst of daily life.[40] By way of this slow pace, the world's complexity has time to re-emerge, as it does in Maria's apartment. This scene is particularly noteworthy for its evocation of a convivial life around the table, and for the meaningful connections between neighbors and friends. Although brief, it offers a glimpse of Le Vele that upends the notion of its infernal isolation from the rest of the city. Here, private space is also public, and the neighborhood can gather around the table for nourishment and play. Maria's apartment is the place where, with Donna Haraway (2008, 17), we recognize as "companions" the people with whom we share bread. *Gomorrah*'s micronarrative of conviviality suggests that, within Le Vele, and alongside the logic of the Camorra, there also exists a quality that Petrini (2007, 241) lauds in elaborating the importance of food justice, a "logic of *giving freely* where there is no utilitarian exchange, but a mutual giving of knowledge, hospitality, opportunities, tastes, visions of the world, and educational elements." This kind of knowledge is fundamental in Campania, where the agricultural and culinary traditions are an enduring part of regional and global culture. However fleeting, the moment around the table echoes through *Gomorrah*, albeit usually in more tragic ways. Franco's final insult to Roberto as the young man decides to leave the toxic waste disposal business is culinary, "go become a pizza maker," and it occurs as Franco waves his hands at rows of terraced earth, that dirt on whose health contemporary Italian society in many ways will rise and fall.

While conviviality did not last in the cinematic narrative, and Maria was betrayed by someone to whom she extended hospitality, there was a strong, embodied experience of geniality in the process of filming on location in Le Vele. The crew's relationship to Le Vele demonstrated that the space of hospitality extended beyond individual apartments, as they immersed themselves in a location that most Neapolitans—not to speak of outsiders—strategically avoid. From the stories Aquino, Bonfini, and De Lazzaris told me, we might infer that the early scene in Maria's apartment most closely reflects the experience of the crew on location in Scampia: largely an experience of unselfish teamwork, and an experience that the rest of the film suggests is sorely lacking where the Camorra reigns. Yet this level of imbrication in a landscape scarred by criminality did not come without its costs. Garrone (2009, 120–21) recognizes that the crew was "used," observing that while people often think that cinema takes advantage of people, here he was "pleased" to see that sometimes the roles can be reversed. Scriptwriter Maurizio Braucci (2009, 108) suggests that the film "inherited" many of the contradictions that reign in Scampia, at times making mistakes, sometimes doing good. There were accusations that the film must have paid "pizzo," or protection money, to be able to film in Le Vele (although they deny this). As I was drafting this chapter, Gennaro Aquino was the object of an investigation into his involvement, as location manager, with the television series *Gomorra*. He and other members of the production company Cattleya were accused of having paid rent to a Camorra boss to film in a villa (Abbate and Tizzian 2014).

Yet how does one make a film about the Camorra, in Camorra territory, without entering into a gray area, when the entire landscape is gray? This might sound like an apology for the production crew, but they are unapologetic in describing their experience, and this is part of the way in which the production returns to dirt. Here, film industry, film production, and film set encounter the material and symbolic dirt that composes *Gomorrah*, where ecologies, politics, narrative arts, and dirt come together to make a film. Here, we cross the threshold into what Pasquale Verdicchio (2011, 115) calls the "uncomfortable space" where all participants, including viewers, are "co-responsible agents."[41] De Lazzaris describes getting dirty on set, and she outlines arguably gray practices that linked the production with the landscape of Le Vele. Yet how to haul heavy equipment through the dirty stairwells of an aging apartment complex without getting dirt on your hands? And how to film stories about this space on location without collaborating with its inhabitants? Armiero (2014, 176) has argued that the environmental justice movement in Campania has had to engage in a practice that he calls, following Jason Corburn, "street science," or that we might, as a rough equivalent, call "dirty research." Armiero elaborates:

> Lay people know through stories, smells, smoke and experiences; they have drawn maps of contaminations and illness; they have collected medical records which testify to years of exposure to toxins; nevertheless, they aim at translating [. . .] that knowledge within a scientific discourse. Hence, activists'

knowledge, or as Corburn defines it, 'street science' does not deny the necessity of official science, rather it seeks to influence the agenda of scientific research; what is denied is the neutral character of science and technology and the theoretically apolitical nature of the researcher. (176)

In analogous fashion, also discussing the crisis in Naples, Iovino (2014b, 152) argues that: "Here, each thing that lives, from the earth to our bodies' cells, is connected to all the rest, and the culture that wants to make us perceive these elements as distant is a culture of guilty abstractions." Rather than remain guilty of abstraction, the crew of *Gomorrah* risked guilt by association by entering Le Vele and befriending many of its residents. They chose to rely on the networks of residents rather than on the police (as film crews often do), because, as Braucci (2009, 107) explains, "this would have created a filter with the people, who are unfortunately used to institutional disinterest. That's what made Scampia what it is today."

In a moving essay about her native city of Naples, Iovino (2014b) observes her position as a "situated" scholar, recognizing the material positioning of her thought and her gaze. Her thought, "situated" though it is, moves between Naples (where she grew up), Turin (where she lives and works), and the world, through the wide reach of her scholarship. Nomadic and located at the same time, she and her work return frequently to Naples to observe and analyze the toxic crisis, a crisis of ecological and sociopolitical citizenship, and so her abstract and equally Neapolitan notion of situated analysis bears lengthy citation here. Such thinking, she writes:

> cannot help but mix with its object; not to 'pollute' it with a point of view, but to show the depth of the connection between our discourses and the biological, material, ecological reality in which we are situated. As a theoretical physicist, the American Karen Barad, has written, "we are part of that nature which we seek to understand." And thus the only way to truly understand it is not to feign an artificial neutrality, but to identify ourselves in it knowingly, and to listen to its voices. Every form of knowledge depends on this immersion, on this *situation*. [. . .] A *radical* knowledge, which assumes the ethical responsibility of the point of observation. (151, emphasis in original)

The hospitable potential of Maria's apartment is initially neutralized as the war of secession between families leads her to lock herself inside, and then destroyed when camorristi murder her just outside her door. But the network of relationships that the production crew relied upon to shoot those scenes of Maria created something different: a collaborative, if ideologically complex, network of cinematic storytellers able to recount a tale of hospitality in Le Vele. When Maria is murdered, in fact, the crime scene is shot in part from above, a position that perhaps would have required De Lazzaris to accept the aid of residents to help lug some camera equipment to an upper story of one of the buildings. *Gomorrah* builds its grim visual landscape on another kind of story, the kind of radical, situated knowledge that for Iovino is critical to ethical responsibility: the kind of knowledge that comes from accepting the hospitality of others.

Both *Gomorrah* the book and *Gomorrah* the film help recount the stories that explain the crisis in Le Vele, and the ways in which the wider urban crisis connects to political and ecological emergencies, to food, water, air, and dirt. In her study of Hurricane Katrina and the devastation left in its wake, Tuana (2008, 189) argues that "the knowledge that is too often missing and is often desperately needed is at the intersection between things and people, between feats of engineering and social structures, between experiences and bodies." This kind of knowledge, although partial, temporally bounded, and controversial, was gleaned by the crew of *Gomorrah* and the residents of Scampia as they worked together to make a film. Roberto Saviano immersed himself in Camorra culture to write his overtly political book, yet he did so while disguising himself as a member of the System and now must live under police protection. The filmmakers, as collective, instead entered Le Vele specifically as narrators—not investigators—ready to relate stories of their encounters. Living at the intersection of cinematic narrative power, institutional power, Camorra power, and a culture of dispossession, the film helps perform the critical work Stacy Alaimo (2010, 22) attributes to her theory of trans-corporeality: it encourages us "to imagine ourselves in constant interchange with the environment and, paradoxically perhaps, to imagine an epistemological space that allows for both the unpredictable becomings of other creatures and the limits of human knowledge." One of the key words used to describe the experience on the *Gomorrah* set was "freedom." De Lazzaris said that, unlike in a military-style hierarchy that reigns on certain sets, everyone working with Garrone feels free to offer an opinion (and this included inhabitants of Le Vele). Bonfini agreed that Garrone never forgets that theirs is collective labor, and that everyone in the crew is an important collaborator. This democratic, nonhierarchical style of filmmaking works in opposition to the "thwarted citizenship," both social and environmental, of citizens in Le Vele.[42] In admitting that making a film means getting dirty, the *Gomorrah* crew acknowledges the territorial, social, environmental, and biophysical matter that links their daily life to that of the residents of the on-location shoots, even if some parts of this shared materiality only last for the duration of the film. Working as collectives, eating as collectives, playing cards together, carrying film equipment together, watching films together, are all ways to contest a global consumer culture that makes people, places, and things disposable.

I have now been reading the *Ecomafia* reports for a number of years; on my shelves are reports ranging from 2011 to 2017, and I have been following the toxic crisis since Saviano's *Gomorrah* was published in 2006. As I wrote this chapter, I mentioned to Serenella Iovino my dismay at the fact that the numbers reported for dumping in Campania remained staggering. In the 2017 report, Campania was still by far the biggest regional destination for illegal waste disposal: 936 documented infractions; 1,123 complaints; 28 arrests; 463 sequestrations of property. With characteristic optimism, however, she pointed out that more numbers mean, in some cases, that more of the stories are being told. Iovino (2009, 346) argues that an "ethic of narration" is "an ethic of invention: the invention of a future. [. . .] It is only by mirroring itself into narration that a society may change." And in fact in 2015, a new twist was added to this unfolding narrative: Law 68 in the Italian penal code at last criminalized *ecoreati*, or crimes against the environment. The 2017 Ecomafia Report now records that a series of cases are working their way through the courts, and celebrates: "after so many years, finally an *Ecomafia* report with a positive spin and a precise goal: to continue on the right path" (10). The preface suggests that, at last, there is "light at the end of the tunnel" (11).

Some of that light is reflected through the lenses of film cameras. More investigations, more prosecutions, more awareness—more films, more narratives, more ethical notions of a possible future. Cinema is complicit in stories of toxicity, and cinema also keeps these stories alive. Getting your hands dirty rather than getting a manicure. Getting your hands dirty while making something, rather than burying your head in the sand. Telling a dirty story, that others might be inspired to write a new history of dirt in Campania, an interspecies geo-history that can help make Campania "felix" again.

Notes

1. Gennaro Aquino, interview by author, Rome, April 14, 2013. All information from Aquino was collected during this interview.

2. Greta De Lazzaris, interview by author, Rome, March 28, 2013; Paolo Bonfini, interview by author, Rome, May 21, 2013. All information from De Lazzaris and Bonfini was collected during these interviews.

3. Garrone (2009, 112) insists that "expression is more important than information," and says that while in the film *Gomorrah* there is a "component of social condemnation, it is only one aspect of its various motivations." De Lazzaris confirms that for Garrone, the film's purpose is not political condemnation. The film scholar Pierpaolo Antonello (2011, 378) agrees that "the core of Saviano's social denunciation and which forms the general rhetoric of the book is totally bracketed off in the film."

4. Filmmakers for Conservation is a non-profit organization, while both the Center for Environmental Filmmaking and the Center for Media & Social Impact are projects of the School of Communication at American University in Washington, DC. The Code was created after faculty at the centers conducted a global survey of 175 filmmakers and filmmaking companies, and also carried out interviews and other research (Engel and Buchanan 2009, 1).

5. See the Tempesta Film website for information about EcoMuvi (http://www.tempestafilm.it/en/ecomuvi/). Thank you to Laura Di Bianco, who introduced me to EcoMuvi through her work on Italian ecocinema.

6. Corbett and Turco (2006, 3) hypothesize that this unwillingness to discuss environmental impact is rooted, at least in Los Angeles, in the public visibility of the industry. Environmental problems can create "image" problems in the moving picture industry: "there is a very strong sense that individuals and entire companies succeed or fail based on highly volatile public perception. The public at large does not think of the motion picture industry as polluting or otherwise environmentally harmful, so any publicity related to environmental initiatives within the industry would, in that view, draw attention to the existence of environmental problems that apparently need solving."

7. Citing Corbett and Turco's report, Richard Maxwell and Toby Miller (2012a) emphasize that, in the Los Angeles area, "the motion picture industry is *the biggest producer of conventional pollutants,*" rivaling the aerospace and semiconductor industries in its energy consumption and greenhouse-gas emissions (271–72, emphasis in original).

8. Serrecchia, interview by author, Rome, March 7, 2013.

9. While recognizing that "war, politics, deforestation, and climate change contributed to the societal collapses that punctuate human history" and noting that "the reasons behind the development and decline of any particular civilization are complex," Montgomery (2007, 5) suggests that in the case of the Greek, Roman, and Mayan civilizations, "the history of their dirt set the stage upon which economics, climate extremes, and war influenced their fate. Rome didn't so much collapse as it crumbled, wearing away as erosion sapped the productivity of its homeland."

10. Pratesi (2010, 9), founder of the World Wildlife Fund in Italy, emphasizes further that "no place exists in our country that can be considered 'natural,' that is to say having the appearance and components it would have without the modifications of man."

11. Other activities of the ecomafia include illegal building and excavation. Following on the success of this neologism, as I noted in the introduction, the organization has outlined new categories in order to condemn, specifically, the "agromafia" (illegal activities related to farming), "zoomafia" (illegal trafficking of animals and betting on races and fights, among other things), and "archeomafia" (trafficking in cultural goods). See www.legambiente.it/temi/ecomafia for more information on these emerging categories.

12. It should be noted that for Roberto Saviano (2007, 38–39), the name "Camorra" is a generic term used by judges, journalists, and screenplay writers, whereas members of the organized crime families in Campania instead refer to themselves as part of "The System." Nevertheless, from outside "The System," the term "Camorra" is meaningful in indicating a geographically specific variant of Italian organized crime.

13. For more on the pathways of illegal waste in Campania, see the annual report published by Edizioni Ambiente and curated by the Legambiente that meticulously collects the "stories and numbers of environmental crime."

14. See Gabriella Corona and Rocco Sciarrone's (2012, 14) article on "Il paesaggio delle ecocamorre" ["The landscape of the ecocamorras"] that appears in a special issue of the journal *Meridiana* entirely dedicated to the theme of the ecocamorra, or the "ecomafia" in the region of Campania. The authors argue that the area around Naples represents an "anti-model" of development, manifested in the deteriorated urban and social environment and in violence against people but also against nature and things.

15. David Harvey (2014, 54) argues that capital must be understood by taking into account "the drug cartels, traffickers in arms and the various mafias and other criminal forms of organization that play such a significant role in world trade." These illegal players in the economy affect the politics of dispossession, he underlines, insisting that "it is stupid to seek to understand the world of capital" without taking them into account (54). See also Zygmunt Bauman's (2004, 63–67) assessment of criminality in the "waste of globalization."

16. Although aesthetically many of Garrone's shots seem to frame post-industrial landscapes, Rob Nixon (2011, 8) points to the problematic designation of landscapes as "post-industrial" since toxic contamination is never "post": "industrial particulates and effluents live on in the environmental elements we inhabit and in our very bodies, which epidemiologically and ecologically are never our simple contemporaries."

17. For more on these complicated ties, see Saviano (2007) and Corona and Sciarrone (2012, especially 21–31, including the rich bibliography cited in the footnotes).

18. The ship's captain, a black French-speaker, makes this hypothesis likely; the globalized illegal waste stream, however, travels in many different directions. Saviano (2007, 294) cites a 2003 investigation, known as "Midas" because of a Camorrista's assertion that "trash is gold," charting territories in Albania and Costa Rica being prepared for dumping. Of the global diffusion of waste, he writes that "every channel is open now," mentioning Romania, Mozambique, Somalia, and Nigeria in particular as destinations for hazardous substances. He also mentions the 1,000,000 tons of high-tech waste from Europe dumped yearly in China (291). Corona and Sciarrone (2012, 26) refer to Legambiente's investigations that reveal China, India, Pakistan, Congo, Nigeria, and Senegal as destinations for dumping from Italy. They emphasize, too, that no Italian region is completely external to the illegal waste traffic.

19. In relation to the aforementioned landscape of global capital, it is significant that each segment of the film revolves around troubling financial transactions: beside toxic waste dumping, there is the fashion industry supported by underpaid, overworked laborers (the story of Pasquale); the drug market and its reliance on minors to transport merchandise (Totò); the Camorra's own privatized social welfare plan, whereby families of incarcerated camorristi receive financial assistance from the bosses (don Ciro); and the enterprising and ultimately doomed attempt to independently access drugs and weapons in Camorra territory (Marco and Ciro).

20. Michael Covino (2009, 73) comments on the film's "dirty" aesthetic, noting that: "Even though set in southern Italy, on the Mediterranean, it's shot in somber colors: washed-out grays, blues, and browns. The movie looks dirty and feels dirtier."

21. In the song "'A peste" [The Plague], Avitabile's Scampia is characterized by the stink of sweat, by its "quagmire" [pantano] and stink [fete]; the singer makes colloquial references to the drug trade. The text of the first stanza is quoted at the beginning of an article by Mancino (2008, 12).

22. Part of a law known as the 1949 "Fanfani Plan," INA-Casa, the *Istituto Nazionale delle Assicurazioni* (National Insurance Institute), was supposed to reduce post-war unemployment by expanding construction and providing low-cost housing in urban areas (Ghirardo 2013, 136). For more on the INA Casa initiatives, in particular in Rome, see John David Rhodes (2007), *Stupendous, Miserable City: Pasolini's Rome*.

23. Ghirardo (2013, 164) elaborates: "with a handful of exceptions, low-cost housing through the late 1980s became a field for architectural experimentation in which designers deliberately rejected Italian traditions for living in cities and inhabiting housing in favour of an abstract and indifferent, decidedly anti-urban modernism. Exasperated by poor maintenance, lack of services, and poverty, all too often the neighbourhoods and housing became and remained squalid ghettoes."

24. Maria Buratti (2011, 103) describes Le Vele as "the relic of a shipwrecked project of urban development."

25. For an exceptional study of the earthquake in Irpinia and its material-cultural resonance, see Iovino's chapter on "'Three Earthquakes" in *Ecocriticism and Italy* (2016).

26. Chubb (2002, 216–18) describes the complicated relief efforts after the quake and the problems exacerbated by suspicion, fear, mistrust of the government, and incomplete communication, in particular with the peasants near the epicenter. In more general terms, Nancy Tuana (2008, 205), writing of the aftermath of Hurricane Katrina, notes that: "The poor are less likely to be able to evacuate. They are less likely to have the cash needed to leave and to live elsewhere. And when displaced, as thousands of New Orleanians have been, they have fewer marketable skills, financial resources to cushion them, and so forth, and hence fewer options."

27. Laino and De Leo (2002, 10–11) point out that many studies view Scampia as having one, monolithic social class, but that instead differentiations should be made: there are representatives of the middle, lower-middle, and marginal proletariat classes, as well as nomadic Roma and commuters who come to work in the neighborhood.

28. In his article on Le Vele in films directed by Garrone and Francesco Rosi, Anton Giulio Mancino (2008, 12) argues that the housing projects unite "malavita, mala-architettura e mala-politica" [lowlife, evil architecture and evil politics].

29. Saviano's (2007, 210) book contains a chapter titled "Cement," and he suggests (in language that mirrors Aquino's) that: "The clans' power remained the power of cement. It was at the construction sites that I could feel—physically, in my gut—all their might."

30. Chubb (2002, 229–30) argues that the creation of "special centralized authorities" to aid in reconstruction lacked supervision and "created a fertile terrain for corruption, waste, and infiltration by organized crime." During the second phase of earthquake reconstruction (starting in 1984), many building consortia received tens of billions of lire without undergoing normal checks and without having to respect normal planning regulations. In this phase, many Camorra clans penetrated the reconstruction efforts (see Corona and Sciarrone 2012, 18–19).

31. See Corona and Sciarrone (2012, 18), who explain that in 1983, Antonio Bardellino, then capo of the Casalesi Camorra clan, formed General Beton, a concrete company that aimed to take advantage of post-earthquake reconstruction funds. Although the toxic practices in the countryside around Campania are relatively recent, it is relevant to note that organized crime has long benefitted from its relationship to dirt, and specifically to the "rich rural world around Naples" (24). Corona and Sciarrone recall that there is documented

evidence that everything—from the market for renting agricultural lands, to selling animals, to producing fruits and vegetables—was linked to networks of illegality.

32. In 2010, it was discovered that a highway connecting Palma Campania and the communities of Vallo di Lauro—a strategic roadway to be used for evacuation in the case of the eruption of Vesuvius—was built with toxic waste (specifically, asbestos) (*Ecomafia* 2014, 136–37).

33. The *Ecomafia* report for 2014 recalls its identification of the Land of Fires in 2003, calling the triangle formed by the towns of Qualiano, Villaricca, and Giugliano the "dump of Italy for decades" (134). The report explains the Camorra's practice of waste disposal: "Here, by night, they burn trash, releasing an extremely dangerous smoke. Black, which comes from combustion of illegal waste" (134).

34. I discuss the trope of invisibility in *Gomorrah* and in a number of recent documentaries about the ecomafia in the article "Trash Is Gold" (Past 2013). For more on Campania, the ecomafia, and cinema, see also Angelone (2011), "Talking Trash" and Bondavalli (2011), "Waste Management."

35. Bozak (2012, 158) points out a further irony, underlining that many digital devices are "made according to the enduring principle of planned obsolescence but are at the same time composed of materials (plastics, glass, compressed metals) engineered to endure."

36. Maurizio Braucci (2009, 107), who collaborated in writing the screenplay for the film, confirms De Lazzaris's recollections, affirming that Garrone works by way of an "in-depth knowledge of places, through long chats with the inhabitants, or simply by spending time there. In Scampia, after spending time there constantly, the crew filmed for a month and a half in one of the Vele, occupying it and, I think, creating positive relationships with the inhabitants. It was the first time something of the kind had happened there." Braucci actively participates in other efforts to contest institutional and governmental neglect of Scampia, including a three-year theater project titled "Arrevuoto" that produced plays in Scampia and central Naples starring youth from the neighborhood.

37. De Lazzaris explained that Garrone also spent significant time at Le Vele before filming began, and Bonfini recounts that he originally accompanied the director to the housing complex to make arrangements for the crew to film there.

38. In a famous anecdote, Garrone recounts that residents of Le Vele filmed one of the fictitious homicides on their cell phones as the film crew was recording. The cinematic "murder" was posted on YouTube and resulted in police interrogations. Later, one camorrista claimed responsibility for the "murder" (Petitti 2014).

39. I have written elsewhere about the ways these documentaries strategically express protest. See Past, "Trash Is Gold" (2013) and "Documenting Ecomafia" (2016a).

40. See Dana Renga's (2013, 135) chapter on Garrone's film for more on the "mundane regularity of quotidian existence" in the film.

41. Verdicchio (2011, 115) argues strongly for the "co-responsibility" of *Gomorrah*'s viewers, insisting that "the enormous amounts of toxic waste that require disposal are the by-products of our consumption; the drugs that are manufactured, imported and trafficked are to meet our demand; and the criminality that is a result of these is also partially our own."

42. The term "thwarted citizenship" is Iovino's (2009, 339), and refers to the fact that "in Naples more than everywhere else in Italy" there has been "a joint denial of territorial balances (sense of place) and of social interdependence (sense of citizenship). It is here that the link between citizenship and territory has been fractured."

3

POSTHUMAN COLLABORATION, COHABITATION, SACRIFICE: *THE WIND BLOWS ROUND*

I SAT DOWN WITH A SMALL CROWD OF *crewmembers in the offices of Aran-ciaFilm to discuss the production of* Il vento fa il suo giro (The Wind Blows Round, 2005). *Anamaria del Grande, who has worked closely with director Giorgio Diritti on his subsequent films, made some phone calls to see who was available to speak to me while I was in Bologna. A host of people generously responded: Mario Chemello, one of the film's principal producers; Roberto Carta, an assistant director; Rocco Lobosco, assistant production manager; Katia Goldoni, production secretary; and Pierangela Biasi, makeup artist. Generous in their willingness to recount their experiences filming in the remote, depopulated Piedmontese Alpine village of Ussolo (the town had seven elderly inhabitants that winter), they spun lively stories of conflict and cohabitation, in what was an ambitious and, as they tell it, often improbable experience in collective cinema. In fact, although each had a specific job title in the production, every crewmember was also contractually a co-producer, a move that technically meant they worked for free until the film made enough money to pay them back, but also meant that the entire group felt committed to "their" film's success.[1] Regarding their roles as co-producers, the interviewees laughed as they explained that everyone did a bit of everything—from cooking, to cleaning the shared living space, to making runs down the mountain for groceries and props, to feeding goats, pigs, and sheep and taking them out to pasture. "It was a meeting of the wills," said Katia Goldoni. "The project united everyone's energies."[2] My recordings of the interviews, which spanned hours on a rainy afternoon in March, are punctuated by frequent laughter, amicable interruptions and additions, and a general sense of conviviality.*

Along with their passion for the production, all of the parties to the collaboration also candidly disclosed some of the difficulties of making a film in an isolated Alpine location, with limited financial and material resources and crowded living conditions. One of the most difficult stories they told me opens a complicated perspective on the intensity of cinematic cohabitation, as well as the imbalance of power that can result when a film crew rolls into town. For a scene near the end of the film, an angry villager gets revenge on the French family by killing two of their goats and hanging them from a stone archway. In order to shoot the scene, the production asked a local abattoir, where two goats awaited death, to temporarily suspend their death sentence until their corpses were needed for the film. The plan incensed a member of the crew—a critical member—who threatened to walk off set. A series of meetings ensued, with impassioned discussions about what to do. At last, an agreement was reached: the entire crew would participate in a sort of final blessing for the goats, and the scene would go on. When the moment for the scene arrived, the goats were killed and given to the production for filming.

This is a posthuman story of collaboration, cohabitation, and sacrifice among the players who constitute a cinematic cast of characters.

Philosopher and cognitive ethologist Roberto Marchesini's (2009) scholarly work is dedicated to theories of the posthuman, via which he argues forcefully that human culture emanates from the human's hybridization with the nonhuman, including technology and nonhuman animals. According to the traditional humanistic framework, he contends, humans employ a solipsistic creativity to bend technology to their needs. This belief demonstrates an arrogant conviction of self-sufficiency, when in actuality all human abilities result from a "dialogue with the nonhuman," not the "abstraction of the human from the world" (163).[3] The humanistic view suggests in godlike terms that the technosphere is created in our image, and thus furthers the cause of human exceptionalism with regards to all other beings. Such a worldview is, argues Marchesini, "misleading and dangerous" (165). A posthuman approach, instead, argues that technology is no mere tool: rather, it enables "technopoiesis," or creativity that emerges from a process of hybridizing with technologies. Marchesini elaborates:

> It is incorrect to see the technopoietic act as a creative process effected by the human in solitude, a direct emanation of qualities inherent to the human. Technopoiesis is the result of the encounter with the nonhuman, an integrative and not a disjunctive outcome. But not only this: every technopoietic

emergence increases the process of conjoining the human with the nonhuman, and in this sense it opens the human-system (rendering it more hybridizable and at the same time more unstable). The technosphere does not create a world tailored to humanity, but rather makes the human ever more needful of the world. (160)

The hybridization with technology parallels our relationship with nonhuman others, with whom our culture and lives are also intimately intertwined, and upon whom we depend for survival, companionship, and inspiration. Marchesini's theories of the posthuman help suggest how making cinema, a markedly technopoietic dance coordinating technologies, landscapes, and human and nonhuman actors, can constitute an opening to the world and, beyond this, a becoming with the world.

As an innovative, collaborative cinematic production, *The Wind Blows Round* helps implement the critical work Marchesini (2009, 165) proposes, that of "inverting the usual reading of the partnership with technology, and of admitting that every technological emergence renders the human-system less anthropocentered." Making the film enabled "performative shifts" (*slittamenti performativi*) for cast, crew, and inhabitants of the Valle Maira, and in many ways nudged along a cinematic process of de-anthropocentering (171). In practical terms, these "performative shifts" meant that mountain residents learned to live side by side with the cinematic apparatus. The mostly urban crew, in turn, discovered how to coexist with goats, pigs, and sheep, and helped take care of the nonhuman cinematic cast, including feeding the pigs and herding goats up the mountainside to graze in high-altitude pastures. All of the humans, locals and non, participated in creating a deeply dystopian narrative that critiques insularity, xenophobia, and the unwillingness to open to human and nonhuman others.

Equally, however, making the film involved the production's direct engagement with the violence that underpins our industrial food systems, our cultural machines, and life in the Italian (but not exclusively the Italian) countryside. Negotiating with an abattoir, filming dead goats as part of a story of intolerance and cruelty, *The Wind Blows Round* also shifted in material-performative ways toward Piedmont's history of violence. In her chapter about the northwestern Italian region in *Ecocriticism and Italy*, Serenella Iovino (2016, 130) identifies a violence "inscribed in these territories" that she describes as "not merely the ostentatious historic and 'mythic' violence of war, but also the mundane and whispered *pre-historic* violence in which everyday war and land are mingled—the slow, vegetal violence of patriarchal hierarchies, the violence of destitution and of seclusion from historical processes. This violence is not only the violence of soldiers, but also that of vinedressers and peasants."

Iovino's chapter about Piedmont focuses on Nuto Revelli's documentation of the Cuneo region, which is where the village of Ussolo (the setting for the film, fictionalized as Chersogno) is located. Revelli, a partisan and writer, created a vast archive of oral histories with the peasants of Cuneo. In these moving tales, Iovino (2016, 138) finds the seeds of stories of resistance and liberation, but she also traces the "intergenerational, interspecies and gendered violence of patriarchal hierarchies" calcified in the region's geology and its family structures.[4] Created specifically out of histories, geographies, bodies, and matter in the Alpine region, *The Wind* both takes an incisive look at one place, and plays a part in a form of deeply engrained biopolitical conflict that touches vulnerable bodies everywhere.

In the process of representing the long-intermingled human and more-than-human histories of the mountain region, and while tending to the nonhuman cast and calling on dead goats to tell the story, *The Wind Blows Round* thus necessarily faced the material-ethical question of human relation to our more-than-human kin. The film can be viewed productively through the lens of posthumanism's collaborative notion of "technopoiesis," but it is also a project that reveals some limits of the humanist imagination and human failings when it comes to sharing the planet with other species, and most particularly with goats. In theoretical terms, posthumanism and animal studies meet here, and in my engagement with both fields, I want to keep present the fact that real creatures and real lives are on the line. Pick (2011, 2–3) expresses the potential limits of posthumanist thought when she suggests that much posthumanism proceeds "internally," seeking to question and destabilize the human self. She recognizes her debt to such thought while insisting that her work intends to move "in the opposite direction, externally, by considering the corporeal reality of living bodies." Such an ethical, more-than-human impulse is the driving force behind the "animal question" that Matteo Gilebbi (2014, 93) synthesizes as "a broad, philosophical debate that erodes the purportedly tidy, sharp division between the human and the nonhuman, calling into question a widely accepted anthropocentrism and mankind's supposed ontological privilege." An analytical philosophical position on the animal question was clearly delineated by Paola Cavalieri (2001, vi) in her book *The Animal Question: Why Nonhuman Animals Deserve Human Rights*, which argues that "among those entitled to that minimum of equality and equity that allows one to live a life worth living, there are many nonhuman beings whom we currently treat as little more than mere things."[5] The analytical philosophical position has tended to stem from a rights-based approach, but other frameworks, like the one articulated by Jacques Derrida, focus on a creaturely capacity to suffer; others still have advocated for the radical connectedness of all beings, sentient or not. The wide-reaching, interdisciplinary conversations in the area of animal studies are difficult to gloss, but Cary Wolfe (2009a, 567) helpfully delineates some underlying principles: "Rather than treat the animal as primarily a theme, trope, metaphor, analogy, representation, or sociological datum (in which, say, relations of class, or race, or gender get played out and negotiated through the symbolic currency of animality and species difference), scholars in animal studies, whatever their home disciplines, now appear to be challenged not only by the discourses and conceptual schemata that have shaped our understanding of and relations to animals but also by the specificity of nonhuman animals, their nongeneric nature."

Such encounters between discourses, conceptual schemata, and real nonhuman animals happen frequently in the philosophical and material zone in which this chapter moves, along with the film production itself. Marchesini, who is not only a philosopher, vividly demonstrates the potentials of a hybrid existence that maneuvers between the pragmatic and the speculative, and as such, his writings are particularly important here.[6] Besides his prolific scholarly publications, Marchesini directs the *Scuola di Interazione Uomo-Animale* (SIUA, or School of Human-Animal Interaction) that uses an approach it dubs "cognitive zooanthropology" in order to reformulate human relationships with nonhuman animals, including cats, dogs, and horses.[7] To this end, the center offers courses in "zooanthropological pedagogy," and Marchesini's publications here include titles like *Il galateo per il cane* (*Good Manners for Dogs*, 2011). When I visited Marchesini at the SIUA offices outside of Bologna to discuss a translation project, I met a group of co-collaborators that included four humans, a turtle, and a rabbit. Here, speculative posthuman philosophies meet what Donna Haraway might call material kinship figurations, and philosophers, turtles, and rabbits directly face the delicate question of living together. These encounters of humans and nonhumans and of philosophies, pedagogies, and practices help foreground the material, ethical stakes of the animal question that Haraway's (2008, 42) work resolutely articulates: "we are in a knot of species coshaping one another in layers of reciprocating complexity all the way down. Response and respect are possible only in those knots, with actual animals and people looking back at each other, sticky with all their muddled histories."

Which lives matter? As I have already outlined, along with a posthuman notion of human debt to the nonhuman world and the ethical and material entangling of our fates, the animal question also brings to light a human tendency to discount and often to exploit nonhuman animal life. And as we have seen, this dark side of the animal question is raised in *The Wind Blows Round* as a production and as a narrative, especially in the bodily form of the two dead goats. The human tendency to anthropocentric hubris operates according to a logic of sacrifice that "produces the Animal," as Haraway (2008, 78) argues, following Jacques Derrida. She elaborates: "Sacrifice works; there is a whole world of those who can be killed, because finally they are only something, not somebody, close enough to 'being' in order to be a model, substitute, sufficiently self-similar and so nourishing food, but not close enough to compel response" (79). The contested notion of "sacrifice" resonates throughout the work of leading scholars in contemporary philosophy who approach the animal question. For Haraway, "sacrifice" becomes a cognitive tool that allows justified killings. For Giorgio Agamben (2004), rather, sacrifice is the horizon of the sacred that the biopolitical machine *denies* to that disposable being, the "*homo sacer*," whom it kills. The *homo sacer*, who "is situated at the intersection of a capacity to be killed and yet not sacrificed," is "outside both human and divine law" (48). "Unsacrificeable," he "may nevertheless be killed by anyone" (67). Through the operation of the biopolitical machine, this "sacred" man, whose death parallels that of the animal, "has been separated from its context" and becomes "incompatible with the human world" (61). Most critically, for both Haraway and Agamben, the notion of sacrifice hides the material conditions of suffering and death, conditions covered by what Agamben calls "sacrificial veils" that allow human and animal life—some humans, and some animals—to be extinguished with impunity. As Matthew Calarco (2009b, 77) clarifies, figuring out who is "sacrificeable" and who is "unsacrificeable," or even posing the question of "who does and does not belong to the moral community is one of the most problematic foundational gestures in the Western metaphysical tradition and is indicative of its imperialistic tendencies."

Given its entanglement in a posthuman world and its material and narrative abilities to represent this encounter, the technopoietic cinematic apparatus would seem to offer a means to raise the veil on this gray zone of sanctioned violence. But cinema, which has a powerful potential to build ethical lines of collaboration and empathy with the nonhuman world, is also guilty of exploiting that world for its technopoietic ends. In short, cinema, too, is built on animal death. This is true of celluloid, as Scott Mac-Donald (2013) explains:

> Though few of those who appreciate celluloid cinema are conscious of it, the filmstrip, at least on one level, encapsulates the way in which modern life and the natural world are imbricated: the light-sensitive silver salts that create a visible image when exposed to light are suspended in a thin layer of gelatin, one of the chief ingredients of which is collagen. Collagen is produced by boiling the bones and tissues of animals. Celluloid, the base on which the emulsion is layered, is made from cellulose. That is, the 'life' we see on the screen is a kind of re-animation of plant and animal life within the mechanical/chemical apparatus of traditional cinema. (18)

As one of Kodak's patents for manufacturing gelatin reveals, its film stock relies on boiling the skins, bones, and hides of cattle, pigs, and sheep (La-Roche, Roy, and Brand 1999), specifically some of the species of nonhuman animals that are the subject of the domestic conflicts, or conflicts of cohabitation, in *The Wind Blows Round*. Because of financial and productive challenges, this particular film was created in digital and printed later on 35 mm for distribution. In theaters, then, the cinematic images were quite literally projected through layers of animal and plant matter. In the digital age, even in a production that chooses not to use celluloid filmstock (or one that, like *The Wind*, uses primarily digital), animal death still underpins filmmaking, since digital processes rely on the extraction and burning of fossil fuels to power the cinematic machine (as I discussed in Chapter One), and on stearic acid, which comes most frequently from animal byproducts, to stabilize digital machinery against heat. As Anat Pick and Guinevere Narraway (2013, 3) affirm, "animal life is quite literally the stuff of images."[8]

Animal life and animal death, which provide the material underpinnings for the technologies that create *The Wind Blows Round*, also undergird the stories it spins of conflict and cohabitation. The film recounts the tale of a French family of goat herders and cheese makers (the Héraud family) who relocate from the Pyrenees to the small village in the Occitan Alps. Initially people and goats are greeted (if hesitantly) as saviors in a town where historic agricultural practices have been forgotten, and where empty, dilapidated houses loom over forbidding gray cobblestone streets. Over the course of nine months, however, the initially generous welcome turns dystopic, as villagers enforce the limits of their hospitality. Goats and Frenchmen alike are reviled as smelly, disruptive, disrespectful of geographic and social boundaries, and no longer welcome in Chersogno. The ethical fabric that should have been woven, according to Haraway's (2003, 50) companion species philosophy, "from the silk-strong thread of ongoing alertness to otherness-in-relation," quickly and tragically unravels, and so near the end of the film, the Hérauds and their goats pack up and leave.

According to Michael Lundblad (2009, 496), recent scholarship in animal studies has "prompted fundamental reconsiderations of nonhuman and human difference, otherness, and subjectivity." In this chapter, I propose that *The Wind Blows Round* effects a series of "performative shifts," both narrative and lived, whereby such fundamental reconsiderations take place. However, it cannot and does not ask these questions innocently. Potentially transformative and deeply implicated in a biopolitical world that tends to disregard animal life and animal death, posthuman cinema faces challenges on multiple fronts. From the perspective of its creative, collaborative production process, to the composition of its filmic narrative, to the engagement of two dead goats for its filmic cast, *The Wind Blows Round* vividly articulates important questions about human ethical responsibilities, and aesthetic and ethical contradictions, in a posthuman world. The fictional Chersogno and the real Ussolo challenge the very foundations of domestic life—that life shared with "domesticated" nonhuman others in the space of a common "domus"—when the house is marked by death.

Death in the Afternoon: Cohabitation, Violence, and Goats in the Western Alps

Late in the film, Philippe Héraud strides across a gray, rainy Alpine landscape, and a close-up shot pans from the left to stop on his face, which bears a grim expression. An eyeline match frames what he is looking at, closing in on two dead, white goats, throats bloodied, upside down. In a subsequent shot, we discern that they are hanging by their hooves from the stone doorway of a dilapidated building. A cut to a longer shot contextualizes the scene just behind the rustic village church. A meditative soundtrack with eerie vocals plays in the background.

The church, bathed in rosy afternoon light, is framed from above as a helicopter circles the village, creating a promotional tourist video. A dizzying shot swings around and captures an ambulance, a stretcher, emergency workers, and policemen. The helicopter lands, and the camera focuses on a

Figure 3.1. Death in the Afternoon. Screen capture, *The Wind Blows Round* (2005), directed by Giorgio Diritti.

confusion of people gathered around the same stone doorway where the goats had hung. A stretcher carries away the lifeless body of Roberto, a young man from the village, with a noose around his neck.

Three tragic deaths. One suicide, two murders. Two real deaths, one fictional death. Three incommensurable events. The death of the two goats, murdered vindictively by someone to protest the French Héraud family's intrusion into village life, and the death of Roberto, a young man whose cognitive disability gives him a marginal status in the village, are set out in a clear relationship of causality. Someone kills the goats, the final straw that convinces the Héraud family to leave Chersogno, and the departure of his beloved friends triggers Roberto's suicide. The sequence of these tragedies and their common location in the stone doorway behind the church trace an ethical line linking all of these failures of cohabitation and extending the moral status of victimhood to goats and humans alike. But the death of this human and these two goats are not equal.

In her remarkable *Creaturely Poetics,* Anat Pick (2011, 106) argues that cinema is a "zoomorphic stage that transforms all living beings—including humans—into creatures."[9] Cinema's "immediacy and materiality" (106) make it a creaturely form, for Pick, and focusing on bodies in film allows her to think the human "outside Cartesian abstractionism, as rigorously material" (6). Calling on creaturely "embodiment" to examine the "corporeal reality of living bodies," she traces a "relationship between vulnerability, existence, and beauty" that "necessarily applies across the species divide and so delivers us beyond the domain of the human" (3). Her observations relate in profound ways to *The Wind Blows Round*, where, in the dystopian narrative, creaturely vulnerability and the suffering of the Héraud family, Roberto, and the two goats are shared across species boundaries. In this way, *The Wind* recognizes some of "the permutations of necessity and materiality that condition and shape human life" (5). In its focus on embodiment, the film draws close to the kind of "creaturely poetics" Pick describes. Reading the film through the refractions of the "creaturely prism" (Pick's chosen lens) that carry outward toward its production, we know that vulnerability was not apportioned equally across species boundaries. Whereas Giacomino Allais, the actor who played Roberto, could rise from the stretcher, loosen the noose from around his neck, and return to his extra-cinematic existence when the shoot concluded, the goats, without their consent, were sacrificed for the film.

As I proceed in this knotty chapter, admittedly with trepidation, I engage with the film's powerful narrative, all the while keeping those two real goats in mind. All films exist, to some degree, at the encounter of the material and the ephemeral, troubling any distinctions between the fictional and the real, but for *The Wind Blows Round*, these encounters are particularly charged. The histories of seasonal herding and the Alpine pastoral landscape in the beginning of the film might evoke nostalgia for a way of life that is being progressively compromised by the advance of modernity. Akira Mizuta Lippit (2000, 1) argues that it is "a cliché of modernity: human advancement always coincides with a recession of nature and its figures—wildlife, wilderness, human nature, and so forth." Animals, he argues, become more "spectral" than "sacrificial," receding "into the shadows of human consumption and environmental destruction" (1). The Héraud family's decision to relocate to the Alps—they are distancing themselves from a nuclear facility that interrupted their pastoral life in the Pyrenees—in fact seems to constitute an attempt to reject that recession of nature, to return to a place where animals are not spectral. The depopulated village in the Valle Maira, in Piedmont, is one where modernity's encroachment seems to have been scant, and from which most humans have consequently disappeared.

The film's title, *Il vento fa il suo giro*, suggests nostalgia for the past. *Il vento* also circulated with an Occitan title, foregrounding the language spoken in those remote mountain valleys and in much of the film: *E l'aura fai son vir.* The circular notion of "blowing round" refers to the *rueido* that, according to an elderly villager in the film, was a collaborative practice developed during World War II to hide hay from the German troops who had begun burning haylofts further down in the valley. In a metacinematic sequence near the end of the film, the villager recites this happy story of collaboration to a videographer making a promotional spot about the region. Recognizing the critical role of hay for the animals who would provide milk, butter, and cheese, the inhabitants of the valley helped one another "per il bene di tutti e di ognuno" (for the good of each and every one), a sentiment that supposedly extended to the nonhuman world. In this idyllic recollection, memories of the past cast a rosy light on relationships in the rural valley, where the circularity implicit in the concept of the *rueido*, likely from the root for "rotation," demonstrates an awareness of the common fates of all those who take part in the cycle of valley life. Violence, in this view, was a historical incursion from the outside, perpetrated by "the Germans" against this otherwise coherent, if impoverished, collective. Memories of the *rueido*, in the form of pictures on people's walls, village ceremonies, and conversations, become a mantra affirming the ethical ties binding villagers to one another and to the surrounding peaks and valleys.

The idealized language of the *rueido* might be understood as rightly recognizing the significant role played by agriculture, and specifically goats, in human history generally and in the mountains specifically. Both agents and instruments of cultural and environmental history, goats to some degree allow Alpine villages like Ussolo/Chersogno to come into existence, and they shape its boundaries.[10] The relationship between humans and goats is a long one. David E. MacHugh and Daniel G. Bradley (2001, 5382) argue that: "accumulating archaeological evidence indicates that goats, in the form of their wild progenitor—the bezoar (*Capra aegagrus*), were the first wild herbivores to be domesticated." Together with sheep, pigs, and cows, goats were important protagonists in the shift in human history from food collection to food production, altering human social and economic structures as well as animal lives (DeMello 2012, 86–87).[11] Recent research suggests that goats demonstrate intentional communicative behavior when humans are watching them, a trait scientists used to think applied only to companion species relationships such as those linking humans to dogs or horses. The study, which sees the scientists reconsidering communication between heterospecifics of all sorts, shows the entangled multidirectionality of the human-caprine web (Nawroth, Brett, and McElligott 2016, 1–2). Other recent (and highly idiosyncratic) research on the part of a person who calls himself "GoatMan" found author Thomas Thwaites (2016) spending three days in the Swiss Alps "becoming" goat. Wearing prosthetic goat legs and a goaty helmet and jacket, Thwaites grazed with a herd, ate grass, (perhaps) narrowly avoided a fight for dominance with the alpha male, and climbed mountains. The author justifies the logic of wanting to be a human-animal hybrid by citing the long history of myths and cave paintings recognizing such crossings, and the compelling existential questions such hybrids raise. Given the human's storied, multispecies past, he posits that, "historically speaking, it's almost odder to *not* want to become a goat" (38).

The collaborative history also maps onto the sublime beauty of the Alps, where the relationships between humans, goats, and rocky high-altitude pastures are delicate and consequential. Classified as a minor ruminant, domestic goats are perfect inhabitants of Alpine (and other "marginal") landscapes: adaptable and sure-footed, they can live in harsh climates and traverse rough terrain, climb trees, and graze close to the ground, navigating pastures that other animals cannot (De Rancourt et al. 2006, 176). Their grazing helps maintain the integrity of the land by minimizing the fire risk and their foraging preferences, if managed well, can keep back invasive weeds and actually contribute to biodiversity in the mountains (Verona 2006, 29–31).[12] The pathways via which goats and sheep travel in the Alps create significant social and cultural networks, shaping culinary traditions, holidays and feasts, architectural structures, sartorial choices, the legal system, and landscapes.[13] These collaborations between humans and their domestic partners enliven the beginning of the film, when the rural community unites to welcome the French family by preparing a house for the humans and a connected stable for the goats, then feeding them, sharing their pasture land, buying their goat cheese, and opening themselves to entanglement with non-Italian and nonhuman others.

Yet the pastoral memory of the *rueido* also oversimplifies many aspects of the agricultural past, a past in which goats have also been complicit in creating conflict. Because of their aforementioned agility and eclectic, efficient dietary habits, goats have also historically helped fuel discord.[14] In Italy, goats have been agents of environmental change, as intensive grazing contributed to deforestation as early as the Renaissance (Pratesi 2010, 110). They have also been subjects of the law, as shifting Italian states alternately legislated in favor of nomadic grazing, allowing herds of goats, sheep, and cattle to move freely up and down mountain slopes, or against it, asserting private property rights and allowing for fences (176–77). The Fascist government in Italy waged a war on goats, claiming that they were guilty of destroying Italian forests.[15] They levied high taxes on the animals, leading some peasants to kill their goats and consequently lose their supplies of milk and cheese, not to mention the affective kinship bonds they often shared with the animals (Armiero 2011, 129–33). Other herders chose to leave the mountains, contributing to the depopulation that marks the fictional Chersogno and the real Ussolo. In *The Wind Blows Round*, whose plot addresses disagreements over private property, discussions of grazing rights show that goats are not simply part of a harmonious cycle of mountain life, but also fodder for the discord that sounds insistently throughout the story. This version of human-caprine history suggests that the wind blowing round can also refer to a kind of karmic retribution for inhospitable behavior and misremembered histories.[16]

Thus as I argued above, memories of collaboration like the one featured in the discussion of the *rueido* also mask the violence present in the agricultural world, which historically scarred the landscapes of Piedmont where the film takes place, even as the landscapes scarred the bodies of its inhabitants. During the time when Italian Fascists, Germans, and partisans fought battles in the mountains, historians chronicled the violence of both war and mountain life. As Marco Armiero (2011, 162–66) argues, the Partisan Resistance in the mountains was marked by deprivation, hunger, and danger of death by avalanche, storms, or cold. So perilous were the mountains that, as partisan leader Nuto Revelli wrote, "we were on the verge of killing ourselves as alpinists instead of as fighters" (Armiero 2011, 164). Even more pervasively, though, in Piedmont interlocking forms of structural violence invested the bodies of women, children, animals, the poor, and the land itself. This is a violence that, as Iovino (2016, 142) explains, comes "from within and from without: from within, with its interlaced forms of oppression and hyper-separation, with its archaic and anti-pastoral 'war of the poor'; from without, with the reckless attacks carried out by industrial development, which is itself a 'progress' without liberation, a state of expanded hierarchies subjugating both humans and land." In spite of the rhetoric of collaboration that frames the narrative, the film provides evidence of systemic violence in the rural world: in the tense relationships between people and the land, in the harsh beauty of the Alpine heights, in the village's isolation and the villagers' fear of outsiders.

And finally, once again taking the goats into account, we must recognize that, having been used by humans for meat, milk, skins, and fiber, goats have long been key players in the human use and exploitation of the animal world. For example, MacHugh and Bradley (2001, 5382) note that they have been described in utilitarian terms as perhaps "the first 'walking larders,'" a formulation that relegates creatures to the status of animate furniture, not heterospecific kin. In *The Wind Blows Round*, the two goats killed to "star" in the film raise the curtain on the human exploitation of the animal world. Already destined to die in the slaughterhouse, the two goats, whose death was repurposed for the film, were always already fated to be sacrificed for human ends. On some level, the death of the goats requires us to acknowledge the constant human dependence on nonhuman animal death, the fact that "to eat is to kill and to deplete resources for others" and "to live is necessarily to live off another," as Kari Weil (2012, 117) explains succinctly.[17]

Whatever the history of agricultural violence and animal sacrifice, the death of these two goats was intolerable for Philippe and his family, whose livelihood and day-to-day existence revolved around their nonhuman companions. As screenplay writer Fredo Valla explained, although "in the rural world there is much violence," the death of these two goats in the film's narrative constitutes evidence of a "surplus of violence," a "cruel act of disparagement."[18] In a shot following Philippe's discovery of the slaughtered animals, he stands at the edge of a herd of cattle that belongs to the antagonist, Emma, who likely killed his goats. Appearing to momentarily contemplate revenge, he instead closes his eyes, then strides off. A subsequent shot depicts the family's truck winding down the mountain road, reversing the journey with which the film began. The Héraud family's departure from Chersogno after finding the two dead goats signals a refusal of this unacceptable violence, the family's decision to retreat rather than retaliate.

Yet even more pressingly, this violence was unacceptable to Roberto, the cognitively disabled man who had become an extended member of the Héraud family. Roberto first appears in an early shot in the village, lying on a bench in front of a house on a cold day when Philippe comes on a reconnaissance mission to look for a house and pastures to rent in Chersogno. Roberto's position is similar to that of a dog chained in front of a house who, a few scenes earlier, barks at the Frenchman. On this and other occasions (as when Roberto drinks from a trough), the camera implies his association with a nonhuman world both intimately linked to human domestic space and systematically excluded from it. The village, in fact, denies Roberto full admittance to the human domestic sphere; over the course of the film, the links between Roberto and the Héraud family become more marked, signaling the family's parallel animalization in village life. The Héraud children are accused of smelling like goats; an angry resident accuses Philippe of being a "vulture;" and holiday travelers turn up their noses at the sight and smell of animal excrement in their village as the goats return from pasture and the pigs eat in a village stable. Gradually, the Chersognesi erect and enforce the boundaries of what Agamben (2004, 75) calls the "anthropological machine," a belief system that "each time decides upon and recomposes the conflict between man and animal." Pushing Philippe and his family, along with Roberto, toward the "animal," they demonstrate their own hypocritical fear of a regression to animality, even as they celebrate their collective past, characterized by the smells, sounds, and practices of cohabitation with nonhuman others. In the process of securing the borders of their humanity, the residents of Chersogno leave Philippe and his family, Roberto, and the goats in a fragile position of alterity. And as villagers push the Hérauds to the margins, Roberto comes closer to them, riding with Philippe and his daughter on the tractor, dining at the family table, and joining them in the stables to help take care of the goats.

Drawn together because of their marginal status and eventually exiled from the community in death (Roberto and the two goats) or because they choose to depart (Philippe, his family, and the rest of the herd), the Héraud family, the goats, and Roberto expose what Iovino (2010b, 55) has called a "'wilderness zone' inside the civilized or 'tame' area of humanity-as-normality." Philippe, who many of the villagers come to see as mad; the goats, who they revile as dirty; and Roberto, who they marginalize for his disability, are all cordoned off from village life by a human perspective that enforces the dualisms—culture vs. nature, human vs. nonhuman, normative vs. nonnormative—that underlie what Iovino defines as "the traditional taxonomy of the human subject" (55). Such dualisms are predicated on the values of "rationality, autonomy, and agency," as Cary Wolfe (2008, 110) shows, rather than on a notion of shared suffering or vulnerability. Aside from fetishizing human rationality and human beings who are abled in normative ways, these views that disregard the "radical asymmetries and heterogeneities among all the different life forms" also discount the entanglement of humans and nonhumans that characterizes life in Chersogno and elsewhere (115).[19]

The Chersognesi's implicit fetishization of human rationality becomes most evident in their attention to language, a significant element of the film. At the time of its creation, *The Wind Blows Round* was said to be the only film ever made in Occitan, or the *lingua d'Oc*. Fausto, a cosmopolitan villager whose musical career has taken him around the world, frequently discusses philosophy with Philippe. In one of their discussions, the former suggests that language—human language, and specifically the Occitan language spoken in the film—offers proof that people have lived together companionably for thousands of years. The film, which is now a cinematic archive of the disappearing Italian dialect (part of the casting call involved seeking speakers of Occitan), nevertheless offers a counterpoint to Fausto's assertion.[20] The harsh disagreements that characterize town hall meetings, the gossip and diffidence that follow the arrival of the newcomers, all expressed in the Alpine dialect, neither signal harmony nor deliver justice. Rather, they articulate an unwillingness to admit new (or readmit old) guests, or to open the borders of their hospitality. Human language, here and elsewhere, is one of what Wolfe (2008, 118) calls the "historically and ideologically specific set of coordinates" that, like politics, philosophy, or law, radically foreshortens "a more ambitious and more profound ethical project: a new and more inclusive form of ethical pluralism that it is our charge, now, to frame."[21]

And in fact Philippe objects to the notion of language's role in cementing community, insisting that culture is born through living together (*convivenza*), day after day. More poignantly, Roberto in fact never says a word in the entire film, and his silence is pregnant. This alien status with regard to language is significant because Roberto instead lives daily with Philippe and the goats, sharing space, eating and drinking together with them. Through this extra-linguistic conviviality, *moving* together, sharing screen space and family space, possibilities are opened for "new lines of empathy, affinity, and respect between different forms of life" (Wolfe 2008, 110). This is a movement between species, between goats, pigs, adults, children, French-speakers, Occitan-speakers, and those who do not speak at all. Philippe and the goats frequently (if perhaps inadvertently) trespass on properties where they are unwanted, partly because, in the rugged Alps, the borders of private property are shifting and ill-defined. Free movement, in fact, is one of the important challenges that Philippe, Roberto, and the goats pose to the rigidity of Chersogno's vision of itself.

Roberto's trespassing across borders is even more distinctive, however, and does not simply transgress property lines. On several occasions, a long shot frames Roberto running through green mountain pastures, arms splayed and gently flapping, playing at being a bird, or an airplane, and thus interloping on territories beyond the human. If the *rueido* is the collective mantra of the village, one evoked in the film from the opening to the close in a variety of forms, Roberto's "flight" is instead a posthuman, embodied mantra, a becoming-other that opens the self to unexpected dimensions. As he flaps his arms in the fields, Roberto's child-like play recalls the mimetic act that, for Marchesini (2014, xviii), underlies human culture and originates in hybridization with other species (or, in Marchesini's language, the heterospecific): "The tendency to represent both the form and the movement of the other, through movements of the body in the postural stasis of yoga or in the kinetic movement of dance or kung fu, determines on the one hand the incorporation of the heterospecific and on the other the anthropomorphic interpretation of it. In mimesis we thus witness a process of threshold [*soglia*], the hospitality of otherness, and not a simple homologous representation of the phenomenon." While the Héraud family lives in Chersogno, Roberto extends what Marchesini calls a "centrifugal" hospitality, being hosted *by* the other through his participation in new dimensions of being, and a "centripetal" hospitality, reorganizing his own existence to welcome others: hosting them. In his winged flight, he enacts his willingness to host alterity. These shots, captured in slow motion, in turn become one of the film's methods of incorporating a different cinematic language and time, of hosting an alternative perspective. When the guests Roberto hosts, and who also host him, are betrayed by Chersogno's conditional hospitality, his world collapses.[22]

When Roberto dies, the community gathers to mourn him. In the cinematic narrative, there was never such a gathering for the goats. Lippit (2002) notes that animals have long been considered "incapable of a proper death" because they (or so philosophers from Epicurus to Heidegger have claimed) lack an awareness of death. More specifically, according to this anthropocentric line of thinking: "Language brings consciousness and with it, the consciousness of consciousness and its absence, or death. In this light, to have language is to have death" (11). Yet by deliberately aligning his death with the death of the goats, Roberto on some level makes those lives grievable as well, his wordless suicide showing that those without language can suffer and die, too. When the villagers gather at the church to honor Roberto's life, they begin to recognize, albeit stutteringly, the faulty logic of their conditional hospitality. This kind of hospitality is embodied in the *rueido*, which in its re-adoption by villagers came to be a logic of consumer-ist reciprocity whereby the guest expects to get something in return: I'll give you hay if you give me milk, eggs, and cheese.[23] It does not, however, take into account the sense of utter loss that results if a guest (centripetal and centrifugal, in Marchesini's formulation, both host and hosted), who asks for nothing, perishes, leaving a hole in the social fabric. After three tragic deaths, the small *fictional* Italian village at last begins to learn that human and nonhuman histories shape, trouble, and alter one another. As Graziella Parati (2014, 319) suggests, villagers finally discern that "nostalgia has no future unless it becomes an inclusive narrative, able to value the role that former traditions and languages play in the creation of a community that can sustain different kinds of cultural proximities." Within the cinematic narrative, misunderstanding goats and misunderstanding human beings are tragic analogues. But outside of the diegesis, what of the film crew, and what about the inhabitants of the Valle Maira?

Domesticity, Nomadism, and On Location Filming

Philippe and a group of villagers tour the house the latter are willing to rent to him. In the dark stone dwelling, light falls on dust, spider webs, and stacks of hay. Wandering through the complex assemblage of rooms, Philippe first shows enthusiasm when they enter the dark stables: "C'est magnifique."

The oldest Héraud daughter crouches in the stables, milking goats by the light of a yellow bulb that casts a warm glow over goats and hay. Suddenly, the sound of breaking glass, and she and the goats start as several jars of mag-gots fly through the window, breaking open on the hard ground.

As goatherds, Philippe Héraud and his family engage in a profession that is 11,000 years old, and part of a long story of the domestication of nonhu-man animals.[24] Transhumance, or the nomadic practice of herding ani-mals seasonally from low-altitude to high-altitude pastures, is "certainly Mediterranean" in origin, and has long had a role in carving pathways and crossing borders between Provence and the western Italian Alps (Verona 2006, 14). Although the Héraud family planned to settle in Chersogno and was not embarking on the journey of long-distance herding, the work they undertake still relies on shared grazing lands, goats and dogs moving on human roads and Alpine paths, and shifting seasonal movement, follow-ing many of the same nomadic practices of transhumance. Thierry Toscan, the actor who played Philippe, "interned" with a local farmer for several

Figure 3.2. Domestic Space. Screen capture, *The Wind Blows Round* (2005), directed by Giorgio Diritti.

weeks before filming to learn how to work with the goats. During the filming process, Toscan was accompanied in his adopted profession by an eclectic cinematic troupe. In creating the film, the herding routes were traversed by goatherd, goats, dogs, cameraman, director, assistant director, boom operators, non-professional actors, and more, who fanned out across the landscape while forming a new, posthuman herd. However familiar herding might be in Alpine histories, though, the herder and the herd (and here, the film troupe) also provoke anxieties: inhabiting the mobile border at the encounter of here and there, guest and host, home and away, the nomadic impermanence of film crew and seasonal herder challenges the stabilities of all of these categories.

But the notion of domestication also locates the sometimes-smelly question of the animal right under our noses: although herders (and film crews) are nomadic, domestication, from the root "*dom-,*" is about being at home (in Latin *domus*). From the beginning of the film, the camera captures spaces of domesticity that are shared by humans and nonhuman animals. In Philippe's first appearance in the film, he approaches a two-story house and is greeted by a large black dog. Behind the dog lie a doghouse and chicken coop, and several chickens roam in the lower right frame. Human and nonhuman occupants, it is clear, share the architectural landscape of Chersogno. The crumbling house in which the Héraud family settles is spatially dispersive, unlike the elegant, tall, rectangular order of Fausto the musician's home. Whereas the professional clarinetist lives in a structure whose walls and boundaries are clearly delineated, the Héraud family residence comprises two rooms in one building, an open courtyard with a water trough, a stable attached somehow to a kitchen, and a cantina where they age their cheeses: it spreads across a wide area, and includes nonhuman spaces alongside the human ones. The camera never clearly demarcates the extent of this amorphous property, and in fact the Héraud family's domestic life extends across town: they play hide-and-seek throughout the village, drawing passersby into the game; they wash themselves at the open trough, in view of one of the "main" streets; the children bathe in other people's bath tubs; Philippe reclines in pastures with goats milling about him as if in a living room. The uncontained fluidity of this nomadic domestic space is one of the key problems of the film: people complain about unpleasant odors, excrement in the street, a dead animal discarded in a place where people hike. They consistently seek to push back the abject excess that at times accompanies agricultural practice, even while they enact revenge by further sullying these spaces, launching maggots into the goats' stable, for example. Yet in spite of their distaste and discomfort, living alongside nonhuman animals essentially shaped human society as we know it and certainly life in Chersogno; the film plays with the ironies that abound when rural mountain villagers forget their roots in the agricultural past.

Acknowledging that "human civilization would not be what it is today if it were not for animal domestication," Margo DeMello (2012) discusses the mutual dependence of humans and nonhuman animals. These are not relationships between historic equals, although the degree to which they should be seen as largely human-driven continues to be subject of debate. DeMello points out that "today's domesticated animals are so highly bred and engineered for human benefit that they could never again survive on their own," and notes that if dependency has been bred into our relationship to nonhuman animals, "its corollary—dominance" is also integral to these rapports (95). Weil (2012, 55) posits that in histories of domestication, the domestic is counterposed to the wild (and slave to free) in a charged distinction "that carries a host of gendered, raced, and otherwise hierarchically organized associations." But although power relationships between humans and nonhuman animals may be unequal, recent scientific evidence points away from the notion that animals were exclusively bred to strategically meet human needs. Rather, the process involves the mutual transformation of humans, nonhuman animals, and the terrain that hosts them. Domestication was, scientists believe, likely "a symbiotic and dynamic relationship between humans and animals independent of either's forethought or conscious intent and that potentially ascribes agency to both" (58).[25] Philosophical ethologist Dominique Lestel (2014, 64) agrees: "The domestication of humans and animals is conjoined and it is this reciprocity that constitutes the major foundation of hybrid communities."[26] Assuming that human-nonhuman relationships are all about human dominance can lead to "anthropodenial," or an underestimation of our shared characteristics and needs (Weil 2012, 58).[27]

In her study of transhumance and shepherding, Marzia Verona (2006, 238) describes the life of herder and herd in evocative terms: "The herder is always at the home of others: in the mountains and on the street, along a river, in a prairie, in a field. Often an unwelcome guest."[28] Although she casts the sheep/herder relationship as antagonistic, Verona's descriptions of nomadic pastoral life actually indicate the political, social, and material entanglement of the lives of herders and herds, and their inherent relationship of dependence. More significantly, her notion of the herder as an "unwelcome guest," equally applicable to goatherd and goats in *The Wind Blows Round*, helps unpack the tensions between hospitality, domestication, and nomadism, as it directly negates what Marchesini (2015, 180) calls the "reciprocation of roles" between heterospecifics. Stopping short of calling for a reciprocal exchange of goods, that relationship of dependence that characterizes conditional hospitality, Marchesini suggests that a heterospecific guest must merely be *recognized* by the host: "A guest, in order to really be a guest, has to have space for dialogue, even before having rights; his presence has to be recognized" (179). When we play with a dog or watch a cat explore a garden, Marchesini argues, we witness familiar actions that are fruit of our common evolutionary heritage, our "common ancestors." In this way, the philosopher argues that a dog (but presumably also a goat, or a pig): "is not a stranger, his way of being is within us and our hosting him lies in recognizing an *existential house common to us and him*" (184, my emphasis). Both homeless and at home everywhere, the herder and the herd *should* be recognized and welcomed as guests in the existential house that is the fictional community of Chersogno, just as the film crew, actors, and goats are guests in the existential house of the historic town of Ussolo.

In this conflict between domesticity and nomadism, the cinematic narrative and the filmmaking practice dovetail. The crew of *The Wind Blows Round* lived in Ussolo on and off for over nine months, in a process of cohabitation that was at times convivial, at others conflictual. Creating the film thus entailed a process of "domesticity" whereby the film crew also came to be at home in the remote Alpine village. Yet during the months of filming, a certain nomadism also prevailed, as crewmembers drove all over the valley in search of props and non-professional actors (including goats); unpaid crewmembers came and went as their schedules and budgets permitted; the entire group left at the end of certain seasonal shoots and returned for new rounds of filming.[29] Although they initially planned on having a crew of 10–12 people, *The Wind Blows Round* eventually had 40 crewmembers who were all "indispensable," according to producer Mario Chemello. Lodged in a rustic hotel in the town where shooting took place, the human crew lived alongside the pigs and goats, and the rhythms of agricultural life—grazing, milking, feeding the animals—became their rhythms. The production team, explained Chemello, additionally had to work around the schedules of non-professional actors who had to leave to milk their cows. It was an experience "at the limits," said production secretary Katia Goldoni, in which long hours were dedicated each day to the tasks required by the hybrid cine-domestic life. Most of the young volunteer co-producers, now more established in their careers, could not imagine repeating it. Yet all of them spoke of a transformative encounter, and a sense of loss when filming concluded. This experience was closely intertwined with the nonhuman actors who lived next door. Goldoni spoke of a feeling of "fraternity" with the pigs she helped care for; makeup artist Pierangela Biasi loved taking care of the goats. Biasi mentions a special relationship that developed between Thierry Toscan (Philippe) and the sheepdog. She says, in short, that the animals were part of the crew.[30] Goldoni suggestively said that the experience of caring for the crew's nonhuman creatures was like "learning to fly," a characterization that evokes the hybrid mimetic practice Roberto engages in throughout the film. In their daily cinematic practice, between shooting, grazing, cooking, milking, playing, there developed what Haraway (2004b, 144) might call a "congeries, or curious confederacy" of filmmakers, valley residents, goats, and pigs.

As I indicated earlier, the biggest challenge to hospitality in the film's narrative came from a villager named Emma, who owned a herd of cows and vigorously protested the incursions of Frenchmen and goats in her life. The crew, according to Chemello, encountered similar resistance from some of the valley's inhabitants, a few of whom showed open hostility (even to the point of calling the *carabinieri*, or Italian military police) at what they felt was an invasion of their privacy and a disregard for their quiet mountain existence. The crew recognized that they upset life in a mountain village that, as Biasi recalls, was used to "their silence, their rhythms. We bothered them, even if we behaved well." Yet Chemello underlines that while "there was some hostility, there was far more generosity." This generosity was particularly noteworthy considering that, as assistant director Roberto Carta explained, "the whole valley participated in a film in which their culture came under scrutiny (and it's not like the film ends well). That's very courageous."[31]

The actor who played Emma, Caterina Damiano, is significant in this regard. Cast in arguably the least flattering role in the film, the nonprofessional actor was, according to Carta and Goldoni, "sweet, a bit shy." In the "backstage" documentary that accompanies the commercial DVD, Damiano explains that in her extra-cinematic life, she worked as a housewife and a *collaboratrice domestica*, an expression that refers roughly to a housekeeper, but literally translates as "domestic collaborator." This cozy-sounding turn of phrase tends to describe work that is part of a shadow economy, frequently done by young, female, immigrant laborers.[32] As a type of labor, it is an example of profound, "in-depth transformations of the system of economic production" that, as Rosi Braidotti (2011, 22) articulates, "are also altering traditional social and symbolic structures." Braidotti, who labels the moment in economic history "postmodernism" (reconfiguring the aesthetic definitions preferred by some critics), spells out that: "in the West the move away from manufacturing toward a service and information-based structure entails a global redistribution of labor, with the rest of the world and especially the developing countries providing most of the underpaid off-shore production" (22–23). Such changes, she says, mark the "decline of traditional sociosymbolic systems based on the welfare state, class, and labor" (23). While she recognizes the power differentials that remain unresolved, Braidotti here sees an opening for feminists, nomads, and ethics. As a category of laborers, "domestic collaborators" and the new mobility they imply (a mobility that affects economic, social, cultural, and familial structures) underlie Braidotti's theory of the nomadic subject, defined as a "threshold of transformations" (25).[33] Embodied in the figure of Caterina Damiano, who self-identifies as a "domestic collaborator," the nomad and the threshold meet. Damiano aligns herself with a category of mobile laborers, essentially opening her life to contiguities with generational, ethnic, racial, and legal others without leaving her mountain valley. Volunteering to act in the film, she repeats and reinforces this openness-as-process, even as she stays in place.

According to Braidotti (2011, 26), nomadism does not in fact require actual physical movement, but rather confirms the "potency and relevance of the imagination, of myth making, as a way to step out of the political and intellectual stasis of our times." Through the creative realm of imagination, Braidotti underlines that her nomadic subject resists essentialism and flows through being, but without needing to leave her home: "Not all nomads are world travelers; some of the greatest trips can take place without physically moving from one's habitat" (26). In sharp contrast with the role she plays in the film, the actor Damiano signals the willingness of valley inhabitants to collaborate with the posthuman production, and specifically to be "domestic collaborators," "at home" (literally and figuratively) with the cinema that had come to inhabit—and also criticize—their valley. This openness to heterogeneous, technopoietic existence (being at home with cinema and with goats, cows, and pigs), the nomadic flowing through a space that most of the actors had inhabited for their entire lives, constitute an ethical horizon that resonates with Matthew Calarco's (2009b) notion of "agnostic animal ethics." Calarco's proposal, which he outlines in response to Paola Cavalieri's rights-based approach to the animal question, urges a poignant, empathetic process of nomadic transformation in the face of the Other: "Following Levinas, ethics can be generally defined as an interruption of my egoism coming from the face of an Other that transforms my being in the direction of generosity. In other words, ethics combines responsivity to the face with an enacted responsibility" (78). Responsivity and enacted responsibility, those qualities lacking in the cinematic narrative of *The Wind Blows Round*, were at many moments part of the filmmaking process. Both production crew and actors described a complicated, ongoing process of adaptation to geological, meteorological, and nonhuman Others. My interviewees in Bologna discussed the fact that, although they are aware of imperfections in the final film, they were so deeply involved in its creation that they cannot see its faults. For those nine months in Ussolo, residents of the valley and members of the film crew put narrative and nonhuman Others first. Like Calarco's agnostic ethics, making *The Wind Blows Round* involved: "a disruption of my perseverance in being that deeply affects and transforms my entire existence such that the Other becomes my priority" (78). And yet in spite of their openness to hosting the Other, two goats died for the film. What, then, of domestic collaboration? What of justice?

Cinema, Goat-Song, and Heterogeneous Justice?

A group of men and one woman sit around a table in a dark room, discussing whether or not they should help Philippe and his family relocate to Chersogno. The camera pans around the table, and the chiaroscuro and stern, rugged faces—many bearded—recall a Biblical scene that might have been painted by Caravaggio.

Throughout the film, villagers gather to pass judgment on the events unfolding around them. Whether in assemblies of the town council, around kitchen tables, or encounters at the local bar, it is clear that the inhabitants of Chersogno, like the film narrative itself, are negotiating positions on tricky questions. Given the cinematic context of sacrifice (and sacrificial goats), the chiaroscuro that illuminates the faces around the table in the above-described scene seems to carry a Biblical moral charge as well. The meeting space resonates with the material and cultural histories linking humans and goats, animals pictured in ancient cave paintings and petroglyphs as a sacrificial animal, and considered in Christian symbolism to represent sinners who have fallen from grace (Hinson 2015, 45, 11).[34] Yet negotiating justice around such a table, the stern envoys are not likely deliberating on the ethical weight of the nonhuman—the fate of the goats. As Calarco (2009b, 81) has argued, "Contemporary ethical discourse and practice do not take place in a vacuum, but emerge from out of a series of background practices and beliefs that have placed the interests of most animals outside the scope of moral and political considerability." The villagers' concerns, although piqued by goats and their droppings, are markedly anthropocentric, and frequently egocentric. The same might be said of much of the history of filmmaking.

Earlier, I discussed the fact that cinema has a long history of disregarding animal life, but film viewers are no doubt familiar with the assertion, often found at the end of Hollywood films, that "No animal was harmed in the making of this film." In the United States, the American Humane Association's (AHA) Film and Television Unit sponsors animal safety monitors

Figure 3.3. Heterogeneous Justice. Screen capture, *The Wind Blows Round* (2005), directed by Giorgio Diritti.

on set; this practice was established in 1939 after a horse was forced to leap off a cliff, falling to his death, for a scene in the film *Jesse James* (Malamud 2012, 70–71). The above-cited reassurance, found at the end of many films, was first used in 1989. Randy Malamud (2012, 71) explains that the AHA's goal is to "safeguard animals on-set." More specifically, the AHA states that it aims to monitor "the welfare of the live animals used in film production, and to that end, we refrain from commenting on content" (qtd. in Malamud 2012, 71). Animals can die or be treated in atrocious ways in the film's diegetic world, in other words, as long animal actors are not harmed. In Lippit's (2002, 9) terms, such an assertion reassures viewers that "cinematic realism [. . .] is not contiguous with outside reality." As such, it "protects, as it were, the interior, diegetic dimension of the film from the outside world" (10). Yet, as Malamud points out, that AHA assurance does not "protect against a rhetoric of violence" (71). I should note that no certification analogous to "no animals were harmed" exists yet in Italy, although animal rights activists do raise objections to animal deaths onscreen, and some Italian films include a version of the AHA disclaimer in their closing titles.[35]

This chapter and this project more widely aim to show that the cinematic membrane is more permeable, and the cinematic apparatus more complex, than an assertion claiming "no animals were harmed" would like to guarantee. In filming *The Wind Blows Round*, the "domestic collaboration" linking filmmakers, professional and non-professional actors, goats, sheep, cows, pigs, and film crew caused stories on set and stories onscreen to intermingle, and in this final section I wonder whether this contamination of the Alpine reality with the cinematic narrative means something significant when we consider the death of the two goats. Once again, I approach this question with some anxiety. I am moved by the humility of eminent scholars who admit their fallibility when confronting the massively complex and ethically urgent animal question. Calarco (2009b, 84) writes that: "It is a risk to focus on animals, even when this focus is open-ended and generously agnostic. It is a risk to constrain our thinking to focus on the specific history of animal subjection and resistance, even when that history is viewed in conjunction with other histories of struggle and oppression. There are no guarantees that we have gotten things right here." And Haraway (2008, 79) confesses, as she launches into a discussion of the relationship between humans working with animals in laboratories: "I am afraid to start writing what I have been thinking about all this, because I will get it wrong—emotionally, intellectually, and morally—and the issue is consequential." I draw courage from their hesitancy, because Calarco and Haraway powerfully show us that these are risky questions worth asking.

First, it is significant that the death of the two goats in the film *is* a tragedy in the narrative, provoking the Héraud family's departure and Roberto's suicide. The goats' death evokes the very etymology of the word "tragedy," which is commonly held to mean "goat-song" in Greek.[36] In the diegesis, beyond the French family's departure, the three deaths also incite reflection. After the town gathers to mourn Roberto, one young resident, Massimo, the son of a cattle farmer and friend of the Hérauds, opts to stay in Chersogno. In the film's final frames, he lights a fire in a large stone fireplace and crouches in front of it, tending the hearth. This literal kindling and metaphorical rekindling of the village's past recalls the importance that Marchesini assigns, in his posthuman philosophy, to Hestia, goddess of the hearth (and by extension architecture and domesticity). Crouching in front of the stone fireplace, Massimo suggests a disposition to re-embody the Otherness that the village failed to accept in Philippe and his family. In such a way, he incorporates Roberto, the Hérauds, and the goats into his imagination and his future. Marchesini (2014, xx) explains the convergence of the domestic Hestia and the nomadic Hermes (god of travelers and patron of herders, among other things) in a way that resonates with *The Wind Blows Round*, since his account incorporates notions of nomadism and domesticity, and also the other-in-flight that Roberto represents: "Otherness does not precede the relationship of threshold, the place that makes the natures of Hestia (welcoming) and Hermes (pilgrimage) converge. In the moment in which the agapic situation of the with-self is recognized, the bird-in-flight becomes a companion who can show another dimension of being and figure this dimension as a possible and thus translatable condition. The phenomenon becomes epiphany, annunciation, and no longer shows itself in the form of a bird that flies but of a with-self-in-flight." In Marchesini's view, it is specifically the *becoming-animal,* the becoming-Other, that allows the nomad to be a "threshold of transformations" (Braidotti's term). Such a becoming, in the film, will change Massimo's relationship to Chersogno, and thus at least hypothetically open toward a less essentialist future.

In this regard, the production itself and its reciprocal opening—together with the Alpine valleys in which it was set and filmed—toward self-reflection and hospitality seem significant. I have already mentioned the creative contract that admitted all of the film crew as co-producers. This strategy, according to Goldoni, meant that "I did my work for myself but also for others." Carta agreed that people were working "to make *their* film." As they labored together, the hybrid community of filmmakers, valley residents, novices and experts, professionals and non-professionals created a choral production that acknowledges and celebrates its horizontality, or what Haraway (2004a) might call the "ontological choreography" that made it possible. This is not a universally positive process since, like in the formation of Haraway's companion species, "Both people and their [here cinematic] partners are co-constructed in the history of companion species, and the issues of hierarchy and cruelty, as well as colleagueship and responsibility, are open and polyvalent, both historically and morally" (316–17). But again in parallel to Haraway's companion species, in *The Wind,* cinematic ontological choreography performs an active "yearning for more livable and lively relationships across kinds, human and non-human" (317).

The Wind Blows Round was not only creative in its production process, but also in its distribution phase, which did not proceed according to the typical industry procedure. In describing the 2005 release of the film, Stefania Tulli (2008, 21–22) writes that in spite of having won recognition at numerous festivals, Italian distributors did not want to risk too much on a film "that talks about goats and herders." The producers decided, instead, to opt for a grassroots distribution strategy, calling on regional film commissions and art house cinemas to distribute the five prints of the film. This highly regional approach worked, as reflected by the fact that the film ran for eight months straight in Milan's Cinema Mexico.[37] Most significantly, many members of the crew—actors and director, producers and makeup artists—accompanied the film as it was screened in and around the Occitan valleys where it was shot, participated in question and answer sessions, and discussed its contents with people who recognized themselves in the narratives that unfolded onscreen. Chemello recounts that: "A debate of collective self-awareness began and continued for months. So many thank-yous, people saying, 'you showed me what we really are, mountain dwellers: culturally, historically, our mentality.'" The conclusion of filming, in this case, was not the end of a relationship that developed during the on-location shooting, but the beginning of a conversation about the future of mountain villages and the consequences of remaining excessively tied to tradition—or of mischaracterizing it. Valla, whose idea for the screenplay was based on events that happened in another Alpine valley (and who lives in a valley nearby), notes that because of this there has been a "maturation of thought" in the valley.

Valla insists that this continuity post-location shooting has important ethical implications for cinematic behavior vis-à-vis location shoots as well. "When the film is finished, often the director no longer maintains relationships with people. During the film, there are relationships of friendship, of debate. It is good that they persist, because otherwise the film is an act of exploitation. That is not right." In Chapter Two, I discuss the ecological and material exploitation that can characterize on-location shooting; Valla underlines (and here his language echoes that of Garrone working in Naples) that the cinematic machine often "wastes" human resources as well. In its distribution strategy, *The Wind* carefully sutured audiences and crewmembers into a common cinematic community, honoring the reciprocal respect that was necessary to make the film, and it created continuities with the extra-cinematic world during and after its release.

At the same time that it went about the business of forming community, *The Wind Blows Round* considers the implications of violence: the potential violence of the cinematic machine, the exclusionary violence of certain kinds of rural thinking, physical violence against self and against nonhuman others. An important question, then, is whether this recognition of structural violence can help open the way to structural change.

Calarco (2009a, 138) suggests that ethical philosophy must challenge exist-ing hierarchies, imagining "alternative ways to think about ethics that are decidedly nonhierarchical, nonperfectionist, and nonexclusionary." As a creative, hybrid cinematic production, *The Wind* nods toward becoming something like what Wolfe (2008, 122) has called "a shared trans-species being-in-the-world constituted by complex relations of trust, respect, de-pendence, and communication." The end of the film deconstructs the mem-ory of the *rueido*, as well as the "anthropocelebrative" (Marchesini's term) promotional film being created to advertise Chersogno as a tourist destina-tion. In its final minutes, *The Wind* instead proposes another kind of ethics, based on Roberto's flight (which we see in flashback one final time after his funeral). The slow-motion images of Roberto flapping his wings exist in a world entirely apart from the negotiations, cited at the beginning of this section, around the village table. Clearly lit, unshadowed, lacking dia-logue, Roberto's flight evokes a notion of unselfconscious difference, along with that centrifugal hospitality that extends its reach to the frames and the spaces and beings around him. According to Haraway (2008, 90), "multi-species flourishing requires a robust nonanthropomorphic sensibility that is accountable to irreducible differences." Roberto's flight, which expresses that irreducible difference, repeats itself and does not allow us to forget.

Considering the production process, the tales the crewmembers told me about the goats, which accompany and nuance the story of the mur-dered goats in the film, courageously bring to light animal sacrifice as well as the often-hidden subject of animal slaughter. As Lippit suggested with his notion of "spectral animals," and as Tobias Menely and Margaret Ronda (2013, 27) outline, animal slaughter has become an "increasingly sanitary, monitored, institutionalized, and en masse process." The slaughterhouse hides the bloodshed upon which our modern society relies, making animals into commodities, "segregating the consumer from animal life, enabling him or her to enjoy, in innocence, the animal product like any other com-modity" (28). "No animals were harmed in the making of this film," the AHA's reassurance at the end of many Hollywood films, glosses over the ani-mal deaths that create celluloid and the animal byproducts that stabilize dig-ital equipment. It dodges the rhetoric of violence that materializes in many cinematic narratives. Like the slaughterhouse, it sanitizes cinematic narra-tive and segregates the worlds inside and outside of the film. *The Wind Blows Round* foregrounds animal death, and spectators, actors, and crew must all face the uncomfortable knowledge of our complicity in those deaths.

Wolfe (2008, 122) describes another possible ethical framework for our relation to differently abled and nonhuman others, based "not on ability, activity, agency, and empowerment, but on a *compassion* that is rooted in our vulnerability and passivity," one "freely extended without hope of reciprocation by the Other." This kind of justice is heterogeneous and *specific*, as Wolfe (2009b, 53–54) explains, citing Derrida; it "always involves our confrontation with an ethical situation that is always precisely *not* generic [. . .]; it obeys instead a double articulation in which the difference between law and justice is always confronted in *specific* situations whose details matter a great deal." In making *this* film in *that* Alpine valley, there was a great deal of compassion shared between goats, pigs, cows, film crews, and valley inhabitants. Compassion, of course, as Haraway and others have observed, is etymologically "sharing suffering."

Assistant production manager Rocco Lobosco remembers vividly the assembly to discuss the fate of the two goats. The crew met in the large dining hall, and each expressed an opinion. They took all views into consideration, because, he says, "The balance is very delicate. This could have been a breaking point. A decision could have been imposed. But it was better [this way]."[38] Although inevitably insufficient, the decision to recognize the goats' death meant that their slaughter—for the film, for our industrial agricultural society—did not go unnoticed. Weil (2012, 112) wonders: "Might mourning the dead animal also be a means of counteracting the silence that exists over its loss and a means to acknowledge and possibly work to change the ways that culture is also constructed over its dead body?" In *The Wind Blows Round,* mourning the goats was part of the account of production and distribution that has been recounted and re-recounted in numerous screenings attended by residents of Alpine valleys and members of the cast and production crew, a story recounted to this scholar of Italian cinema on a rainy March day in Bologna. Weil argues that: "We are not only autobiographical animals; we are biographical animals who seek to acknowledge those whose lives have been entangled with ours, whose lives have changed ours" (103). Each of the human lives that contributed to creating the film, each of their memories of Ussolo and their cine-domestic life, are marked by the congeries of creatures jumbled together in that space and time.

No matter what conclusions are tentatively drawn here, though, a torrent of questions follows in their wake. Should *The Wind Blows Round* have filmed two, real, dead goats? If the goats were to die anyway, is it worse that they were killed for visual consumption than for a meal? And if they had

Been destined for dinner, what if those plates had gone uneaten, or those leftovers had spoiled in the refrigerator? Should we even watch films if they are based materially on animal sacrifice? Can we and should we envision a world in which such sacrifices are not necessary, or not allowable? Must we acknowledge that the world as we know it has been built on animal sacrifice? Where are the limits of our ethical responsibility to the nonhuman other? And to human others? If this film has done its work, these and other questions continue to haunt us long after the closing credits roll, and "we" include inhabitants of the Valle Maira, of Piedmont, of the film production crew, of the international community of viewers who saw *The Wind Blows Round* at festivals, in art house cinemas, and in film courses. Haunted or not, we are not absolved of guilt. But if we stage our position as tragedy, as "goat-song," we at least sing it for ourselves and others and do not let it disappear from view. Haraway (2008, 85) argues that "the logic of sacrifice makes no sense and the hope for forgiveness depends on learning a love that escapes calculation but requires the invention of speculative thought and the practice of remembering, of rearticulating bodies to bodies." The film crew, however awkwardly, gathered to mourn those lost goats, and, as Weil (2012, 103) insists, "mourning means attesting to a life."

Notes

1. Citing Jean Rouch, Luca Caminati (2011, 129) suggests that Diritti's approach might be understood as "participatory ethnography" or "shared anthropology," and writes that this method challenges "once and for all the hierarchy of representation implied in any account of otherness and alterity."

2. Katia Goldoni, interview by author, Bologna, March 8, 2013. All information from Goldoni was collected during this interview.

3. All translations of Marchesini's work are my own. Given the hybrid, collaborative scope of his philosophy and the ethical goals of this chapter, I have chosen to translate "uomo" as "human," rather than man, and have used the female rather than the male pronoun in several instances. Marchesini often uses "uomo" (man) and "umano" (human) interchangeably.

4. Elizabeth Leake (2014, 43), focusing on the novels of Piedmontese writer Cesare Pavese, finds similarly that women in his stories are frequently aligned with goats, pigs, and other animals in narratives that repeatedly insist that all of these are sacrificeable, and that "the countryside is the habitual site of violence."

5. *The Animal Question* was originally published in Italian as *La questione animale* (1999). Cavalieri's analytic philosophical approach (she deems this "analytic moral philosophy") has been much debated and nuanced, including in *The Death of the Animal* where a roundtable is staged between Cavalieri, Matthew Calarco, John M. Coetzee, Harlan B. Miller, and Cary Wolfe (2009). While my own approach draws more on the material and

posthuman perspectives of Rosi Braidotti, Calarco, Haraway, Marchesini, Wolfe, and others, nevertheless, I recognize the analytic tradition as an important contributor to the framing of this ethically pressing debate.

6. In this sense, his trajectory recalls that of the career of Donna Haraway, which encompasses zoology, biology, feminism, philosophy, and capers with her dog, Cayenne Pepper.

7. His scholarly works include, for example, *Il tramonto dell'uomo: La prospettiva post-umanista* (*The Twilight of Man: The Post-humanist Perspective*, 2009), and *Etologia filosofica: alla ricerca della soggettività animale* (*Philosophical Ethology: The Search for Animal Subjectivity*, 2016).

8. To quote Pick and Narraway (2013, 3) more extensively, nonhuman animal "byproducts are part of the photographic and media apparatus (from the oil used to power film production, transmission and consumption, to the collagen-containing gelatin of the filmstrip emulsion, or the stearic acid in the plastic parts of computers), and the human labour in front of and behind the camera: animal life is quite literally the stuff of images."

9. Here Pick extends a logic she traces through André Bazin's work. In the introduction to *Screening Nature: Cinema Beyond the Human*, she and Guinevere Narraway (2013, 2) explain why Bazin is important for ecocinema studies: "Bazin situated cinema at the juncture of filmmaker, camera, and the world. The complex relationship between these three points is, for Bazin, revelatory and affirms—empirically and morally—the reality of the world and the realism of the medium."

10. I have also written about goats in an article discussing bodily memories of the interspecies past. See Past, "(Re)membering Kinship" (2014).

11. Joy Hinson (2015, 20–21) suggests that it is possible that goats as a species are Mediterranean in origin, since some of the earliest "ancestral goat fossil remains" were found in Pikermi and Samos, Greece (other similarly ancient fossils were found in Iran). The oldest of these are about 8.2 million years old. The oldest "true goat fossils," instead, are approximately 1.77 million years old and were found in Dmanisi, Georgia together with the remains of an early man, Homo georgicus.

12. Verona (2006, 32–34) refers specifically to the ruminants' ability to improve grass quality for chamois, roe deer, and deer, but she also discusses the return of wolf populations to Italy made possible by the continued presence of herds of domestic livestock. The World Wildlife Fund has been working in the region of Abruzzo to help herders find a path of cohabitation with wolves: with the regional administration and the *Associazione Protezione Animali* (APA, or Association for the Protection of Animals), they promote wildlife tourism and compensate herders for animals lost to predators (34).

13. In her chapter on the "Twenty-First-Century Goat," Hinson (2015, 132–45) discusses the use of goats to harvest argan oil for the cosmetics industry, the many goat festivals held around the world, goat racing, and goat mascots for military brigades and sports teams. Her book, published in the Reaktion Books animal series, is an excellent starting point for considering the natural and cultural history of the goat.

14. In his 1848 *The Book of the Goat; Containing Full Particulars of the Various Breeds of Goats and their Profitable Management*, Henry Stephen Holmes-Pegler remarked that "'the naturally roving disposition and well-known mischievous propensity of the goat are its great drawbacks'" (Hinson 2015, 59).

15. Hinson (2015, 78) argues that goats generally cause deforestation only in areas where humans have felled trees, and says that it is "the combination of human and goat activity that is responsible for the problem, causing goats to come into conflict with people."

16. In an article on the Valle Maira, Graziella Parati (2014, 311) demonstrates that the area has a dense, heterogeneous past, "where influences originating from the African continent have had an impact from the Middle Ages to the twentieth century." In her analysis of *The Wind Blows Round,* she shows that forgetting this part of the past keeps Chersogno from "constructing new proximities that have their roots in past heterogeneities" (318).

17. In her chapter on "sharing suffering" in *When Species Meet,* Haraway (2008, 71) tackles the thorny question of science's use—and abuse—of animals, especially in laboratories. Her arguments encompass the degree to which our relationships with the nonhuman world inevitably result in our instrumental use—not just for science, but also for art—of nonhuman others: "work, use, and instrumentality are intrinsic to bodily webbed mortal earthly being and becoming."

18. Fredo Valla, interview by author, Milan, May 6, 2013. All the information I cite from Valla was collected in this interview.

19. As Iovino (2010b, 54) argues, rather than celebrating or embracing "a simplistically 'harmonious' and 'balanced' worldview," refusing humanity-as-normality allows us to "substitute the concept of dualism with that of complexity." Roberto and his marginal position in the community thus resonate deeply with the connections scholars have been building between disability studies, animal studies, and posthumanism. Cary Wolfe (2008, 110) argues that the former two areas of study are "two of the most philosophically ambitious and ethically challenging" among the "contemporary fields of interdisciplinary cultural studies that have emerged over the past decade."

20. Alpine Provençal, or occitan alpin, is listed as "definitely endangered" in the UNESCO Atlas of the World's Languages in Danger. Piedmontese is also considered "definitely endangered." See http://www.unesco.org/languages-atlas/, accessed July 30, 2018.

21. Language, specifically, and the "linguistic turn" in philosophy, are part of a "dogma" that for Wolfe (2008, 111) is "founded in no small part on the too-rapid assimilation of the questions of subjectivity, consciousness, and cognition to the question of language ability."

22. I will return to questions of hospitality in the next section, but here would note that my notion of "conditional hospitality" comes from Giovanna Faleschini Lerner's (2010, 7) work on migration cinema. Speaking of multiculturalism, which could describe Chersogno's initial welcome of the Héraud family, she notes that such hospitality "places the immigrant consistently in the subordinate position of the guest who needs to be instructed in the laws of the house and is subjected to the authoritative judgment of those that inhabit it." Jennifer Fay (2018, 16) has innovatively adopted the notion of "hospitality" to analyze cinema in the Anthropocene, asking "How might hospitality be understood as concerning not only human rights but also a regard and even a right that humans extend to the earth and the earth back to humans? [...] Is there any hospitality to be found in the image?"

23. Wolfe (2008, 122), also arguing from a Derridean ethical position, posits that: "the ethical force of our relation to the disabled and to non-human others is precisely that it foregrounds the necessity of thinking ethics outside of a model of reciprocity between 'moral agents'; indeed (as a range of thinkers from Levinas and Lyotard to, more recently, Zygmunt Bauman has argued), the ethical act might instead be construed as precisely one that is freely extended without hope of reciprocation by the Other."

24. DeMello (2012, 84) explains that animals are domesticated "when they are kept for a distinct purpose, humans control their breeding, their survival depends on humans, and they develop genetic traits that are not found in the wild." Haraway (2004b, 142) writes that domestication "refers to the situation in which people actively force changes in the seasonal subsistence cycles of animals to make them coincide with particular human needs."

25. As Marchesini (2015, 190) has argued, "When we play with a dog, we think we are the ones who domesticated him, and not that our ancient alliance laid the foundations for what we are today."

26. The notion of "philosophical ethology" has been defined, in a series of special issues of *Angelaki*, as an approach to "human/animal relations not merely as textual plays of language but as domains of bodily comportment and conduct" (Buchanan, Bussolini, and Chrulew 2014, 1). Curating the translation of works by Lestel, Marchesini, and Vinciane Despret into English, Brett Buchanan, Jeffrey Bussolini, and Matthew Chrulew chart a zone of engagement that values "overlapping ways of knowing—empirical, phenomenological, ethnographic, otherwise" (1), and that makes sense of Marchesini's eclectic methodologies and projects that I described at the beginning of this chapter.

27. Weil borrows the term "anthropodenial" from anthropologist Frans de Waal's book *Primates and Philosophers: How Morality Evolved* (2006).

28. The above quote is preceded by this more problematic affirmation that reverses the relationship of dominance: "The herder is a slave. The beasts command, always, with their needs and their demands. You can never abandon them. And then there are laws, bureaucracy, prohibitions that are sometimes absurd and anachronistic. The spaces are never infinite or without borders" (Verona 2006, 238). I take issue with Verona's characterization of the "beasts" who control the lives of the herders and the notion of a master-slave relationship that makes sheep dominant. Such an affirmation both misunderstands domestication and divides herder from herd, when their relationship is actually much more entangled than this would imply. In her entry for the word *bestia* (beast), Eleonora Adorni (2015, 28) argues that the word exceeds Linnaean taxonomies: "the beast [*fiera*] is an impure entity, theriomorphic and beyond the confines of what humans are willing to consider as a neighbor or known."

29. Mario Chemello explained that the crew was there initially from February through March, shooting scenes with snow; then late May through June; and again in September. They returned in October to capture some final scenes (interview by author, Bologna, March 8, 2013. All information from Chemello was collected in this interview).

30. Pierangela Biasi, interview by author, Bologna, March 8, 2013. All information from Biasi was collected during this interview.

31. Roberto Carta, interview by author, Bologna, March 8, 2013. All information from Carta was collected during this interview.

32. In 2012, foreigners accounted for nearly 90% of newly registered domestic workers. The prevalence of foreigners in the informal market means that the number of domestic collaborators is likely much higher than the 766,000 officially counted by the *Istituto Nazionale della Previdenza Sociale,* or National Institute of Social Security (see Barbiano di Belgiojoso and Ortensi 2015, 1124). A search on Google scholar for "collaborazione domestica" returned many articles whose titles include words like "immigration" and "migration," as well as "informal economy," "submerged economy," "discrimination," and even "slavery," aptly indicating the unstable, marginal associations with this job description.

33. It should be noted that, in the case of "domestic collaborators," the material-economic thresholds of transformation—realized in part, for example, in the national collective agreement for domestic workers of 2007—are limited, considering the "low exit rates" from the domestic sector, particularly for women (see Barbiano di Belgiojoso and Ortensi 2015).

34. Hinson (2015, 45) further notes, regarding the Biblical importance of goats, that the Bible uses ten different words for goat: seven in Hebrew, three in Greek. In the context of goats and judgment, Hinson observes that the Gospel of Matthew says that on Judgment Day

people will be divided between the sheep and the goats, with the goats condemned to eternal damnation for not having behaved charitably (105).

35. A memorable protest was raised against Giuseppe Tornatore's Sicilian epic *Baaria* (2009). In one scene, a cow was slaughtered by having its throat cut; the scene was filmed in Tunisia, apparently because it would have been a crime in Italy according to animal cruelty laws. The LAV, or Anti-Vivisection League, was vocal in asking why the scene was filmed in Tunisia, and why Tornatore did not choose to use special effects ("Bovino" 2009). The LAV regularly makes inquiries about possible animal cruelty on set, and president Gianluca Felicetti called for a regulation against animal abuse in cinema ("Animali" 2013). Some Italian films adopt the AHA formulation: "nessun animale è stato maltrattato per realizzare questo film," but as of yet there is no official certification procedure.

36. The reasons for this etymology are debated: perhaps the original chorus was a group of goat-tailed satyrs, singing to Dionysus; perhaps goats were sacrificed or given as prizes in festivals of Dionysus (see Ferguson 2013, 3–6 and Gilbert 2013, 301 n8).

37. The film's eventual success at the box office also meant, according to Chemello, that all of the volunteer co-producers could at last be paid back for their labor.

38. Rocco Lobosco, interview by author, Bologna, March 8, 2013. All the information I cite from Lobosco was collected in this interview.

4

SILENCE, CINEMA, MORE-THAN-HUMAN SOUND: *LE QUATTRO VOLTE*

*S*OUND RECORDISTS PAOLO BENVENUTI AND SIMONE PAOLO OLIVERO *met me in a noisy bar in Milan to talk about capturing sound for* Le quattro volte *(2010), a film released in English-language markets with no subtitles because it has virtually no audible human dialogue. The recording of our conversation is punctuated by the tinkling notes of a jazz piano, chairs scraping along the floor, traffic noise, ambulance sirens departing from the nearby hospital where Benvenuti and Olivero had been working on another film, someone whistling. Production manager Marco Serrecchia met me at the American Bar in Rome near Piazza Fiume, and in the background a steady stream of hits from the 1980s, most distinctively Belinda Carlisle's "I Get Weak," provides a soundtrack to our dialogue. Every now and then, there is the clink of a glass, or the distinctive thump of the filter basket for the espresso machine. When I spoke with director Michelangelo Frammartino two years earlier in Milan on a hotel patio, workers were cleaning the stone floors with cacophonous polishing equipment. My ears can, at all points, make out the spoken words documented by my faithful digital recorder, but sometimes I have to focus intently in order to not lose the thread. My recordings of these exchanges perform and affirm Frammartino's assertion that "words are sounds in the midst of many others."*[1]

This is the story of the eloquent "silence" of the more-than-human world, and of a cinema that stretches outward to acknowledge it.

In writing about *Red Desert* and the growing environmental movement in Italy (Chapter One), I cited the 1963 Italian publication of Rachel Carson's *Silent Spring* as a watershed, a moment when attention shifted from conservation to the fight against pollution. Carson's ([1962] 1994) landmark text, often lauded for communicating its message in a moving style, condemns deadly pesticides including DDT, aldrin, dieldrin, and arsenic by illustrating the devastating results of their use. From its portrayal of agonized, dying songbirds to dead house and barn cats and post-apocalyptic roadways despoiled of endemic trees and flowers, her work paints a bleak picture of a world doused in industrial toxins. Both the book's title and its famous first chapter, "A Fable for Tomorrow," conjure up the "strange stillness" of a "spring without voices" (2). Carson's poignant evocation underlines that the tragedy of the chemical poisoning of our shared environment is an acoustic catastrophe, among other things. Her work thus suggests that, to gauge the health of ecosystems, one of the things that we need to learn to do is to listen to them more carefully.

More than half a century from the publication of *Silent Spring*, the significance of listening to the more-than-human world has not diminished, but the sounds of spring have changed. One of the reasons we might fail to hear the "voices of spring" in the early twenty-first century has to do with human-caused factors no longer attributable to the mass die-offs provoked by DDT, but rather with questions of sound itself. Anthropogenic noise today reaches nearly every corner of the globe. Urban development; transportation systems including air travel, roadways, and shipping; resource extraction and other industrial activities; and motorized recreation are some of the primary causes of increased anthropogenic sound, even in areas we might expect to be free of such incursions (Barber, Crooks, and Fristrup 2010, 180–81). Chronic noise exposure is "a significant threat to the integrity of terrestrial ecosystems" (180). It can produce a range of extra-auditory effects documented in humans, including sleep disturbance, depression, cognitive impairment, and respiratory disease (González 2014, 344–45). In the more-than-human world, one of the most immediate threats for many species is that of "masking," when noise inhibits perception of sounds like predator footfalls, wing flapping, or alarm calls (Barber, Crooks, and Fristrup 2010, 180–81). Since many nonhuman animals rely on sound for orientating, defending themselves, hunting, mating, and communicating more generally, shifts in the soundscape can dramatically alter their abilities to interact with their environment (González 2014, 344). Beyond the direct effect of noise on nonhuman animals, scientists have also documented noise-driven shifts in "ecological services" such as seed dispersal and pollination (Francis et al. 2012, 2727–28). This means that noise can indirectly change the vegetal landscape, albeit in ways that are unpredictable and sometimes not measurable for long periods of time.[2] Within our bodily space, over time, noise exposure can change the way that we hear things, resulting in temporary or permanent hearing loss, or tinnitus, a perception of sound in the ears when no external sound is present (González 2014, 344). And in the world around us, nonhuman animal species have been found to change the frequencies of their vocalizations as the result of noise pollution (Barber et al. 2011, 1283 and Hempton and Grossman 2009, 184–85). Sound record-ist Gordon Hempton (2009) reports that his recordings of birds in captiv-ity were unrecognizable to ornithologists working with the same species in the wild, noting that because of anthropogenic noise, the "avian choir is not just shrinking, but forgetting its repertoire" (185). In Italy, Damiano Benvengù (2018, 37) cites recent Italian studies affirming the importance of birdsong as an indicator of biodiversity, warning that more than half of the species that regularly nest in Italy are at risk. Thus the voices of spring may actually be singing a different tune in the Anthropocene, if we are able to hear them over the din of our own acoustic production.

Like Carson's vivid notion of a silent spring, the very material con-sequences of noise pollution help us to picture a force that is frequently thought of as immaterial, or is "overlooked" in Western cultures where the visual tends to dominate. Sound, after all, is invisible, and in the absence of a recording device, it dissipates in space over time. But it also depends inherently on matter to move, requiring air, earth, water, or another sub-stance to transmit its waves. Once it enters a human body, sound travels through air, eardrums, and bones, and causes synapses to fire. Sean Cubitt (1998, 95) elaborates on the fact that it is impossible to: "distinguish between the vibration of the air, the vibration of the eardrum and the bones (the feet, after the ears, are our most sensitive receptors, especially of bass notes; the collarbone and chest respond to more airborne sounds), and the neurobio-logical events which, in consort, provide us with the mental event of sound perception." Sound waves quite literally move something inside us, even as our bodies absorb and reflect them; they show, as Cubitt articulates, "no respect for the sacrosanctity of the epidermis in Western philosophy" (95). As we acknowledge the multiple pathways of sound through our bodies, so should we recognize the many trajectories of our own, anthropogenic sounds through other bodies, part of an exchange of vibrant (and specific-ally vibrating) materiality.

The material effects of sound and the material pathways via which it travels resonate in ecocinema studies, where they indicate yet another way that film impacts and circulates in a world beyond the screen. In film analysis, Christian Metz (1999, 357) points out that the distinctions we draw between on- and off-screen sound, part of a series of divisions between "primary and secondary qualities" of the cinematic apparatus, are at best approximate, since a sound is either "audible or it doesn't exist." Elaborating on and challenging the traditional categories, Metz argues that: "When [sound] exists, it could not possibly be situated within the interior of the rectangle or outside of it, since the nature of sounds is to diffuse themselves more or less into the entire surrounding space: sound is simultaneously 'in' the screen, in front, behind, around, and throughout the entire movie theater" (357). The attempt to locate sound in space draws analysis off screen and into the theater, where it mingles with the noises produced by audiences and technologies; it also nudges criticism into the spaces where film crews, recording technologies, and the more-than-human world speak in a myriad of voices. Like in a body, in cinema, sound travels throughout the space, touching and responding to the organic and inorganic surfaces that it encounters. What we call "silent cinema" in English is called "cinema muto" in Italian—not without sound, but rather mute, refraining from speech. This lexical difference underlines a fact that scholars of early film have frequently remarked: cinema was never silent, whether we think of the world on set or the projection in a theater. Although cinema did not originally record diegetic sound, even "silent" film sets were lively places that buzzed with the noises of the cinematic apparatus. John Belton (1999, 379–80) has described the evolution of cinematic technology, an evolution designed to lessen noise and distortion on set: encasing cameras, quieting the buzz of lighting systems, building quieter sets, reducing pickup on microphones.[3] From the need for such innovations, we can derive an idea of the humming and buzzing of the technologies that powered early filmmaking. Off set and in the movie houses, alongside theater noise and musical accompaniment for the images onscreen, the cinematic apparatus made noise, voicing its techno-industrial presence as celluloid ticked through the projector.

Today, the booming vibrations of surround sound focus our attention on the conventional cinematic soundscape of dialogue, sound effects, and music (Théberge 2008, 66).[4] In some ways, the noise emanating from the speakers also performs a masking function that diverts attention from the more multiplaned soundscape of film technologies, theater patrons, and non-cinematic noise (air and auto traffic, sirens, wind and rain, to name a few) that also vibrates the airwaves around film viewers. As Randolph

Jordan (2010) explains in his work on audiovisual ecology in cinema, contemporary technologies like THX attempt to perform "space replacement," or a complete standardization of theater architecture so that any place-based acoustic signature is eliminated. This, the theory goes, would allow for the perfect reproduction of whatever a film seeks to communicate via its soundtrack. But watching a film always means participating in intersecting sonic experiences (21–23). The quest for "sonic purification" can never entirely succeed in a space that admits crunchy popcorn, drinking straws, and human bodies.

In spite of the fact that sound has always been a part of what is now unequivocally our audio-vision, though, in many ways it has occupied a secondary position with respect to the image, in part because most Westerners are not as well-versed as listeners as we are as viewers. This in spite of the fact that comparative evolution tells a story of the critical importance of sound across species: auditory organs evolved before the ability to intentionally produce sound; many species hear a broader range of sounds than they can produce; and hearing still functions in sleep and hibernation (Barber, Crooks, and Fristrup 2010, 180).[5] Nevertheless, film theorists and ecocritics alike note human failings when it comes to listening to the more-than-human world. In film studies, Metz (1999, 358) argues for a sort of material-aesthetic bias, suggesting that there is a "conception of sound as an attribute, as a nonobject, and therefore the tendency to neglect its own characteristics in favor of its corresponding 'substance,' which in this case is the visible object, which has emitted the sound."[6] In the Italian case, this bias was underscored by a practice of post-synchronization, or dubbing voices in studio, that was legislated by the Fascist Regime and for many years continued to be standard cinematic practice.[7] As Antonella Sisto (2014, 8) has explained, in Fascist Italy, "all films, national and international, were dubbed into a 'standard' Italian, a studio-fashioned, affected, theatrical language that existed, vocally and linguistically, only at the movies." Such a practice, she insists, distances sound from image and creates a cognitive gap in spectatorship (9), and can at least potentially further extol the visual object. More dangerously, in its erasure of linguistic and vocal difference, Sisto argues that dubbing can constitute a "vocal/sensorial and cultural cannibalization of the other" (8).

Ecocriticism tends to point out, instead, an anthropocentric bias that directs the ear to listen to human sounds rather than those of the more-than-human world, a failing that has equally exclusionary implications.

Christopher Manes (1996) asserts that: "nature *is* silent in our culture (and in literate societies generally) in the sense that the status of being a speaking subject is jealously guarded as an exclusively human prerogative" (15, emphasis in original). Cubitt (1998, 107) argues for a correspondingly anthropocentric, but even more egocentric listening practice proper to humans, who have, in the process of "becoming rhetorical," "all but obliterated listening as a passive art." Both Manes and Cubitt argue that we would rather listen to ourselves speak than hear what a more-than-human world might have to say. Yet as Eduardo Kohn (2013, 42) has eloquently demonstrated, regarding communication via audible and other kinds of language, "signs are not exclusively human affairs. All living beings sign. We humans are [. . .] at home with the multitude of semiotic life. Our exceptional status is not the walled compound we thought we once inhabited."

Acoustic ecologists advocate for the preservation of disappearing soundscapes, and they also encourage humans to mindfully re-engage with the sonic complexity around us. In *The Sound Book*, Trevor Cox (2014) describes exercises developed by acoustic ecologists to retrain our ears to distinguish the heterogeneity of the world's plurivocal soundscapes. The process of "ear cleaning" (no cotton swabs required!) can include inventing new onomatopoeic words to describe sounds, not speaking for an entire day, exercising breath control, or taking a soundwalk, and is designed to reorient the ears and change the brain's reception of sound (16–21). Whether listening for birdcalls, whispered conversations, pneumatic drills, or jet aircraft, the idea is that we can train our ears to "filter things differently" (21), to hear the vibrations and the voices of the more-than-human world around us with attention to their nuance and at times (as Carson suggests) their urgency. Cinema, too, can effect a process of auditory retraining. As Belton (1999, 384) argues, the "recording aspects of motion picture technology possess dual characteristics: they both transmit and transform." A film production's strategic positioning of recording equipment reflects, he suggests, "a consciousness that sees and (in the sound film) hears and that coexists with what is seen or heard. [. . .] The cinema remains the phenomenological art par excellence, wedding, if indeed not collapsing, consciousness with the world" (384).[8] The process of recording sound for *Le quattro volte* constituted an awakening to the world's eloquence, as Benvenuti and Olivero explained: "When you remove the dialogue, you discover an enormous variety of sound."[9]

What follows here considers the acoustic geographies of *Le quattro volte*, a film that challenges conventions of both cinematic narrative and

sound through a responsive process of cohabitation with the filming locations. The film was made on location in Calabria over the course of three
years, migrating from Serra San Bruno, to Alessandria del Carretto, to Caulonia. It conjoins four different stories: that of a goatherd, a kid goat, a tree,
and charcoal. Drawing on the Pythagorean theory of metempsychosis, or
the soul's passage through human, animal, vegetable, and mineral phases,
Le quattro volte casts human and nonhuman actors in significant roles. The
Calabrian countryside onscreen is the very landscape of Magna Graecia
where Pythagoras lived and the Pythagoreans were based,[10] and its acoustic
qualities speak through a soundtrack that Benvenuti and Olivero captured
on location without using directional microphones. *Le quattro volte* affirms
the eloquent, disanthropocentric sound of "silence," or the broad soundscape that the human ear attuned to rhetoric tends to filter out. It quiets human voices in order to allow spectators to heed the articulate enunciations
of the more-than-human world.

The Sound of One Goat Sneezing: Air, Visualized

*An initially all-gray frame gradually clears, revealing smoke emanating
from large, dark smoldering mounds. The sound of wind whistles with the
movement.*

*In a large village church, sunlight filters through high windows and the
camera captures particles of dust suspended, and gently moving, in the air. A
very low, resonant rumble gives the impression of being underwater.*

*In a dark stable, a group of kid goats plays while their mothers graze on
the mountainside. They jockey for position on top of an iron washtub, and a
small brown and white one temporarily wins. From her position on top, center frame, she suddenly sneezes, spraying a cloud of spit.*

On a number of occasions in *Le quattro volte*, the mountain air is less than
clear. In the instances described above, dust, smoke, and spit cloud the
onscreen view, directing our attention to something interstitial, the space
between more solid objects. As these substances occupy the screen and
gradually (smoke) or suddenly (sneeze) dissipate, they show that air, too,
takes up room (as Giuliana recognized in *Red Desert*), and that the space in
between "things" is not empty at all. In this way, the film renders visible the
invisible, and points to its strategy of filling in, philosophically, ethically,
visually, and acoustically, those areas easily disregarded or forgotten by a
bourgeois society more apt to keep its eye on the consumable prize.

Figure 4.1. Sneezing Goat. Screen capture, *Le quattro volte* (2010), directed by Michelangelo Frammartino.

This fullness of space resonates with the philosophy of sound in *Le quattro volte*. Normally, on a film set, at the end of the day, sound recordists document the "room tone" or "presence," capturing the sound of that particular environment without dialogue. This process acknowledges the unique sonic characteristics of a place populated by sundry beings and things, since as sound waves travel around a location, they resonate differently depending on what they encounter along the way.[11] By filming the "presence" of an environment, sound recordists ensure that "silence" in that space has a quality that reflects its material makeup. More specifically, recording a room's presence underlines that when we talk about "silence" in cinema, we generally do not mean absence of sound. In a finished film mix, barring exceptional occasions, room tone occupies the space under dialogue or fills in when no one is speaking; a complete absence of sound might be used to upset convention, but otherwise can simply make it seem that theater equipment is malfunctioning.[12]

Benvenuti and Olivero discussed their work recording sound on sets in Milan, where many audiovisual artists are employed to make commercials. They explained that, when filming commercial spots, they skip the step of recording a room's "presence," since all that counts are the spoken lines and the music: "the rest doesn't exist, the environment [*ambiente,* which also can be translated as 'presence'] doesn't exist." In this sense, the anthropic, consumerist focus of the Milanese commercial world evacuates acoustic context, promoting a single message that lacks the multidimensionality of the lived world.[13] Working in Calabria, Benvenuti and Olivero once again did not have to record an environmental "presence" at the end of a day of filming, but this time because the goal of *Le quattro volte* was constantly that of capturing the broad soundscape. There was no anthropic vocal foreground positioned against an acoustic backdrop that needed to be convincingly "not empty." Rather, the pair sought to create a soundscape that could apprehend, as they explained, the "relationship between all of the acoustic subjects, almost equally. Even speech was equal to the rest." "Presence" was therefore not being recorded in order to fill a potential lack, but rather to represent the fullness of a sonic landscape whose vocalizations were primarily more-than-human.[14] Benvenuti and Olivero emphasized that their goal was to record the entire visual field, and to do so with attention to detail, or specifically to the separate sounds of various (principally nonhuman) actors in the plane. To achieve this, they generally worked with one mobile microphone, and then with as many as eight other mikes positioned across the landscape. The film's final mix reflects this diffusion of recording devices. In the first scene after the opening title, a long shot of a mountain meadow, a herd of goats arrives over the crest of a hill in the distance. On the soundtrack we hear wind, a fly buzz by, the bells on the goats' collars, birds tweeting, a dog barking, footfalls, a distant thumping. Not all of the distances of framing and volumes seem to perfectly correspond: the dog's bark sounds closer than the dog, initially, and the rest of the sounds seem diffused through the space. This phenomenon is repeated throughout the film, when sounds in the back of a deep frame are audible, and sounds presumably closer to the camera (human voices in particular) are not clear. The proximity of a mobile subject, whether wind, goat, or waving grass, to one of the microphones means that the actor, wherever she might find herself in the visible frame, can occupy a significant and discernable position in the acoustic landscape.

The recording strategy that Benvenuti and Olivero developed to capture the soundscape shifts the position of both film crew and spectator. They described, with awe and a hint of nostalgia, the degree of patience and respect producers, directors, and other members of the crew had for recording sound. The producers granted them an extra five days at the conclusion of filming to continue their meticulous sound work, a gesture unheard of for a low-budget film. Benvenuti and Olivero's innovative and extensive attention to recording practice also leads to a novel experience of acoustic playback, one that requires interpretive attention. In Hollywood cinema, Cubitt (1998) has examined the spectacular effects made possible by digital theatrical playback, like the helicopters that swoop from the back of the theater to the front screen in *Apocalypse Now.*[15] These effects, he explains, formulate an "ideal audition, a sonic architecture whose centre is carefully calibrated to coincide with each seat in the house" (116). He characterizes this centered listener as a "Cartesian subject" who "earns its sobriquet of neo-classicism by its return to the unification of the subject as its prime concern" (116). The subject described by Cubitt is in fact doubly Cartesian, as sound engineers commonly use Cartesian coordinates, or points along two- or three-dimensional axes, to situate their imagined listeners in space. In a more philosophical sense, however, the sense in which this subject is "neoclassical," the Cartesian subject indicates Descartes' separation of humans from animals, mind from body, or reason from matter; such dualisms celebrate man's ability to master nature by segregating him from the (supposedly) non-cogitating world. Not surprisingly, this version of Cartesian thought has been a focus of ecocriticism, which seeks to show that such divisions and hierarchies are untenable.[16] In *Le quattro volte*, the non-hierarchical origin of sound, which comes from throughout the visible space (and beyond), effects an acoustic de-centering of the subject. This disanthropocentric process continues to resonate in Frammartino's decision to not use surround sound in the majority of the film.[17] The director's choice, which he historicizes by explaining that Pythagoras taught from behind a curtain (a detail to which I return below), further calls into question the conventions of contemporary film and helps perform the work of shifting the spectator toward the periphery.

As I emphasized before, sound cannot materially reside in the space of the film screen, but rather envelops the audience, regardless of where it originates in the theater. Even sound from a Milanese commercial "moves not only the volumes of the air, but the mass of the body," as Cubitt (1998, 117) articulates. Yet some kinds of sounds, those designed with that Cartesian listener in mind, are engineered to give the spectator the illusion of the central importance of his own position, all the while choosing what it is he is supposed to hear. The work of directing the ear is "undertaken on our behalf," explains Cubitt, when a soundtrack hierarchically clarifies dialogue or other acoustic details. Unlike deep-focus or wide-screen technologies, which might allow our eyes to roam across the visual space in spite of an implied directionality of the gaze, "the constructed nature of the soundtrack constricts audition" (114).

Ironically, then, *Le quattro volte*'s soundscape, which does not envelop the audience at the outset *as* surround sound, but rather emerges from behind the screen, allows for a more flexible and subjective acoustic experience. It provides a wide auditory field with distinctive sonorous details, each one of which can be heard, if the ear so desires, in its particularity. In that opening frame depicting the mountain prairie, it is possible to listen across the plane, to choose to privilege the sound of wind, goat bells, or insect chirps, without the soundtrack strongly suggesting which is most important. Like a screen occupied entirely by smoke or dust, or sprayed with mucous by a kid goat, the acoustic space is filled with sonic details that carry equal weight.

Cubitt (1998, 120–21) suggests the potentials of a sonic design that does not constrain the ear but rather makes room for this kind of horizontal listening:

> An image in motion will always capture your look, inscribe you into a direction. But sound, as long as it is not contained by headphones or an individuated space, must be approached, walked into, penetrated, and, in walking into it, as your body subtly moulds the acoustic around it, the sound will penetrate you. Even as it does, the openness of this space, its architectural quality, becomes apparent: that an open soundscape is a world in which others exist as well as yourself. This combination of intimacy and publicity is the space of the dance, and of all the richness of communication and mutuality of which the dance, however pensive, however irrational, however self-involved, is capable.

Le quattro volte's soundscape invites viewers into what Donna Haraway (2008, 25) defines as a "dance of relating," a dance between film production and cinemagoer where ears and eyes are unconstrained by acoustic convention. Like the relationship Haraway describes with her dog Cayenne Pepper, this film "is about co-constitutive naturalcultural dancing, holding in esteem, and regard open to those who look back reciprocally" (27). Only here, "respect" is not only based on "*respecere*," looking back, but also reciprocal listening. The film leaves ample room for other voices to come to the fore, whether singing crickets, bleating goats, chirping 35-mm projectors, or teeth crunching popcorn.

In this horizontal acoustic space, the goat's sneeze, which was probably "the sweetest, most delicate" sound Benvenuti and Olivero recorded, is a biosemiotic tool that can open the film's sonic perspectives. Both delightfully familiar and unfamiliar, the sound of a sneezing goat suggests a common human/caprine tendency to react, bodily, to our surroundings. Regarding goats and sneezing, animal behaviorists, who characterize goats as "vociferous" creatures, hypothesize that a certain high-pitched goat sneeze is an "alarm vocalization" that warns the rest of the herd of danger (Miranda-de la Lama and Mattiello 2010, 2), although illness and nasal worms can also cause them to sneeze. The baby goat in the film seems to be happily at play, but Frammartino points out that goats often fear the goatherds and by extension other humans, so perhaps this sneezing kid is actually issuing a warning to her companions. Of course, we may not fully understand the meaning of goat vocalizations. Daniel Gilfillan (2016) reminds us that we can never truly "inhabit" the audio receptors of other species, and thus we can only make theoretical assumptions about other animals' production, transmission, and reception of sound. Uncertainty regarding the significance of the baby goat's communication does not negate its importance in the more-than-human horizon of the film, though. Assuming that I cannot know the experience of the baby goat might lock me into the idea that I am stuck at one pole of "absolute otherness, irreducible difference, incommensurability" with respect to the beautiful creature onscreen (Kohn 2013, 86). Yet making some "provisional guesses" about trans-species meaning allows for what Kohn (2013, 86–87) calls "living thought," a creative, shifting way of knowing that is always, necessarily mediated. Hazarding such guesses with cinematic sound enlivens them even further. On location and for spectators, the sound waves created by that goat sneeze vibrate the bodies of a posthuman herd of animal, vegetable, and mineral actors. Those waves shift stubborn bodies and certainties, and reveal that we are "emergent ephemeral waypoints in a dynamic process" of cinematic relation (87).

Non-Anthropocentric Sound: The Dog's Footfall

Panorama of the mountain meadow. A dog runs around the perimeter of a herd of goats, barking. As he passes near the camera, his footsteps in the grass are audible. Later, when he runs down a narrow forest path in front of the goatherd, and later still when he runs up a paved road, we once again hear the soft padding of his feet.

The non-hierarchical soundscape that I have been describing in *Le quattro volte* at times gives way to more focused sound: a bleating kid goat, for example; a resonant drum in the village procession; a church bell or a bell around a goat's neck; a dog's bark. Both in terms of the final rerecording mixing and in the sounds we hear in the frame, it is important to emphasize that not all sounds in the film were captured on location. Although the

Figure 4.2. Dog's Footfall. Screen capture, *Le quattro volte* (2010), directed by Michelangelo Frammartino.

production crew worked meticulously to collect sound from the filming locations across Calabria, their artistic strategy did not preclude modifications to the soundtrack at the mixing stage. When I asked about the Foley sound listed in the credits, Benvenuti and Olivero explained that during the post-production mixing in Berlin, an editing stage in which they took part, various sounds were "reinforced."[18] The only "pure Foley" sounds in the film, though, were the soft thud of the dog's footfalls: "A dog walking on grass makes no noise. [. . .] But the dog had a specific presence."

In my earlier discussion of the material effects of sound, I outlined a kind of "acoustic footprint" of anthropogenic noise on the planet. A footprint is a physical impression left on the ground by the passage of a foot, an impression that can become fossilized in geological layers and read long afterwards as a history of passage. It records a presence and signals an absence: the passage of a material being with weight, whose departure leaves behind a trace. It also tells a story of the cohabitation of species and the "multiform, at stake, unfinished, consequential" companion relationships that characterize lives lived together (Haraway 2003, 30). Donna Haraway (2003, 66) notes that the guardian dogs, sheep, goats, and herders that migrated in Africa, Europe, and Asia "have literally carved deep tracks into soil and rock," companion footprints that are comparable to the "carving of glaciers." In contemporary understandings of human impact on planetary processes, the notion of the "footprint" has become a commonplace. A "carbon footprint," for example, refers to the measure of carbon emissions for an individual, organization, or community; an "ecological footprint" takes into account human resource use more widely.[19] In this usage, too, a footprint implies both a presence and an absence, but the stories these traces tell are often less convivial. Humans (especially Western, and most especially American) leave traces of our passage on the planet by consuming resources at precipitous rates, leaving our mark while we subtract those of others: liquidating minerals when we use petroleum, rainforests when we clear them to graze beef cattle, beef cattle when we eat them, and onward. Our carbon or ecological footprints, then, are carved into the landscape at the expense of other substances and beings.

In their article on noise pollution and ecological services, scientists Francis et al. (2012, 2733) warn that the "spatial footprint of noise, the anthropogenic soundscape, will only increase because sources of noise pollution are growing at a faster rate than the human population. These data suggest that anthropogenic soundscapes have or will encompass nearly all terrestrial habitat types, potentially impacting innumerable species interactions both directly and indirectly." As in the case of our carbon and ecological footprints, a significant acoustic footprint created by humans risks engendering crisis in the rest of the listening world. Barber, Crooks, and Fristrup (2010, 183) have discussed the ways that nonhuman animals not only listen to one another's footfalls and vocalizations, but also listen *across* species boundaries to evaluate their environment (a gray squirrel, for example, takes advantage of information garnered from the communication call of the blue jay), in what the scientists characterize as "acoustical eavesdropping." This cross-species communication leads the group of researchers to observe, a propos of the impact of human-created noise, that: "It is clear that the acoustical environment is not a collection of private conversations between signaler and receiver but an interconnected landscape of information networks and adventitious sounds; a landscape that we see as more connected with each year of investigation" (183). The dog Vuk's footfalls allow us to eavesdrop across species, to listen to a sound that would normally be too quiet for human ears to make out.

To think of sound, or noise, leaving a "footprint," is to emphasize an at least potentially enduring relationship between those impermanent waves and the objects they touch. To allow for an "acoustic footprint" is to trace the residues left behind by things that seem immaterial, writing a history through stories and vibrations, not always a legacy carved in the earth. Thinking the "acoustic footprint" of those canine footfalls offers another pathway to re-think cinematic sound with *Le quattro volte*. The canine presence evoked by the Foley sound gives the dog's footfall weight, and emphasizes that this non-human subject has narrative substance in the film, drawing it into the post-human realm where nonhuman actors feature, including in the credits.[20] It directs our audiovision to a protagonist whose role is roughly equal to that of the goatherd in the first, "human" section of the film. Behind the scenes, liter-ally and in the extra materials that accompany the DVD, this significant role is borne out by the story of a crucial long take starring Vuk, a border collie and canine actor from Milan. In the take, which lasts 9 minutes and 45 seconds, Vuk's role required him to bark at a religious procession as it leaves the village through a stone archway; follow the procession for a bit, then return; pull a stone from under the wheel of a small utility truck, parked on a slope, allowing the truck to roll backwards into a fence penning in a herd of goats; then herd the freed goats into the town through the archway.[21] While offering evidence of the human challenges of collaborating with nonhuman actors on set (it took 16 takes to get the shot, according to the DVD extra materials), this scene performs the emptying of the village, and the film, of human protagonists.[22]

Vuk's Foley-created footsteps, however, also resonate with the film's historical past, a past mirrored in the production's choice, mentioned earlier, to favor stereo and not surround sound. Frammartino (2011, 146) explains that this decision was made to honor the aforementioned legend that Pythagoras taught from behind a screen, blocked from the view of his students: "The teaching came from a sound whose source you could not see, an invisible source. For this reason his disciples were called 'acous-matics.'" The "acousmatics," one of two major groups of Pythagoreans (the others were the "mathematics"), were followers who learned "acousma," or the doctrines and precepts of their invisible teacher; according to the Ox-ford English Dictionary, they followed these precepts "unquestioningly," "rather than studying his scientific proofs and demonstrations."[23] The word "acousmatic" can also be an adjective, referring either to characteristics of these Pythagorean followers, or more widely to any sound without a visible source. In this latter sense, the word has been adopted by film scholars to focus attention on sound rather than vision.[24] And in fact "acoustics" more generally shares this root with "acousmatics," giving unseen film sound, in a manner of speaking, a Pythagorean-Calabrian origin.

The dog's footfalls are technically the opposite of acousmatic in cinemat-ic terms, since we see the canine trotting by; they were created in studio to counter the human tendency to dismiss the more-than-human in the frame. Yet Cubitt (1998, 107) suggests an understanding of acousmatics that draws Vuk's footfalls closer to those Pythagorean listeners. In the human historical process of becoming rhetorical, there is, he argues, an "empirical lack of a passive and receptive, acousmatic practice of listening—to the phonemes, the stresses, the shape, the tone, the weight of a voice speaking. We are too active for that, and cannot wait to replace that other voice with our own." To the intellectually negative "unquestioning" acousmatic listeners of the OED, Cubitt substitutes the double terms "passive *and* receptive" (my emphasis), suggesting that listening to the sounds from behind the screen might ultimately be a way to let another in, to allow our silence to open toward other speaking voices. And since the dog's footfall originated in a studio, where sound was added to the image to encourage an experience of audio-visual attentiveness to Vuk, it is in another sense acousmatic, since we do not see its *actual* source, the technical and technological processes that created it. As observers and listeners, thus, we allow that acoustic footprint to be imprinted on us—and it is a footfall that advocates for a nonhuman world, but is made through that world's collaborative relationship with cinema.

Vegetable and Mineral Sounds: A Posthuman *Carboneria* for the New Millennium

The screen is black. On the soundtrack, we hear a low rumble, a high-pitched but quiet crackling, and a distant thumping.

A stone barrier is placed on the opening of a tomb, shutting out the light. From the dark screen, once again, a resonant thumping emerges, and twice, kid goats gently bleat.

Night falls on a baby goat sleeping beneath a tree, and the screen fades to black. Sounds of trickling water, wind, and a woody creaking enliven the darkness.

Large, wooden logs gradually cover vertical openings in the frame where light shines through a wooden structure, causing the frame to go black. Now, the sounds of thumping are closer, apparently created by logs being piled around the black space.

The four sections of *Le quattro volte* are divided by black screens that are in turn accompanied by a rich, generative soundscape. These black screens serve as what Gilles Deleuze (1989, 200) calls the "interstice between two images," taking us from episode to episode in the film.[25] In Deleuze's

Figure 4.3. Carboneria. Screen capture, *Le quattro volte* (2010), directed by Michelangelo Frammartino.

theory, a black screen carries a potentially "genetic" value: "with its variations and tonalities, it acquires the power of a constitution of bodies" (200). In fact from the first black screen emerges the goatherd; immediately after the second, a baby goat is born; after the third, the focus turns to the tree; and after the fourth, charcoal appears. The dark screens thus seem to call forth not just images, but also substances, matter. They are of particular importance in a film whose soundscapes are as significant as the images.

The recurrent thumping across three of these four scenes, a thumping heard elsewhere in the film, has an apparent diegetic source in the episode of the *carbonai,* or charcoal burners.[26] To make charcoal, workers build a large, half-spherical mound of logs with a flue in the middle. The mound is covered in straw and dirt, and small holes are opened around the base to provide air to light the fire. A *carbonaio* climbs a long, sloped ladder to the top of the pile, dropping wood in the chimney to feed the flame. He uses a long paddle to tamp down the surface of the pile, cutting off air so that the wood within burns at a slow, high temperature (around 500–600°C) (De Luca 2000, 85). There are several moments in the film where we hear the sound of the paddle as if from a distance, including that early scene in the mountain meadow. Although the charcoal burners were located in Serra San Bruno and the goatherd in Caulonia, two Calabrian locales that are many kilometers distant from one another, the thumping sound provides continuity across space and weaves an acoustic geography suturing together goatherd and charcoal burners, goats and charcoal. Benvenuti and Olivero reported discovering, in the process of listening to the film, a range of sonic similes. Insisting that "Calabria has a sound all its own," the recordists singled out the sound of the goatherd's shoes and of 150-year-old doors and latches as particularly beautiful. They also mention analogies between sound recorded on a microphone that was entombed in a cemetery and the thud of wood being thrown to the ground in the charcoal burner's enclosure. These sounds, the varying tones of matter hitting matter, are in their turn reminiscent of the soft thumping sound in the black interstices, and also summon to mind the pulse of a heartbeat.

The fact that sonic metaphors in the film evoke a heartbeat take the audience to a sort of degree zero of observation, a place where we recognize the continuities between our bodies as receptors of sound and participants in sound-making. Cubitt (1998, 95) writes of the interactions between bodily sounds and the world around our permeable borders: "pounding of the pulse, whooshing of the bloodstream, the high whine of the central nervous system. All hearing is made up of the interference between these bodily sounds and those that enter it from without, traversing it with vibrations and electro-chemical flows." In the day-to-day world, where the noisy acoustic footprint of the Anthropocene accompanies us most anywhere we go, it is difficult to discern the sounds produced by our own bodies. Yet there are ways to experience our corporeal utterances. Acoustic ecologists and other scientists at times conduct research that requires silence in order to isolate other sounds; to this end, some universities and research facilities have anechoic chambers (literally, "free from echoes"), or rooms carefully insulated from outside sounds, which also absorb speech and other sounds generated within them (Cox 2014, 210–12). Acoustic engineer Trevor Cox (2014), who regularly works in the anechoic chamber at his university, visited a sensory deprivation chamber where, besides being in a silent space, he was also in pitch-blackness (and floating on a shallow pool of saltwater). In both anechoic and sensory deprivation chambers, Cox explains that there is an "impressive" and evidently unnerving feeling of sensory confusion that sets in because of the odd room tone, or lack thereof. More intimately, once ambient sound is mostly eliminated, in its absence, we can hear, with distinct and perplexing clarity, the vocalizations produced by our own bodies. One such auditory phenomenon is "pulsatile tinnitus," when our hearing discerns the blood pumping through our veins. Cox writes that: "Normally, this blood movement is quieter than the everyday external sounds passing down the ear canal, but in the flotation tank with earplugs, this pulsing sign of life became audible" (220). *Le quattro volte*'s dark, generative screens are accompanied by sounds that recall the movement of life through our veins. In the dark, in the cinema, in the face of a black screen from which there emerge thumping and liquid sounds, we are thus encouraged to contemplate our own bodies as sources of sound, attuned to the idea that we, too, are part of the acoustic landscape of cinema.

Yet the fact that this cinematic heartbeat emanates from the paddles and logs of charcoal burners, or *carbonai*, draws the story of *Le quattro volte* in the direction of Italian national-popular history, too. Any Italian, or any Italianist, thinking of "*carboneria*" likely has in mind not the charcoal burners of Calabria, but rather the *Carbonari*, members of a secret society that took root in Italy in the nineteenth century to push for the cause of unification.[27] Although the origins of the society are cloaked in legend, it is likely, considering initiation ceremonies, symbols, and other available evidence, that the society was based on the Freemasons and was intended to arouse anti-French sentiment in southern Italy (Rath 1964, 353–56).[28] The society initiated members at a number of different "grades" or levels, perhaps as many as nine (362–63).[29] For the first and largest of these levels, much of the initiation ceremony was conducted "in the symbolic language of the medieval charcoal burners and vendors who most *carbonari* believed were the real founders of their society" (365). During the highly symbolic ceremony, initiates were called into a "baracca," or hut, which was in an area called the "forest," where the grand master presided over a hewn block of timber; part of the initiate's first declaration to the grand master was an affirmation that he had been "carrying wood, leaves, and earth in the forest" (357). Later, the initiates rambled blindfolded around the forest and passed through fire, eventually taking an oath with their hand on a hatchet (357–58).

By way of metaphor, by popular association, and through its material entanglement with fire and wood, *Carboneria* links charcoal-making and charcoal burners to the myth-making that accompanied Italian unification. The initiation ceremony, which further involved spiritual declarations promising faith, hope, and charity, may otherwise bear little resemblance to the daily life of a charcoal burner, or to the scenes in the film showing their work. Nevertheless, the final episode's passage into the film's mineral phase of existence proposes what could become a new iconography for a posthuman Italian history: its focus on the charcoal, rather than on the human charcoal burner, retools national history as a story of regional knowledge, attentive listening, and eloquent matter. In new material histories, the kinds of histories examined by material ecocriticism, agency "is not to be necessarily and exclusively associated with human beings and with human intentionality," but rather is "a pervasive and inbuilt property of matter, as part and parcel of its generative dynamism" (Iovino and Oppermann 2014, 3). Both as film production and film narrative, *Le quattro volte* demonstrates its willingness to honor the generative dynamism of the nonhuman actors it records, and to admit these actors' vital roles in a collaborative, alternative history.

Such attentiveness to nonhuman matter is part of the history of *Carboneria* in its sense as charcoal-making. Barbara De Luca (2000), a folklorist who studies the ways that *carbonai* articulate knowledge of their work, cites an interviewee, Bruno, describing the delicate process of balancing air and fire to create good charcoal.[30] If there is too much flame, he explains, you end up with ashes. Watching and smelling the smoke, the charcoal burner knows if the pile is burning well, but sound is also important in this process (I quote in Italian here to capture the onomatopoeia of the regional Cansiglio dialect): *"se l'è bén carbonizà te sente anca dal rumore: cri cri, che al canta bén"* (if it has burned well, you can also hear it in the noise: *cri cri*, it sings well [85–86]). De Luca points out that sensory (and in particular auditory) knowledge is critical, since the charcoal burners cannot see the fire burning in the middle of the pile. She also notes that fire is frequently characterized as a living being in the language of the charcoal burners: it moves, climbs, walks, goes up and down, is guided, escapes. Further, the charcoal pile (called a *poiàt* in dialect) has bodily parts, including a mouth, a belly, and feet, and needs to be fed, cared for, dressed (87). Also notable here is the notion that the charcoal and the flames that create it sing with a "cri cri" sound, a sound that also speaks on the film's soundtrack. Charcoal burners speak the language of charcoal, and they learn to listen to, and articulate to one another (and to folklorists), the messages communicated by the biofuel. In this kind of *Carboneria*, as Serenella Iovino and Serpil Oppermann (2014, 9) have suggested, "the human agency meets the narrative agency of matter halfway."

In the process of filming charcoal and its production, sound recordists and film directors, too, become attuned to the voices of nonhuman subjects. The high-pitched crackling that I described as part of that first black screen could also be approximated with a "cri cri," and in fact seems to be the sound of wood crackling in a fire. These are sounds that Benvenuti and

Olivero described as some of the most detailed of those they recorded, and the intense and rapid transformation of matter required their close attention. When the camera filmed the scenes of the charcoal-making process, including some close-ups of the dark, hot coals, both camera and microphones were at a safe distance from the intense heat. Later, in the extra days conceded by the production for collecting sounds, the recordists returned to Serra San Bruno and were able to capture the sonorant wood from much closer. The singing sound of the coals when they come out of the heat, they explained, fades quickly, and needs to be recorded immediately upon their removal from the mound. In a series of shots in that final episode, we witness the fluctuating sound of matter as it progresses through the transformation from wood to charcoal: heavy, dull, and soft around the edges when it comes from a moisture-filled log; then lighter, higher-pitched, and tinkling when it becomes charcoal.

From a substance that evokes sounds of a living heartbeat, we thus arrive at one that creates a sound recalling a goat's bell, continuing to interweave a tapestry of sonic and material metaphors across the episodes of the film. This final transformation is entangled with a moment in the first episode, when the goatherd finds a goat's bell on the ground in the forest, tucks it in his pocket, and walks around the small village signaling (by way of his acoustic footprint) that he has become goat.[31] These sonic metaphors, here generated by way of the tingling pitches of ringing bells and singing charcoal, are not just poetic; they help provide what Iovino and Oppermann (2014, 3) characterize as "a more accurate (and also more ontologically generous) picture of reality," where history is not moved only by a human subject "posited in isolation from the nonhuman—but a material-semiotic network of human and nonhuman agents incessantly generating the world's embodiments and events." With the singing charcoal, whose creation evokes sounds of heartbeats and goat bells, *Le quattro volte* voices an alternative history: more-than-human stories that echo beyond the halls of human narrative and comprehend the entanglement of matter and meaning. The sound of charcoal is vividly evoked in language, that lively language of the charcoal burner whose ear listens carefully to the arboreal transformations, and one reproduced by the sound recordist's microphone. It is a voice that speaks from charcoal's recent past as living matter, that past recounted vividly in the story of the tree, just one episode earlier. In human historical terms, charcoal can tell of its employment as a component of gunpowder and its use in blacksmith work, both ways in which it helped to support transportation, revolution, nation-building, and colonialism.[32] It helps tell a story of deforestation, a history that in Italy has caused landslides, soil erosion, floods, and a loss of soil fertility, among other things.[33] It is a voice that speaks of its future as fire, when it will be burned on a barbecue or in a pizza oven or a rural stove to prepare the food that fuels the activities of other beings (Lugli and Stoppiello 2000, 42). And it writes its future as art, when it can trace the lines that an artist might sketch, or provide stories and images for a filmmaker's craft. Listening to the charcoal's voice, *Carboneria* in its original sense asserts the importance of regional, material histories in understanding the past, and charcoal sings matter's vibrant speaking ability. A cinema that attunes its ear to such voices shows, in turn, its openness to the idea that, as Roberto Marchesini (2009, 165) has suggested regarding human collaborations with technology, "every technological emergence renders the human-system less anthropocentered."

Posthuman Conclusions: "Is This a *Silent* Film?"

When I screened Le quattro volte *for a class one semester, my students, having read about the film online, marched into the room demanding with suspicion, "Elena, is this a silent film?"*

Upon beginning to write this chapter, I was carefully re-listening to a scene in the film and excited to discover the sound of a dog barking at an interesting moment. I listened again, and no dog. I paused the film, and a dog barked. Fluffy, excitable Ky, next door, had momentarily become part of my soundtrack.

Rosi Braidotti (2013, 55) writes that her favorite sentence in the English language was written by George Eliot, and comes from the novel *Middlemarch*: "If we had a keen vision and feeling of all ordinary human life, it would be like hearing the grass grow and the squirrel's heart beat, and we should die of that roar which lies on the other side of silence. As it is, the quickest of us walk around well wadded with stupidity." This roar, argues Braidotti (55), is the "Spinozist indicator of the raw cosmic energy that underscores the making of civilizations, societies and their subjects."[34] Braidotti has powerfully insisted that, "Once the centrality of *anthropos* is challenged, a number of boundaries between 'Man' and his others go tumbling down, in a cascade effect that opens up unexpected perspectives" (65–66). In her favorite Spinozist Eliot quote, that waterfall effect is acoustic, a presence that roars with more-than-human vibrant materiality.

Figure 4.4. Posthuman Film Crew. Screen capture, *Le quattro volte* (2010), directed by Michelangelo Frammartino. DVD extra materials, CG Home Video S.R.L.

Ecocriticism and posthumanism posit that there are innumerable ways that our supposedly bounded human bodies and human subjectivities should be opened to the world beyond (and within) the human: by understanding our coevolution with other species, or through the recognition of the different organisms that compose our bodies, to name just two. In the case of *Le quattro volte*, an innovative film that required inventive filming practices, making the film constituted an opening toward the world around the film, a cohabitation of film crew with Calabria's human and nonhuman dwellers. Like during the making of *The Wind Blows Round*, the specialized roles of the small but collaborative crew eventually broke down in the process of becoming-other. All of the crew members with whom I spoke discussed the gradual dissolution of boundaries between the human troupe and the nonhuman world: from their attentive studies of goat psychology (one baby goat imprinted on a cameraman, recalled Benvenuti and Olivero), to their careful observation of the seasonal changes in eucalyptus leaves, to their collaboration in building charcoal mounds for the scenes with the *carbonai*, the film was a process of becoming-Calabrese, in a context where being Calabrese meant more than just being a human inhabitant of the territory.[35] Benvenuti and Olivero remembered with particular fondness the crewmember who, after a long career working in film, began the project with a clear idea of his specific technical role and an unwillingness to do things not specified by his union contract. When he realized that snails were needed for a particular scene in which they would co-star with a goat in the goatherd's kitchen, however, his love for the slow-moving gastropods won out, and he began carefully collecting and feeding snails for the production, giving each one a name. Serrecchia offered this as but one example of how, by the end of filming, *Le quattro volte* had shaped a "great brotherhood" of relations.

The film also moves toward an open embrace of the posthuman by engaging technologies to capture the relationships between eloquent forms of matter. The recordists described testing microphones as they prepared their shots, with the sensitive instruments scattered over the landscape. They could listen to any one of these mikes in their headphones, or the mix of all recordings together. The process, which they described as dynamic, created a sensation of having a disembodied, mobile ear that could move with the microphone, while their bodies were elsewhere, out of the shot. Working on subsequent productions, they described this process as disquieting—as when they were filming in a forest at night and could hear but not see animals passing at a variety of distances—or even dangerous—as when in a crowded market, their ears could be in one place and their bodies might be in the path of a passing truck. As cinematic cyborgs, the sound recordists augment and direct their powers of hearing on our behalf, and in the case of *Le quattro volte*, they do so to give us a horizontal, deep soundscape. They were irrevocably transformed by the process of what Marchesini (2009, 159–60) evocatively dubs "technopoiesis," which is a consequence of "man's capacity to learn from the nonhuman, to import nonhuman references into his ontopoietic dimension." Rather than being a means (as a certain humanist view would have it) for human dominance of the world, cinema instead becomes a means of further entangling ourselves with it.

Keeping in mind notions from cinematic sound theorists affirming the never-silent nature of cinema, whether we examine filming practices on location or projection practices in the theater, we can imagine that the equipment, production crew members, and vehicles employed to make *Le quattro volte* added anthropogenic noise to the soundscape in Calabria. Yet the film nevertheless demonstrated an exemplary ability to listen to the world around it without making its own voice too distinctive, achieving what Frammartino and Serrecchia described as "mimesis" with the landscape. Serrecchia remarked on the important friendships they made with the charcoal burners and local members of the production crew; for many scenes, in particular with the goatherd, they abandoned their vehicles and carried heavy equipment up the mountain on foot; director Frammartino conducted much pre-production work by mountain bike, in order to reach the goats grazing in the mountains. Regarding their rural Calabrian setting, Serrecchia also notes intriguingly that: "the 'Ndrangheta did not even realize we were there." The 'Ndrangheta, the criminal organization active in Calabria, he explained, might have approached him as production manager to ask for money, or to insist that a favored person be hired as part of the crew, or to request that the film production pay a higher amount for some service. Such things often happen, he says, with larger crews. "There, nothing. We were not the cinematic machine. There were twenty of us, always out in the fields with the goatherds . . . invisible. We were camouflaged [*mimetizzati*] in the landscape." This "mimesis" is not simply mimicry, but rather a transformation of all parties in the collaboration. Like other technologies, cinema introduces what Marchesini (2009, 160) identifies as "changes in the anthropo-poietic coordinates, modifying the human dimension in all its ontological aspects, for the very fact of being an operator [*operatrice*] of hybridization and a medium of conjugation with the nonhuman."[36] No party to such collaboration emerges unchanged. The introductions performed in making such a film (meeting goats, charcoal burners, century-old trees, landscapes), show that, as Haraway (2008, 42) has suggested, "Once again we are in a knot of species coshaping one another in layers of reciprocating complexity all the way down."[37] Frammartino described his role as director as one that gradually "weakened," and noted that he "progressively loses control" (deliberately, we might add) of cinematic productions and artistic installations as he cedes space to the desires, ideas, and presence of others.

In a unique but analogous way, the film worked its way into the soundscape in my home office, when Ky's bark from next door seemed to become part of the soundtrack. So, too, did voices from my class become active participants in the film, when students (who overcame their initial rebellion against the notion of "silence" and loved the film) felt free to articulate their own recollections of Italian ancestors who made charcoal, or their concern for the fate of the kid goat, or their marvel at the strategic abilities of snails to escape their containers. So, too, are other films transformed, since *Le quattro volte* has been working its way into each project that Benvenuti and Olivero undertake, as their ears, they say, listen to the world differently now: "There is a life around us that does not exist in the image, it exists only in sounds." So, too, are Vuk and the goats and charcoal burners transformed by the passage of the film production through their lives. The eloquent, audible silence of the more-than-human world creates a space from which we listeners become a part of the fugue of voices speaking in the accents of Pythagoras' Calabria, from behind the screen.

Notes

1. Michelangelo Frammartino, interview by author, Milan, June 29, 2011. Except where otherwise noted, information from the director was collected during this interview.

2. Francis et al.'s (2012) research shows that the impact of noise exposure on the environment was variable: indirectly positive on pollination by hummingbirds; indirectly negative on seedling establishment of Pinus edulis. Their findings indicate clearly, however, the complex ways in which sound impacts the nonhuman world, since "noise exposure may trigger changes to numerous ecological interactions and reverberate through communities" (2731–33). More urgently, Barber, Crooks, and Fristrup (2010, 183) write that their research shows that because of the importance of communication and listening among and across species, "the masking imposed by anthropogenic noise could have volatile and unpredictable consequences."

3. Belton (1999, 379) argues that "the sound track seeks to duplicate [. . .] the sound of an image, not that of the world. The evolution of sound technology and, again, that of studio recording, editing, and mixing practice illustrate, to some degree, the quest for a sound track that captures an idealized reality."

4. Théberge (2008, 66) explains that the analytical division between dialogue, sound effects, and music, a division common in academic study, is based on a technical distinction whereby in production and post-production, these elements are processed separately and only brought together in a final mix.

5. As further evidence of the critical importance of hearing, acoustic engineer Trevor Cox (2014, 19) points out: "we have no 'earlids,' and there is no auditory equivalent of closing our eyes or averting our gaze."

6. Rick Altman (1992, 35, 39) discusses "Four and Half Film Fallacies" that have led to the neglect of sound in cinema studies. These include the mistaken notion that "sound is an add-on, an afterthought, and thus of secondary importance," and the erroneous idea that "sound appears to reproduce the original faithfully," and is a matter of engineering, not art. Altman insists on a more complex understanding of sound that includes attention to its materiality and its ability to "represent." In her welcome book on film sound in Italy, Antonella Sisto (2014, 2) argues cogently that: "The optical regime that governs cinema discourses flattens the film to the screen and poses the spectator as the recipient of visual information transmitted to the brain through the retina. The disembodied eye/spectator becomes prey to voyeurism, fetishism, panoptic[ism], fascination, the gaze (as in feminist and psychoanalytical theory), but mostly suffers from a general Western theoretical negation of other senses, and the body."

7. Sisto (2014, 10) differentiates dubbing (audio translation of foreign films) from post-synchronization (adding soundtracks to Italian films in post-production). Both practices were common in Italy, and direct sound entered the "national cinematographic enterprise" only in the 1980s. Rather than suggest that post-synchronization is an aesthetic limit, Sisto

also argues that Italian auteurs in the 1950s and 60s used post-synchronization in innovative ways, creating "an affective and effective dimension of film sound for the shaping of modern film aesthetics" (13).

8. Belton (1999, 384) argues eloquently for the acoustic and visible impact of the cinematic apparatus on its context: "Though the cinematic apparatus becomes, decade by decade, a more perfect transmitter, reducing signs of its own existence by eliminating its system's noise, it inevitably reproduces not only the light and sound waves reflected and emitted by objective reality but also its own presence, which is represented by the perspective from which these waves are seen or heard."

9. Paolo Benvenuti and Simone Paolo Olivero, interview by author, Milan, May 8, 2013. All the information I cite from the sound recordists was collected in this interview.

10. According to Christoph Riedweg (2005, x), Pythagoras probably left the island of Samos sometime around 530 BCE and emigrated to Croton, which today is Crotone, in Calabria.

11. For more information on recording room presence as compared to the use of directional microphones, see Stephen Handzo (1985, 393–99). Directional microphone placement is almost entirely organized around anthropic action. For example, Handzo recommends that: "the best position for a directional mike is at arm's length in front of the player and just above the head" (394). Room presence, on the other hand, is based on observing the quality of a more-than-human space: "each room has a distinct presence of subtle sounds created by the movement of air particles in that particular volume. A microphone placed in two different empty rooms will produce a different room tone for each" (395).

12. Handzo (1985, 395) explains that "there is never no sound even when nothing is happening on the screen (except possibly when indicating death, memory, a Godardian 'alienation effect,' etc.). The soundtrack 'going dead' would be perceived by the audience not as silence but as a failure of the sound system."

13. Cox (2014, 272) expresses concern about the relationship of sound to consumerism: "It makes me uneasy that our aural environment is becoming peppered with sounds primarily designed to sell products. Globalization of technologies also causes an attendant homogenization of the noises that form the backing track to our lives."

14. The recordists did return to some locations to re-record sound independently of the camera, as, for example, in the case of the long take of the religious procession. They were unable to use the direct sound because the dog trainer was giving commands to the dog Vuk during filming. According to production manager Serrecchia, the recordists also could not often stay after a scene to record the "presence" of a place because they were needed for other tasks, like helping to herd goats. Yet attention to local sounds and the location's presence was meticulous; they had members of the town procession, for example, march through the streets again wearing the same shoes they wore in the long take (Marco Serrecchia, interview by author, Rome, March 7, 2013; all the information I cited from Serrecchia was collected in this interview.).

15. The sound of the helicopters was created by celebrated sound designer Walter Murch, using modified versions of "the sound of a chain twirled against a paper bag" (Handzo 1985, 407).

16. Greg Garrard (2004, 60–63) suggests that the case for the "mechanistic world view" attributed to Bacon, Descartes, and others may be overstated. Yet there is little doubt that we need alternatives to the "principles of internal or external opposition" that emerged as a result of "Descartes' famous mind-body distinction" (Braidotti 2013, 55–56), whether these

alternatives be posthuman and Spinozan (Braidotti 2013), process-relational (Ivakhiv 2013, in particular 42–48), non-anthropocentric (Iovino 2010a), etc.

17. In visual terms, the camera's framing of deep space runs parallel to Benvenuti's and Olivero's acoustic work. Monica Seger (2014, 292) has convincingly argued that the engagement of deep space on the cinematic screen in *Le quattro volte* constitutes a Deleuzian de-centering, whereby "Frammartino challenges viewers to no longer place the human centre-frame, but rather see it as one form of life among many."

18. Given the traditional and rather rigorous divisions between production and post-production, especially as regards sound, this participation in the rerecording mixing stage is highly unusual for sound recordists. Arguing that film budgets generally privilege the visual over the aural, Handzo (1985, 400) writes that: "the reality is that sound quality is the first thing to be sacrificed once the production falls behind schedule and all that matters is to get the shot." That the recordists participated in post-production mixing thus offers further evidence of *Le quattro volte*'s commitment to the acoustic landscape and to collaboration among members of the crew. Benni Atria, the film's image editor, was in fact originally a sound editor, and helped build the film first thinking of sound, and then of the image (Frammartino 2011, 147).

19. See definitions and usages in the Oxford English Dictionary, www.oed.com.

20. The closing credits list: "The dog Vuk; The silver fir of the Pollino; The goats of Caulonia; The charcoal of the Calabrian sierra." For more on the closing credits and the film's posthuman ethics, see Elena Past, "(Re)membering Kinship: Living with Goats in *The Wind Blows Round* and *Le quattro volte*" (2014). The DVD extras dedicated to the long take involving Vuk note that the canine actor was awarded a special jury prize at Cannes for his role in the film.

21. See also Frammartino 2011, 146–47. The primary challenge for Vuk was to perform all of these actions in sequence, but another significant issue throughout the film was the fact that he reportedly did not like goats.

22. Seger (2014, 295) points out that we cannot see the truck crash into the goat pen, but we do hear it: "Guided by sonic clues off screen, we are able to rely on visual memory, on no-longer-visible imagery, to map out the spatial parameters of the concurrent actions taking place."

23. Identifying an "internal tension" in the Pythagorean school that dates from about 450/440–415 BCE, Riedweg (2005, 106–7) explains that the "acousmatics" were those "for whom the master's 'oral sayings,' primarily concerning sacrifice and worship, were central," and that this group rigorously followed rituals and taboos. The mathematicians, instead, "considered their chief task to penetrate Pythagoreanism scientifically and to further develop it."

24. See in particular Michel Chion (1994, 71), who explains that: "Acousmatic, a word of Greek origin discovered by Jérome Peignot and theorized by Pierre Schaeffer, describes 'sounds one hears without seeing their originating cause.' Radio, phonograph, and telephone, all which transmit sounds without showing their emitter, are acousmatic media by definition." See also Vivian Sobchack (2005), "When the Ear Dreams: Dolby Digital and the Imagination of Sound."

25. Deleuze (1989, 200) explains that the "new value of the black or white screen" shows that, "on the one hand, what is important is no longer the association of images, the way in which they associate, but the interstice between two images; on the other hand, the cut in a sequence of images is not now a rational cut which marks the end of one *or* the beginning of

another, but a so-called irrational cut which belongs neither to one nor the other, and sets out to be valid for itself" (emphasis in original).

26. The forests of the Serre region in Calabria have long been a space for metallurgy; Francesca Lugli and Assunta Alessandra Stoppiello (2000, 41–42) report that the first documentation of metalworking in the region dates to 1094, and that metallurgy has always been connected to the production of charcoal. While ironworking fell out of use in the eighteenth century, a small number of charcoal burners continue to live and work in the area today.

27. Although the growing society attracted people with different political goals, and although those goals changed according to contemporary political events, Rath (1964, 366) argues that "the one common political goal unanimously professed and upheld by every Carbonaro was to give unity, liberty, and independence to the Italian people and to expel all foreigners whether French or Austrians, from the Apennine Peninsula."

28. Christopher Duggan (2008, 58) agrees that the origins of Carboneria are uncertain, perhaps beginning in Scotland, the Jura, or the forests of Germany, but that the structure and style were "heavily Masonic."

29. Rath (1964, 363) writes that the patriot Giuseppe Mazzini achieved the sixth grade and believed there to be three more.

30. De Luca's research focuses on charcoal burners in the Cansiglio, a Prealpine plateau that straddles the provinces of Belluno, Treviso, and Pordenone.

31. For more on the goatherd's transformation, see also Past 2014, 242–43.

32. Volcanologist Haraldur Sigurdsson (1999, 4) explains that gunpowder was invented in the thirteenth century, and that "the explosive formula of 70% saltpeter (sodium nitrate), 15% charcoal, and 15% sulfur was discovered by the Chinese and introduced to Europe by Roger Bacon in the early fourteenth century with revolutionary impact—helping to blast apart the feudal system and making armored knights history." Gunpowder, then, marries the southern Italian history of charcoal and volcanoes (the latter of which are the subject of the next chapter). In their study of charcoal-burning sites in Liguria, Montanari, Prono and Scipioni (2000, 79) explain that by studying the "tree taxa" used in charcoal production, they identify "biogeographic, palaeovegetational and palaeoethnological data which can usefully support those coming from archive." Thus charcoal and the trees it comes from preserve the stories of ancient forests, geographies, and cultures, and the field of "applied anthracology," which studies these charred remains, can benefit from examining well-preserved charcoal from either wildfires or hearths, kilns, and other anthropic contexts (80–81).

33. For more on the history of deforestation in Italy, see Vecchio (2010), "Forest Visions," and Pratesi (2010), *Storia della natura d'Italia.*

34. In fact Braidotti (2013, 55) explains that she loved George Eliot before knowing that the author had translated Spinoza, "my favorite philosopher."

35. Serrecchia, Benvenuti, and Olivero all described with particular respect the long months director Frammartino spent on location getting to know goats and goatherds, so that he might understand what kind of scenes could be realized with some cooperation from the film's bleating protagonists.

36. Or in slightly different terms proposed by Haraway (2008, 229), we can observe in the behaviors of the film crew a nonmimetic alignment with their surroundings that is profoundly transformative. Haraway offers the example of the cross-species "unintentional movements" that French ethnologist Jean-Claude Barrey observed when people ride horses: "'Human bodies have been transformed by and into a horse's body. Who influences and who is influenced, in

this story, are questions that can no longer receive a clear answer. Both, human and horse, are cause and effect of each other's movements. Both induce and are induced, affect and are affected. Both embody each other's mind.' Reciprocal induction; intra-action; companion species. [. . .] The nonmimetic attunement of each to each resonates with the molecular scores of mind and flesh and makes someone out of them both who was not there before."

37. This citation, too, opens itself to "techno-poiesis," since, by "species," Haraway (2008, 41) explains that she refers to: "landscapes, animals, plants, microorganisms, people, and technologies."

5

VOLCANOES, TRANSGENERATIONAL
MEMORY, CINEMA: *RETURN TO THE*
AEOLIAN ISLANDS

ON A SUNNY, COOL SUNDAY IN MARCH, *I sat in the grass at the Villa Doria Pamphilj, a sprawling park located on one of the hills of Rome, with director Giovanna Taviani. Giovanna is at home in Rome, eternal city of Italian cinema, but also in San Miniato, Tuscany, where she grew up with her "fathers," the renowned directors Vittorio (her father) and Paolo (her uncle) Taviani, and on the island of Salina, one of the seven major islands in the volcanic Aeolian archipelago where her extended family has long vacationed, and where she had a role in the film* Kaos *(1984) as a girl.*

As our interview concluded, her cell phone rang: on the other end was Franco Figliodoro, the islander and actor who stars in her film. While they chatted, I gazed out over the Roman landscapes and recalled, idly, the park where Maddalena Cecconi (played by Anna Magnani) goes on an illicit date with Alberto Annovazzi (Walter Chiari) in Luchino Visconti's film Bellissima *(1952). Sitting in the Roman park with Giovanna, the lines between cinema and reality blurred.*

The next month, Giovanna helped me organize a trip to Lipari to meet Figliodoro (his nickname means "golden boy") and the volcanic landscapes of her documentary, Fughe e approdi *(Return to the Aeolian Islands, translated more literally as "Escapes and Landings," 2010). Over the course of a week, I encountered (by design and by chance) naturalists, historians, librarians, volcanologists, film scholars, documentarians, actors, volcanoes, pumice cliffs, marinas, bays. All of them have been transformed by the passage of cinema over and through the Aeolian Islands, and their voices accumulate in images, words, and sounds in my notebook, recorder, and camera. The hissing voice of the fumaroles on the island of Vulcano, and the low grumbling of Strombolian eruptions, are firmly lodged in my imagination.*

On the island of Lipari, over a plate of spicy pasta all'eoliana, Figliodoro and his American partner Janet Little told Ed and me stories of Franco's cinematic past. The recorder picked up the sounds of forks clinking as we debate the talents of Sean Penn, Johnny Depp, and Daniel Day Lewis, and hear about Figliodoro's sighting of Burt Lancaster and his encounter with Antonio Albanese. Figliodoro's first cinematic appearance was in Kaos, and from the Taviani brothers and their kindness, he says that he learned about "a new kind of energy." Nourished by tomatoes and capers that taste of rich volcanic soil, we were also fed by memory, and united in our love for cinema.

As I begin this chapter, my mind weaves connections with the preceding ones: the wind is blowing round. Antonioni reappears here, because his film L'avventura *(1960) features prominently as a cinematic citation in Giovanna's film. Like in Chapter One, geological time encounters the human rhythms of modernity and cinema. There are goats in this film, like in* Le quattro volte *and* The Wind Blows Round, *and* Return *also shares a production manager, Marco Serrecchia, assistant director, Franco Monopoli, and editor, Benni Atria, with* Le quattro volte, *evidence of the close ties that bind the Italian cinematic community today. Like* Gomorrah, Return *is divided into episodes, and in both films, relationships characterized by both collaboration and conflict interact with a porous volcanic landscape.*

This is a tale of cinematic memory and its entanglement with Italy, especially the Aeolian Islands. It is the story of the vitality in volcanoes, cinema, water, and film crews, and about how the cycling and recycling of energies shapes Italian cinema. Finally, it is a proposal for how volcanic stories can help form disciplinary and material alliances between actors of all kinds.

The volcanic Aeolian Islands just north of Sicily have been frequently documented on film since 1946, when a group of four men sailed from Milazzo to Lipari and formed the group Panària Film.[1] Francesco Alliata, who had experience behind the camera chronicling World War II for the Istituto Luce, developed a waterproof housing for his 35-mm Arriflex camera and, together with his companions, filmed the short documentary *Cacciatori sottomarini (Underwater Hunters)* (Genovese 2010, 26–27). Alliata's pioneering work with underwater photography and his exploration of the Aeolian ecosystems inspired Roberto Rossellini, who helped support the group's efforts, to film on the islands several years later.[2] Rossellini brought the tiny

Sicilian islands into the international spotlight by conveying film crews and real-life dramas onto their shores. The director began filming *Stromboli: Terra di Dio* (1950), starring his new lover Ingrid Bergman, in April of 1949, just before William Dieterle began filming *Vulcano* (1950), starring Rossellini's recently jilted lover Anna Magnani. The ensuing "war of the volcanoes," as it was dubbed in the press, or the tensions between Rossellini, Bergman, and Magnani as they worked simultaneously on location, led international journalists to rush to the Aeolian Islands and chronicle the romantic crisis. The two films, which both featured exciting volcano-driven drama (clouds of sulfuric gas, rumbling eruptions, flying rock, etc.), along with the copious reporting from the islands, also served as location scouting for future films, sealing their fame as destinations for cinematic productions.[3]

Driven by deep, subterranean geological movement, the thermal convection in the earth's crust, volcanoes offer spectacular, visible clues to the energies that underlie existence on the planet. Volcanoes are "the manifestation at the surface of a planet or satellite of internal thermal processes through the emission at the surface of solid, liquid, or gaseous product" (Francis and Oppenheimer 2004, 2). Volcanoes, in other words, are a planet's externalization of internal forces, and their magmatic movement rivets the human gaze. Early scientific accounts of volcanoes, like Lucretius' (1995) description of Etna in *De Rerum Natura* in the first century BCE, draw our eyes to observe the spectacle of eruption. In an anachronistic reading of his text, Lucretius' verse almost appears to offer cinematographic advice:

> It was no middling slaughter
> When the flame-storm rose and swept like a lord through the fields
> Of Sicily; neighboring peoples turned their eyes
> And saw the smoking temples of the sky
> Glitter with sparks. [. . .]
> You must look deeply into these affairs,
> Long ponder every part, keep your scope wide (218)

As one of the most dramatically visible testaments to the fact that our earth is on the move, volcanoes quite fittingly have a privileged relationship to the kinetic language of cinema, that art of moving pictures. Sharing an impulse to mobility and visibility, a cinema that turns its gaze to volcanic landscapes finds a world that speaks its language.

This concluding chapter calls on a film that is really many films, one that cites an extensive history of Aeolian cinema, in order to propose that disanthropocentric film studies inspired by volcanic stories can help

Figure 5.1. Volcano. Screen capture, *Return to the Aeolian Islands* (2010), directed by Giovanna Taviani.

us read the world (and teach the world, if we are teachers) in nuanced and deeply ethical ways. *Fughe e approdi* is a 2010 narrative documentary that recounts director Giovanna Taviani's journey to the Aeolian archipelago, and it chronicles the history of films made there.[4] The film is a voyage in Taviani's memory and in cinematic history: her father and uncle (the Fratelli Taviani, or Taviani brothers) are among the most celebrated contemporary Italian directors, and the film charts her complex past as actor, daughter and niece, cinephile, and film scholar.[5] Her family vacationed on the island of Salina when she was a child, but the Taviani brothers also made films on the islands, most famously situating one of the episodes of *Kaos* on Lipari's pumice cliffs. As the film travels from island to island, telling stories and mapping the archipelago, the footage that punctuates *Return* alternates between Taviani's contemporary digital documentary film, clips from narrative feature films (*Stromboli, Vulcano, L'avventura, Kaos, Caro diario* [1993], *Il Postino* [1994], among others), clips from historic documentary films (*Bianche Eolie* [1948], *Isole di fuoco* [1955], *Alicudi* [1961], and more), still photographs, and home video featuring Taviani and her brother and cousins. Categorizing the diverse archive of footage (different genres, different historical periods, celluloid and digital, varying aspect ratios, black-and-white and color) that appears over the course of *Return* proves difficult, though, because each grouping shifts to admit others. Taviani the documentarian performs as an actor in *Kaos*; Nanni Moretti, director and star of

Caro diario, visits the Taviani family and features in their home video footage; Taviani's father, director of *Kaos,* appears in *Return* to talk about his daughter as a child and to elaborate on his own filmmaking practice. The cinematic layers are affective, artistic, and historic. Memory and history, in *Return,* are both deeply and irretrievably cinematic.

Return to the Aeolian Islands opens with a contemporary shot of Stromboli erupting dramatically. The sea at sunset is alive with movement, as wisps of ash move quietly around the edges of the frame, then a deep rumble sounds in the bass register of the soundtrack, and lava erupts explosively. As the opening titles appear over the continuing eruption, the edges of a filmstrip roll by on the left. This graphic overlay maps cinema onto geography, acknowledging the mobile powers of both images and rocks, and the collaborative relationship that will link them in this film. "Geography," as John Calderazzo (2004, 132) notes, "means 'earth script,' terrestrial writing, the planet's story." As the opening titles foreshadow, here the intertwined stories of volcanoes, islanders, immigrants, and film productions demonstrate the reciprocal relationship linking earth script and film script. Shortly thereafter, the film introduces its palimpsestic strategy, juxtaposing archival film footage in black-and-white with graphic matches of the same landscapes in color, or using innovative eyeline matches in which a character in a black-and-white film gazes on a contemporary landscape in color. *Return* thus documents the archipelago's material past, at times literally lining up and comparing landscapes captured on film 50 or 60 years apart: it frames ecological, and not just cinematic history.

Taviani's cinematic memory archive unfurls as an embodied memory, born in the back-and-forth between human perception, human narrative, and terrestrial writing. In other words, in this film we can understand, as Catriona Mortimer-Sandilands (2008, 270) argues in an essay on landscape, memory, and her mother, that "symbolic reflection and sensual perception" are "specific embodied practices that are not only physically but historically located—enabled differently in the context of different technologies, social relations, and interactions with the more-than-human world." We can see vividly that, as material ecocriticism recognizes, memory "does not only reside in the mind, but rather in the complex interrelations among bodies, minds, and landscapes" (279).

Return offers an intriguing case study of this enfolding of human memory, narrative, and landscape because it is situated on terrain that shifts dramatically in human time: earth that rumbles, spews fire and sulfuric gasses, and emits terrestrial energy in a way that defies human indifference to the natural world. There are many good reasons that we should pay attention to volcanoes, and in fact over the course of human history, the spectacular power of volcanic activity has led humans to observe volcanic landscapes with heightened curiosity and concern. A few of the top motivations: the Icelandic volcanologist Haraldur Sigurdsson (1999, 1) notes that humans study volcanoes because heat and fire "have been of crucial importance to humanity's progress." There is the critical fact that volcanoes change the earth's climate, affecting crop yields and cooling the surface of the earth, wielding the potential to strain the resources of a crowded planet "to the limit" (10). Local explosive eruptions can devastate towns, covering them in ash or burying them in pyroclastic flows. These and other hazards (dangers to air traffic, for example) create a need for volcano observatories (like the *Osservatorio Vesuviano,* or Vesuvian Observatory in Naples) that monitor and predict eruptions.

The force of the body/mind/landscape interrelation also translates into a rich material-discursive tradition of volcanoes, with volcanic energy converting to sometimes-apocalyptic narrative energy. History and myth often correlate volcanoes with war, weapons, and hell; they envision them as the homes of divine and terrible creatures, like the horned red giant known in Japanese mythology as the Oni monster, the Greek volcano and fire god Hephaestus, or the Roman god of fire, Vulcan.[6] The Aeolian Islands are said to be the home of Aeolis, Greek god of the winds, as well as the angry Cyclopes. Archaeologists have confirmed that, for centuries, women and girls were thrown into volcanic craters or buried on volcanic summits in rituals intended to appease angry gods.[7] Although this evidence suggests how the volcanic imagination seems to be coded as stereotypically masculine, driven by images of warcraft, weaponry, and angry male gods, volcanoes also have a "feminine" side. Hawaii's Kilauea volcano, for example, is home to Madame Pele, a goddess of fire, who according to legend had a quite literally steamy relationship with Kamapua'a, god of water (Calderazzo 2004, 35). Tahitians also have a volcano or fire goddess, Pere (Sigurdsson 1999, 19). Poet Giacomo Leopardi (2010, 300) imagined that Vesuvius buried Pompeii with ash and flaming lava that erupted violently from her "utero tonante," or "thundering womb." Lively volcanic narratives open possibilities for unexpected alliances, and the force and heat of volcanic power inspire stories and allow for agencies that can be male, female, or neither; human or nonhuman.

Volcanoes are compelling subjects for the final act of this book, then, not just because they are riveting geological forces, but also because they enable—even demand—the formation of creative bonds between human and more-than-human actors around them. Islanders and production crews alike are swayed by the vigor of volcanism. Under Stromboli's crater, Franco Figliodoro, a lifelong resident of Lipari and the film's protagonist, says that as a child, "I felt a force larger than myself, saying 'I'm in charge here.' [. . .] The volcano doesn't scare me. It gives me a feeling of serenity. I listen more."[8] Over the course of *Return,* Taviani, Figliodoro, and a small production crew travel from island to island, mapping the archipelago and collecting stories about the cinematic and volcanic past. Importantly, in the process of filming volcanoes, the directorial role (like in *Le quattro volte*) yielded some of its centrality to other players; the production crew relied on all kinds of knowledge, and any number of experts, to navigate (and not just metaphorically) the waters around the islands. The contemporary segments were filmed in October, when island weather is uncertain and waterspouts and whirlwinds are common. As production manager Marco Serrecchia explained, even more critically than starring in the film, Figliodoro was "one who knew those places like the inside of his pockets: the winds, the passages, the channels, the dangers, the behavior of the islands."[9] In this and other ways, the film narrates its reliance on a broad range of sources that, in an inclusive process of montage, creates a new kind of story. Fishermen, women, volcanoes, legends, films, and histories all have important roles to play in *Return*. In these volcanic landscapes, and in the suturing together of volcanic films, we find evidence of what Serpil Oppermann (2013, 28) describes as feminist ecocriticism's embrace of "heterogeneity," where "difference and otherness (in the sense of race, class, sex, gender, species) are indexed on a non-hierarchical ideology and appear as non-disjunctive categories." Here, volcanoes are not just powerful exploding mountains, but also fertile landscapes and sites of fragile, natural-cultural heritage.

The Aeolian Islands, with their moving landscapes of shorelines and active volcanoes, are a place where the inherent mobility and porosity of human identity is particularly visible. The alliances formed in making the film—alliances that see collaborations between old and new film stock; humans, goats, and volcanoes; young documentary film crews and elderly island inhabitants, among others—are dynamic and generative. *Return to the Aeolian Islands* arguably screens something that in cinematic terms resembles Braidotti's (2010, 209) "nomadic ethico-political project," because by way of its polyphonic archival form, the film offers a multitude of ways for human and nonhuman agents to "experiment with different modes of constituting subjectivity and different ways of inhabiting our corporeality." It also offers us new ways to think about cinema.

Walking through Volcanic Landscapes: "I Want to Get Out!"

A high angle shot in black-and-white from the film Stromboli *frames confining, dusty streets flanked by low walls, dirty, plastered buildings, and closed courtyards. An increasingly anxious Karen (Ingrid Bergman) runs through the narrow spaces repeating in panicked tones: "I want to get out! I want to get out!" The camera pans right to follow her flight, then the film cuts to color and to Taviani's footage. An elderly woman in a housedress, leaning on a cane, is identified in a title as Angelina. She makes her way slowly from the back of the frame toward the camera. Her progress leads her down a long, narrow street flanked by white plaster walls on one side and rough stone walls on the other. Green trees and the crater of the volcano cap the end of the narrow street. In a sound bridge from the previous scene, Karen's desperate voice overlays the shot of Angelina.*

In the montage that follows, the film returns to black-and-white footage of Karen as she makes her way up to the ashen crater of the volcano, walking into a landscape of sulfuric gasses. Moaning and bowing her forehead to the ground, she asks for strength, understanding, and courage and invokes "Dio misericordioso," "Merciful God."

The human bodies in these two scenes, ambulating at different paces and for different reasons, are both fragile: one is elderly, the other is panicked. Going on foot "returns the body to its original limits again, to something supple, sensitive, and vulnerable" (Solnit 2000, 29). Walking through a volcanic landscape amplifies corporeal fragility, and here, the volcanic landscapes expose very different kinds of vulnerabilities, including their own. Age, social status, fear, and (bodily and cinematic) exposure are just some of the forces at work, and they vibrate through bodies and landscapes. Although Karen initially runs from the volcanic eruption, at the end of *Stromboli*, she climbs the mountain slope in a gesture that appears desperate but also suggests an alliance between diva and volcano. Angelina, who walks slowly down the street in *Return to the Aeolian Islands*, embodies a lifetime of human-volcano relation, one characterized by considerably less drama, but equally marked by intensities and alliances. Karen and Angelina and their stories reveal something about volcanoes (and these Italian volcanoes in particular), and about the different material stories that unfurl through and around them.

Like any other, the Aeolian Islands are a landscape in progress, but as a volcanic archipelago, the flux is discernable in human time. When a volcano erupts, geological time, far from seeming monolithic and immobile,

Figure 5.2. Mobile Landscapes. Screen capture, *Return to the Aeolian Islands* (2010), directed by Giovanna Taviani.

performs a dynamism that refuses what we might think of as the quietude of stone. The four active volcanoes on the Italian peninsula—Etna, Vesuvius, Stromboli, and Vulcano—set Italy apart from other European regions (Bevilacqua 2010, 15–16). They testify to its geological youth (it emerged from the sea less than a million years ago) and to its continued instability (the African plate continues to press northward by about 1 cm a year, shrinking the Mediterranean basin and creating volcanic subduction zones) (Sigurdsson 1999, 34). The Aeolian Islands have been shaped from the Pleistocene through the Holocene, starting 1.3 million years ago and continuing today. The islands of Alicudi, Filicudi, Salina, Lipari, Vulcano, Panarea, and Stromboli are the visible parts of a more complex system, the rest of which is today a submerged seamount (Calanchi et al. 2007, 34). Not only are eruptions common in this dynamic system; shifts in island shape can happen in short time frames. Calanchi et al. (2007, 327) discuss a "competition" between the sea and the volcano on Stromboli, and the scientists note that periods of retreat of the island's beaches (1938–1955 and 1987–2001) are counterbalanced by periods of advancement (1955–1987, 2001–2003).

Eruption and erosion, flows of rock and water form and deform Stromboli's coast, to such an extent that photographs, maps, and illustrations chart an island whose dynamic shape shifting is easily perceptible. Stromboli has been continuously active for the last 2500 years, and Vulcano last erupted in 1888–90, recently enough for there to be early photographs of pyroclastic flows, or deadly, fast-moving currents of gas and rock, running down its sides (57). The volcanic activity on these islands intensifies and accelerates geological time, making it comprehensible in a human lifespan. In this way, it urges conversations between landscapes, memory, and bodies.

In Rossellini's *Stromboli*, the volcano of the title assaults Karen, reminding us of the rather obvious, yet nonetheless critical, fact that volcanoes are dangerous to all forms of life in their vicinity. In an extended, chaotic montage, the mountain hurls flaming bombs (a technical term for large pieces of volcanic rock ejected during an eruption) onto the small village and fills it with smoke and dust, as villagers hurry down to the shore to take refuge in boats. The film's recreation of chaos and panic provides a convincing approximation of how such an event might unfold. Oppenheimer (2011, 22) vividly describes the "variety of weapons" in a volcano's armory, including: "ash and toxic gas clouds, lava flows and the exceptionally destructive, searing avalanches known as pyroclastic currents." Flying bombs and pyroclastic flows are just part of the story of how creatures and volcanoes interact, however. In the atmosphere, volcanic matter has "profound impacts on atmospheric chemistry and on the Earth's heat budget and climate" (54): significantly, as I noted above, it changes the earth's climate and the temperatures of the oceans.[10] On a more local level, the volatile mountains can also cause landslides, mudslides, and tsunamis. Volcanoes can trigger "catastrophic human and economic losses," especially because people often build cities near volcanoes (22). Clouds of volcanic ash, composed of tiny particulate glass and crystals, can make airplane engines fail, or, once they settle back to earth, kill crops and contaminate pastures, resulting in famines. The danger for human populations is significant in Italy. Naples, positioned halfway between Vesuvius and the massive Campi Flegrei volcanic system that, in an eruption approximately 39,300 years ago, disgorged "up to 80 times more magma" than neighboring Vesuvius, is considered to be "one of the regions of the world at highest risk from volcanic activity" (208).[11] The volcano from which Karen runs does not threaten such widespread damage: Stromboli erupts every 10–20 minutes, and has for thousands of years, making it a *somewhat* predictable and less explosive volcano. Yet some eruptions are stronger than others, and 1930, 1985–86, 2003, and 2007 saw periods of more violent activity. The primary risks for humans of living with Stromboli, according to scholars, are larger eruptions, lava flows, the volcano's unstable slopes, and tsunamis triggered by such phenomena (Calanchi et al. 2007, 323). Over the years, the volcano has caused a number of human deaths, including tourists hit by bombs when climbing to see the crater.

As Oppenheimer (2011, 31) asserts, however, volcanic news "is not all bad," neither all catastrophe nor all collaborative cohabitation . On the positive side, Sean Cocco (2013, 14) eloquently articulates that volcanoes "are like great engines that drive the world's vitality." Light dustings of ash from volcanic eruptions nourish agriculture, providing sulfur and selenium to the soil. When ash falls in the seas, it can supply metals and nutrients that phytoplankton need (Oppenheimer 2011, 31). Even landscapes decimated by volcanic fires regenerate, and in Italy, they eventually sustain rich Mediterranean soils ideal for growing grapes, olives, capers, and tomatoes, among other things.[12] Various types of volcanic material accompanied humans in the process of becoming *sapiens*: as Sigurdsson (1999, 3) records, the most primitive stone tools, which are approximately 2.5 million years old, were made from lava, and in later epochs, obsidian. Two major products of volcanic eruptions, pumice and obsidian, have made the Aeolian Islands crossroads of Mediterranean commerce since about 5000 years BCE, during the Neolithic period. Pumice provided the *pozzolana*, a kind of cement made from volcanic ash, that helped the Romans construct the Pantheon and the Colosseum (3). In more recent years, as the film illustrates, Lipari's pumice cliffs made the island a profitable site for commerce, but here the story once again becomes knotty: pumice also led to illness, since the airborne particles released in the process of extraction led to severe respiratory ailments. Rich volcanic soil made the islands (especially Salina) fertile ground for vineyards, but these were subsequently wiped out by the Phylloxera pest in the late nineteenth century. The relative isolation of the islands made them effective quarantines for cholera victims, then prisons for anti-fascists placed under house arrest in the 1930s and 40s, and then a refuge for Mussolini's daughter Edda Ciano after the end of World War II. Phylloxera, a Strombolian eruption in the 1930s, respiratory illness, and house arrest were also the reason for emigration and escape from the islands.

Volcanic landscapes like the Aeolian Islands thus illustrate in countless vivid ways the fact that no landscape remains stable over time, and volcanic films show how this underlying unsteadiness can make humans anxious, but can also support them. Recognizing that "volcanoes are marvelous, but they are lethal," Taviani delved into the vertical layers of geological and human history.[13] Her choral volcanic film performs the fact that, as Jeffrey Jerome Cohen (2010, 57) underlines, "Flow is the truth of stone, not its aberration." In a volcanic landscape, we experience the "ontological vertigo" that Cohen identifies (with a nod to Aldo Leopold) when you "think like a mountain," because this kind of critical inquiry shows both "a geological formation that does not remain still and a creature of unstable history, easily undone" (3). Ontological vertigo aptly describes what Karen experiences when, in the midst of an unhappy marriage, the landscape around her begins to explode. Her urgent desire to "get out" makes sense in both existential and geological terms. Angelina also "thinks like a mountain," though, as she walks slowly through the landscape that has been her home for decades. The stories of give-and-take between human bodies, volcanoes, islands, labor, vines, and illnesses become the "volcanic stories" of *Return*, or the oral and cinematic histories and mythologies that its human and nonhuman inhabitants recount.

Angelina's and Karen's encounter via the film's montage in the scenes described above creates a node: the horizontal pathway via which Karen tries to escape intersects, in the subsequent scene, with the vertical line of the street via which the elderly Angelina, a contemporary interviewee, walks into the frame. The zone of intersection creates a map of historical and geological time, and shows different ways that humans live with volcanoes. It also exposes and begins to trouble the uneven power dynamics created when film crews visit tiny volcanic islands.[14] Angelina's presence in the montage counterbalances Karen's panic with gentle irony. The immigrant Karen, like the movie star Ingrid Bergman, lands on the island of Stromboli as an adult and stays for a relatively short period of time: she lives the volcano as crisis. On the other hand, like many of the other interviewees, the elderly Angelina in Taviani's film spent an entire, long life on the island. For her, the volcano is home, even though she lived through a number of periods of "anomalous" Strombolian eruptions. Film crews and divas erupt into island life, wielding at least some financial power and considerable cultural capital, leaving waste in their wake; as I discussed in Chapters Two and Three, their relationship to the cinematic location is far from innocent in ecological or social terms. Film productions, too, "choose" the Aeolian Islands as locations, while islanders cannot necessarily decide whether to stay or go.

While Karen and Angelina (as well as Ingrid Bergman and Angelina) live very different experiences of volcanoes and of film productions, the cinematic montage unites them in a magmatic sisterhood, a network of solidarity that runs throughout the film. Although all of the films cited by Taviani were directed by men, in *Return*, extended sequences feature female protagonists, from the unhappy Maddalena (Anna Magnani) of *Vulcano*, to the unhappy Karen in *Stromboli*; from Edda Ciano, Mussolini's daughter, to the missing Anna of *L'avventura*, to Monica Vitti, who in documentary footage recalls the time spent filming in the Aeolian Islands. Many of the documentary's interviewees are women: an elderly woman on Lipari remembers the political prisoners on the island during the Fascist era; an elderly woman on Vulcano recalls Magnani's stay there; a group of women recount their mothers' stories of marriage by proxy. Women protest lost loves, rebel against island limits, and spin tales of witches (the flying *maiare*), mysterious fiery-eyed donkeys, and perilous waterspouts. They confess their fear of volcanoes and talk about how, when men migrated en masse to other countries in search of better job opportunities, women stayed and worked. Film clips and still shots of photographs and drawings punctuate their memories and reinforce, in visual terms, their recollections.

Yet it is not simply the presence of all of these women in the film that is of interest here, nor is it the fact that *Return* is a significant cinematic work directed by a woman in an industry where, whether in Italy or Hollywood, women are vastly underrepresented.[15] The constant movement of water and stone and celluloid and flickering light, which drives Karen's ontological emergency and Angelina's slow walk through the streets, parallels the dynamism animating feminist geographies. Dynamism is, according to geographer Doreen Massey (1999, 5), a characteristic of space and place, not just time: "The identities of place are always unfixed, contested and multiple. [. . .] Places viewed this way are open and porous." In parallel with this notion, Massey argues that: "Geography matters to the construction of gender," and summons up canonical traditions of Western thought that align time with the masculine and characterize space as feminine (2). In these cultural codes, masculine time is credited with "history, progress, civilization, politics and transcendence," while feminine space is marked by "stasis, passivity and depoliticization" (7–8). Massey advocates that the kinetic and ontologically mobile affirmation "keep moving!" can be a "gender-disturbing message" that overturns such essentialist notions. She warns that: "The challenge is to achieve this whilst at the same time recognizing one's necessary locatedness and embeddedness/embodiedness, and taking responsibility for it" (11). A volcanic landscape is one in which such a gender-disturbing message cannot be avoided, for volcanic matter is porous, and everything volcanic moves. For the film industry, shooting on a volcanic island challenges the very notion of "location," because it necessarily means embracing location as animated matter.

In *Stromboli,* Karen the unhappy immigrant struggles against place, and the film ends dramatically with her invocation to a merciful God, as she cries out near the crater. Angelina's slow walk down a Strombolian street in *Return,* though, offers an alternative speed at which to "keep moving," a speed that navigates between the desperate pace of the diva, the short duration of the film production's stay on Stromboli, the longer span of a human life lived out on the island, and the palimpsestic time of island geology. Like the films it cites, *Return* too visits the islands for only a short period of time, but its documentary form incorporates voices from behind the scenes and across historical time, the voices and landscapes transformed by cinema and volcanic eruptions. Although moving pictures and their crews sweep through island life, Taviani's documentary sketches the way that film can also chronicle, participate in, and perhaps even create a dynamic locatedness. In the memories of the islanders, pieces of the film remain, and on the filmstrip are imprinted versions of the island that are no more. A moving image can on some level situate itself in the passage between times and places, located *somewhere* while recognizing that place is not still.

Shifting Memories and Cinematic Forgetting

In a series of documentary interviews, elderly islanders hypothesize about what happened to make Karen of the film Stromboli *escape to the crater of the volcano. Angelina observes that Karen left her husband many times. They must not have gotten along, she assumes, because "essa era simpatica" [she was nice]. Another elderly woman (Aimèe) laughs as she guesses that the protagonist of the film disappeared into smoke and sand, eaten by the volcano. An elderly man (Stefano) suggests that, offended by her husband's aggressive behavior, Karen ran up to the crater, but she was saved at the last moment by her repentant spouse.*

As these interviews humorously reveal, not everyone who recalls the filming of *Stromboli* remembers the finished film in the same way. For some, the story had a happy ending; for others, Karen's flight resulted in a fiery

Figure 5.3. Shifting Memories. Screen capture, *Return to the Aeolian Islands* (2010), directed by Giovanna Taviani.

volcanic death. None of them evoke the open-ended pan to a flight of birds over the volcano's crater that actually ends Rossellini's film.

In her voiceover as she introduces this series of conversations, Taviani jokes that although the entire island participated in making the film, "no one ever saw it." This oddity is partially explained by the fact that seeing the film when it was made would have been complicated, because the islands lacked places to screen it. Genovese (2010, 25) points out that when the Panària Film troupe arrived on the Aeolian Islands in 1946, only Lipari and Santa Marina on the island of Salina had electricity. Lipari also had a few phone lines, stores, and a restaurant; the other islands had no light, radio, newspapers, stores, restaurants, or hotels, and of course, no cinemas. When the filming of *Stromboli* began several years later, Ingrid Bergman's house was provided with electricity via large batteries (40). Access to "accurate" memories of the cinematic image was at the time a privilege reserved for a select few. The islanders' stories of Bergman and Magnani implicitly underline their distance from the glamor of Cinecittà, and their exclusion from the technologies that made film possible. Stefano, who remembers that Bergman tickled his leathery bare foot and complimented him for his nice "paws" when he brought her a cold coffee, exemplifies the affectionate (at least here) but colonizing impulse of the cinematic machine.

Return, though, shifts the privilege of institutional cinematic memory as it documents and honors other kinds of recollection. The oral histories of the islanders become part of film history, and the interviewees' choral reminiscences shape future memories. These histories, too, will be uneven, since Taviani's documentary will never circulate as widely as a big-budget film. And the histories it recounts are the product of a cinematic machine that alights on the islands, appropriates stories, and departs. But the stories and meta-stories in *Return* will be reflected and refracted through family histories, classrooms, academic discussions, and film festivals, including Taviani's annual SalinaDocFest that in 2016 celebrated 10 years of bringing films (including *Return*) to the islands. As such, *Return* offers a chance for viewers and islanders to participate jointly in confronting the "deficits" and "unevenness" existing in systems of power, and to perform the "compensative and balancing function" that is part of the potential of narratives (Iovino 2016, 144).[16]

Although they do not describe the film's actual ending, the islanders' conflicting accounts of Karen's fate nevertheless exist on Stromboli; they endure physically in the brains of those who remember them. Whether accurate or not, memory has a material presence in the body. Mortimer-Sandilands (2008, 273) underlines that memory is a physical phenomenon resulting from the movement of neurons: "no two memories follow the same path, and the more often a particular route is followed, the more chemically sensitive particular neurons become to one another." She continues:

> I find this idea quite extraordinarily beautiful: in the act of remembering something, the world is, quite literally, written into our brain structure. And memory allows the body to greet the world with greater physical ease the more often we have a particular sensory experience. Far from a reductionist account that would discard consciousness in favor of brain structure, this account is of a meeting between embodied mind and active world that must include not only physical experience but social relationships, not only sensory data but the interaction between any given sense-moment and what has gone before. [. . .] Histories are uniquely embodied. (273)

The social, technological, and physical relationships that so deeply marked life on Stromboli during Rossellini's time there clearly traced lasting impressions in the physical pathways of the minds of the island's inhabitants—and these are multidimensional memories of encounters with images, people, volcanoes, and technologies. Taviani's film, which works by asking people to re-narrate their recollections and thus retrace those neural pathways, ultimately reinforces the bonds of memory, even if the memories of the film *per se* are imprecise. My own watching, re-watching, and recollecting

Taviani's film's stories of the island inhabitants misremembering *Stromboli* creates a path of memory that parallels and is confused with the memory of seeing *Stromboli* at the Cinema Trevi in Rome sometime around the time I spoke with Giovanna. The historical montage of footage, in other words, creates memory montages whereby discrete memories—separate screenings, separate encounters, separate places—overlap and combine, presumably creating new neural pathways in the very process of activating established ones. Mortimer-Sandilands' eloquent description of the channels of reminiscence suggests memory's deeply personal and contextual nature.

While memory is certainly important in a volcanic landscape, though, forgetting volcanoes has also been a recurrent problem over the course of human history. In the Italian context, as Iovino (2016, 24) points out, before the disastrous eruption at Pompeii, Vesuvius had been dormant for 800 years, and thus "the memory of its agency had simply disappeared from the general narratives about this place—thus, the epistemic (and physical) shock." And then just a couple of centuries after the eruption in 79 CE, Pompeii, buried under hardened lava, was already forgotten again. This fragile, short-lived memory signaled, as Iovino argues, "human amnesia regarding nature's force" (26). Human amnesia is perhaps understandable when confronted with geological time. How do we know which mountains to worry about, when the earth's crust is dotted with thousands of volcanoes, including many under the oceans? Yet remembering geological history may be crucial in Italy and elsewhere if disaster is to be avoided. Volcanologists Peter Francis and Clive Oppenheimer (2004, 17) argue that "it is best to regard as *potentially active* any volcano that preserves geological evidence of eruptions within the last 10 millennia."[17] Vesuvius has not erupted since 1944, and the region around Naples seems to have once again forgotten or at least opted to disregard volcanic memory, since the city's dense population rises far up the side of the slope: more than half a million people live in an area designated a high-risk "Red Zone" (Oppenheimer 2011, 342). This means, Oppenheimer explains, that "most of the people living on or near the volcano today have no direct experience of Vesuvius as an active volcano" (342). When considering how best to mitigate potential volcanic disaster, Oppenheimer describes forecasters' need to weigh the possibilities of inspiring panic, on the one hand, and the dangers of encountering apathy or noncompliance on the other: people might overreact, or they might refuse to react, or both. In either case, aligning and reactivating geological, scientific, and social memory seems to provide a critical tool for responding to volcanic disaster.

Reawakening the memory of a volcano might be easier if we acknowledged that memory is neither exclusively a human phenomenon, nor is any particular memory created solely by forces working within our brains. Our human neural pathways, explains Mortimer-Sandilands (2008, 274), are only part of the memory equation, since: "the act of remembering involves a recognition of a relationship between the body/mind and the external world that is not only determined by internal forces." Deeply embedded in the physical structures of our brains, memories are nevertheless not exclusively located *in us*, but also in the objects, places, and beings that create and activate them. The relationship of embodied memory to the Aeolian setting was discernable in an intriguing story Giovanna told me about making *Return*. The Taviani family owns a house on the island of Salina that they purchased in the 1970s for a song because it was somewhat dilapidated and had formerly been inhabited by an elderly woman, known on the island as Chiccaredda, who was thought to be a witch. Islanders recalled that a young boy would take milk to Chiccaredda, chasing a red ball on his way up the drive. One night, after Giovanna had been working long days to write the screenplay (a process that involved watching film after film), she was returning home in her car after dark when, apparently out of nowhere, a red ball crossed through her headlights. "It was there, I saw it!" she insists, while at the same time imagining that her sighting of the red ball was impossible.

Taviani set both her creative and rational mind to work, and began to tell people about what she had "seen." One explanation that she came up with was that this was her version of Fellini's *8½*, and in the thick of screenplay writing, her brain no longer distinguished between art and reality. She had, after all, been speaking to Chiccaredda for years, since for her the witch represented a sort of creative muse, the presence of all of the people who had passed through the house. Perhaps that red ball was her brain's way of "screening" this artistic reality. For some islanders, on the other hand, including Figliodoro, the ball was quite simply real: they saw no inconsistency between imagination and material reality. Then Giovanna told her story to a group of psychiatrists, who played a clip from a French film that showed a red ball just like the one in her memory. "Have you seen this film?" they asked. Giovanna was sure that she had not. Yet her parents (or at least her "fathers") likely had seen the earlier film, and according to the psychiatrists, hers was a transgenerational, cinematic memory, passed along to her via the pathways of someone *else's* mind. She "remembered" a ball that her parents had seen and housed in their own recollections. In this story, memory remains personal and contextual, but the body in which it is embedded is no longer—or not only—Giovanna's.

How can you retain a visual memory of something you have not seen? Even without sorting out which account is "true," we can hypothesize that the red ball on Salina adds material and narrative layers to the montage of clips that is *Return to the Aeolian Islands.* The anecdote of the red ball, powerful in Taviani's imagination as she recalls the creative period spent conceiving and shaping the film, helps frame a broader theory about memories of the islands, and island memories. The archival approach to cinema that Taviani adopts as a filmmaker and film scholar recognizes and participates in a posthuman transgenerational memory that has deep ties to the volcanic places that comprise it. This cinematic archive is not so much a montage of Taviani's memories as it is a montage of the *place's* memories—memories that are stored on celluloid and digital films and in volcanic rocks and island plants.

This is not to suggest simply that places evoke memories; rather, it is to submit that places and things actually have memories of their own. Thinking memory in a posthuman age means recognizing that hard drives have memory, as do glands and magnets and plants. We see this if we simply draw on different existing definitions of memory, definitions that do not require that the bearer of memory have neural pathways. The Oxford English Dictionary, after all, tells us that memory can be "The capacity of a body or substance for manifesting effects of, or exhibiting behaviour dependent on, its previous state, behaviour, or treatment; such effects; a state manifesting this capacity." Here, the dictionary offers examples of "thingy" memory including magnetic memory or the memory that we can discern in the pituitary gland's ability to remember prior secretions. Then there is the sense of the "capacity of a body or substance for returning to a previous state when the cause of the transition from that state is removed," which is used to describe cables with PVC jackets that "learn" the shape in which they are stored, or Silly Putty, which reduces back down if you stretch and then immediately release it ("memory" 2015).

These definitions seem to pose a distinction between a mechanical and other memory—between a "behavior" and a "thought," or between intelligence and instinct. But although it resonates with a notion of behavioral memory, the memory at work in *Return's* volcanic stories does not require us to insist on these differences. Material ecocriticism has posited that intelligence is not just a human phenomenon, but also a quality of the world.

Ecophenomenologist David Abram (2011, 123) asks provocatively: "What if like the hunkered owl, and the spruce bending above it, and the beetle staggering from needle to needle on that branch, we all partake of the wide intelligence of the world—because we're materially participant, with our actions and our passions, in the broad psyche of this sphere?" In Abram's imagination (which is not, he insists, his alone), mind is a "medium," "an invisible and ceaselessly transforming layer of this world, a fluid medium that permeates our bodies" (124).[18] In intimate relation to mind, memory, too, is distributed across beings and landscapes, and not exclusively human.

In this broader context—in the world in which our minds reside—and specifically in the plant world (where plant "neurobiologists" like the Italian Stefano Mancuso have in fact been making radical and convincing claims about plant intelligence),[19] something like transgenerational memory seems to exist and to be tied to a plant's response to place. Scientists have recently hypothesized the existence of a botanical "transgeneration memory," whereby one generation of plants can pass down the "memory" of an adaptation to a stressor to a generation that has never encountered the stressor before. Molinier et al. (2006, 1046) explain that "owing to their sessile nature, plants are constantly exposed to a multitude of environmental stresses to which they react with a battery of responses." A series of experiments led the scientists to conclude that "environmental factors lead to increased genomic flexibility even in successive, untreated generations, and may increase the potential for adaptation" (1046).[20] Without ever having encountered a particular toxin or stressor, these plants can *remember* how to react because a previous generation successfully navigated the same situation. In other words, memory can be botanical, and botanical memory can be passed across bodies and time. Rather than being personal, exclusive, and corporeally bounded, here memory follows non-neural pathways, participating in a dance of time and place and in the dynamic encounters of bodies in the world.

This scientific possibility was anticipated in the form of a lyrical intuition on the part of one of Italy's great poets, Giacomo Leopardi. A plant, the broom flower, inspired Leopardi to write his memories of the volcano Vesuvius, and to immortalize them in one of his *canti*, "La ginestra o, il fiore del deserto" ("Broom, or the Flower in the Wilderness," 1936). The broom, which is both "solitary" and prolific, spreads its thickets over scorched landscapes, embodying volcanic contradictions and setting the poet's memory to work. As Leopardi (2010, 295) recalls how the lively villas and flourishing gardens of Pompeii perished, he insists that "The noble nature is the one / who dares lift his mortal eyes / to confront our common destiny" —and "common destiny" (*comun fato*) invests humans and broom flowers. Lamenting his contemporaries' regressive enslavement to a kind of thinking that defies reason and truth, Leopardi's poem invokes the plant as victim, as witness, and as wise counterpoint to human folly. In spite of his exhortation to humans to lift their eyes to the future, however, Leopardi and his broom plant are grounded in memories of the volcanic past. "Extinct Pompeii," destroyed by the active volcano's "burning flood, / which advances hissing and unstoppable," existed in "immemorial oblivion" for humans, but not for the broom (305). He lauds the plant's wisdom, addressing her directly when he writes: "you did not presume / that either fate or you had made / your fragile kind immortal" (309). "La ginestra" might express the poet's pessimism regarding human intelligence in the face of nature, but the more-than-human world of the broom demonstrates a form of acumen based in a situated memory of volcanic landscapes. Humans, he argues, have vainly raised themselves "up to the stars" (309), while the broom, which has neither forgotten nor disregarded the volcanic fires beneath it, remains firmly rooted in place. Leopardi uses plant memory to reactivate volcanic memory, showing how it is only by remaining entangled in the porous landscape and in the transgenerational, trans-corporeal ebb and flow of history that humans have a chance.

Returning to the montage of islanders' memories of *Stromboli*, it becomes clear that by *showing* us people who narrate their embodied memories of a significant island event, by framing their voices and bodies as they interact with mountain slopes and cinematic and earthly soundtracks, the fragility of one kind of memory (human narrative memory) is built on the embodied presence of another (volcanic, situated memory). Giovanna's vision of the red ball and her accompanying notion of transgenerational memory help change the stakes of "remembering" the film, or "seeing" it. Though Taviani laughs at the islanders' inexact recollections of Rossellini's film, the film strategically presents different kinds of memories, including celluloid memories of those landscapes and plurivocal memories of film's passage across the islands. Further, both the films and the volcanoes feature as bearers of memory, or what Iovino (2010a) calls the "'warehouse' of common memories to humanity and nature, in which human and natural life are dialectically interlaced in the form of a *co-presence*" (31, original emphasis).[21] In the montage of old and new films, old and new landscapes, which all collaborate to become yet another film, narrative suturing also becomes a process of opening to a wider experience of body and mind. Abram (2011, 127) insists: "There is a profusion of individual bodies; there is the enveloping sphere of the planet; and there is the ongoing, open relation between these. The fluid field of experience that we call 'mind' is simply the place of this open, improvisational relationship." The scenes featuring islanders' "forgetting" Rossellini's film perforate the permeable membrane between landscapes, memories, and cinematic subjects of all kinds.

Learning from Volcanoes

In a scene near the end of the film, Giovanna's father, Vittorio, leans on a white plaster railing recalling why they chose to film a scene for Kaos on the pumice cliffs of Lipari. "You were there, too, Giovanna," he says, and the film cuts to a medium close-up of a 14-year-old Giovanna, tears streaming down her face, as a gentle female voice insists, "You want to go too, don't you?" In the ensuing montage, the Kaos soundtrack plays behind Vittorio's voice, as the film cuts between his explanation of the scene and the children, including Giovanna, who scramble up a steep, dusty white pumice cliff. Perched high on the slope, they leap in gravity-defying jumps down to the sea. As they descend, now the montage (accompanied by the musical soundtrack) captures archival black-and-white footage of women, men, and children at work and at play, flying down similar pumice cliffs, as the friable surface gives way beneath their feet.

Like the scenes framing the previous section, this montage plays with notions of memory. The pumice cliffs are a rich and generative site of volcanic memory: generations of ecological, family, and cinematic history intersect and overlap. Actors and directors age, film stock fades, light changes, colors shift. But the scene also helps to build a cinematic pedagogy, showing part of the process of Taviani's becoming-director. Framing her father on film, and then cutting from a production in which she featured as young actor, Taviani foregrounds the extended process of accumulating knowledge about the islands and about cinema. Here and elsewhere in the film, her father features as teacher and mentor, making *Return* a cinematic bildungsroman.

In *Return*, though, humans are not the only teachers, and the lessons learned are not simply those that regard human arts. Rather, the volcanoes feature as teachers and objects of study, testifying to the long history of these landscapes not just as spectacles, but as part of a growing human

Figure 5.4. Learning from Volcanoes. Screen capture, *Return to the Aeolian Islands* (2010), directed by Giovanna Taviani.

interest in natural science. Volcanoes, in fact, urged theories and theorists forward, as once again their accelerated geological time, their potential for violence, and their ability to carbonize and preserve things long fascinated inquiring minds.[22] Many of these minds were specifically studying Italian volcanoes. Sigurdsson (1999, 36–39) cites Aristotle's writings about Vulcano and Empedocles' interest in Etna, and observes that Callius, Polibius, Cornelius Severus, Strabo, and Pliny the Elder wrote about Stromboli. The landscape in the background of the scene framing Vittorio Taviani is one that has long been in the sights of students of volcanoes. For their volcanic "character," Stromboli and Vulcano in particular have been significant in the history of volcanic eruptions; they give their names to two different kinds of volcanic activity, strombolian and vulcanian.[23]

As I wrote before, knowledge of volcanoes' destructive power may be vital to human survival on the planet. But equally crucial is a more subtle lesson that volcanoes teach, a lesson regarding our entanglement in a world that speaks another language and follows a set of rules that are not human rules. Empedocles, sometimes considered the father of volcanology, was said to have thrown himself into Etna's crater. Hiking up to the top in bronze sandals, legend has it that he abandoned one on the crater's edge, giving away his final resting place. Michel Serres' (2012, 76) lyrical description of the fabled ascent in the book *Biogea* proposes that volcanoes contain a key point of suture between the violence and the generative delicacy of planetary processes, and that this is what Empedocles' final landscape revealed to him: "in the sweat of the effort and his deathly pain, Empedocles is approaching the mystery of the origins, of the big bang of world and human history, of the violence that separates and the energy that reunites things as well as humans. He is approaching the mouth of the volcano that destroys, through hate, the cultivable fields and, through love, causes the fragile relief of the Earth to be continually reborn."

Separation and unity, violence and creation, hate and love, rather than diametrically opposed forces, are here partners in intricate patterns of becoming. Observing volcanoes leads careful students neither to believe in a benevolent, stable mother nature, nor to an apocalyptic vision of our relationship with the more-than-human world, since volcanic landscapes perform the complex character of environmental history. Volcanoes can wipe out human history, and as we know from the outdoor museum at Pompeii, they can preserve traces of it. Their perilous lava eventually gives way to fertile soil that nourishes life on the planet. These subtle lessons, which Leopardi's "wise" broom flower knows, recognize the fragile nature of existence, all the while persisting in commitment to relation.

The landscape of Vittorio Taviani's memory, the pumice cliff on which he and his brother filmed *Kaos*, communicates this volcanic lesson in a nuanced way. While the strombolian eruption at the film's beginning has the sound and drama of a Hollywood disaster film, the pumice cliffs teach the more mobile lesson of a documentary. The pumice cliffs of Lipari are quite fragile, and here overlapping scenes show Lipari crumbling, as erosion and human foot traffic sweep the crumbly rock to the sea. The film's beautiful montage of people sliding down the shifting pumice cliffs offers a visual record of an intensive practice that over the years endangered the fragile shoreline. The pumice mines began operating in the 1700s, when Lipari was an "enormous warehouse" that furnished pumice to all of Europe (Calanchi et al. 2007, 16).[24] It was not until more devastating industrial extraction began, though, that the northern half of the island became "unusable." The pumice cliffs today are substantially reduced from what they once were, having been physically carried away to serve human commerce, construction, and need. Since the year 2000, the Aeolian Islands have been designated a World Heritage Site, and after intervention on the part of the United Nations Educational, Scientific and Cultural Organization (UNESCO), the pumice mines were closed on August 31, 2007, mining machinery seized, and quarried material impounded. National Law 394/1991 bans the resumption of mining activity ("State of Conservation" 2010). Nevertheless, the anthropogenic threat to the ecological health of the Aeolian Islands continues. In a passionate appeal to protect Sicily's UNESCO sites, Gianfranco Zanna (2011, 5) of Legambiente Sicilia condemns cementification, decay, illegal building, but perhaps more insidiously, the propensity to disinterest for natural-cultural landscapes and the tendency to break promises to preserve them.[25] The UNESCO 2007 State of Conservation report in fact suggests that although PUMEX was ordered to cease all mining activities, "some extraction may still be going on at the PUMEX mine in the guise of removal of stockpiled material" ("State of Conservation" 2007). The history of Lipari's pumice cliffs illustrates how intense industrial use of the planet's resources in the Anthropocene can profoundly endanger human lives and radically change the profile of landscapes.

Learning this lesson from the Aeolian Islands seems especially poignant, because the UNESCO designation of the Aeolian Islands as a World Heritage Site is based on island pedagogy. The designation reads as follows: "The islands' volcanic landforms represent classic features in the continuing study of volcanology world-wide. With their scientific study from at least the 18th Century, the islands have provided two of the types of eruptions (Vulcanian and Strombolian) to volcanology and geology textbooks and so have featured prominently in the education of all geoscientists for over 200 years. They continue to provide a rich field for volcanological studies of ongoing geological processes in the development of landforms" ("Isole" 2016).

Yet volcanoes do not only teach lessons to volcanologists, and their lessons are not recorded in geology textbooks alone. Volcanic knowledge is inherently interdisciplinary, first of all. As Calanchi et al. (2007, 12) point out, it is impossible to separate the fields of geology and archaeology on the islands because "the relationship of man with the earth, here more than elsewhere, was intrinsic and intense." Volcanic knowledge is also democratic, spread across species and landscapes and all manner of human knowers. For example, several decades ago, in the volcanic Philippine archipelago, a cohort of citizen scientists was engaged to observe sulfurous odors, strange animal behavior, and drying vegetation, in an effort to help predict volcanoes and earthquakes. In the absence of funds for a more technologically sophisticated observatory, animals, plants, vapors, and citizens were shaped into a more-than-human confederacy of witnesses and observers. On the Aeolian Islands, a host of islanders are working to learn from the volcanoes, and to teach their stories to others. On the island of Salina, librarian Antonio Brundu curates a rich collection of books and articles about the Aeolian Islands, and seems to know them all by heart. On Lipari, Pietro Lo Cascio and Flavia Grita run an organization called NESOS that conducts research on island ecologies and also invites islanders to "Conosci le tue isole" ("Get to know your islands") by joining free, educational excursions throughout the archipelago. The *Centro Studi e Ricerche di Storie e Problemi Eoliani* (Center for Study and Research on Aeolian History and Problems) outlines its candid vision in its lengthy name, and publishes insightful texts about film, history, travel, tourism, as well as Aeolian fiction. Figliodoro knows the volcanoes and seas intimately, observing winds, marine habitats, and volcanic slopes to anticipate danger and diagnose the ecological health of his beloved home. Iovino (2014a, 102) compares such knowledge to lava flows: "Knowledge—human and nonhuman informational interchange with the world—is a form of porosity; it is the way the world enters and conditions habits of living, thus determining the way living beings *in-habit* the world."[26]

As narrative, *Return* shows its porosity as its borders flex to admit the work of other directors, film crews, and historical periods. It participates in island pedagogy, performing a cinematic archaeology of knowledge, juxtaposing films and histories. As production, it also interacted with and learned from eclectic sources: cinematic, geologic, human. Taviani and the crew positioned themselves as students and scholars to learn from the islands, islanders, and films about the islands. Figliodoro, as interlocutor and guide for the film crew, was one of the central teachers, recounting his own long history of listening to and learning from the islands' more-than-human messages. He is a passionate advocate for attention to island ecology. In our conversation, he discussed his concern for a practice of fishing for squid using batteries that leak mercury into the seas, against which he has actively advocated for years. He lamented that the sea, thanks to overfishing and the poisoning of marine waters, has become a "cemetery." "We have been incapable of appreciating the value of our landscape," he says. "We've lost sight of the reason people want to come here." Figliodoro worries about the "violence and arrogance" of those who have sought to profit from their relationship with the islands, and condemns an "oligarchic power" that has led to making poor decisions about their future. One of the lessons that Figliodoro learned from his volcanic home, then, is about the dangerous dance between human hubris, human and nonhuman fragility, and capital.

Human hubris and human greed are major protagonists in the story of volcanoes and volcanic landscapes. Reports to UNESCO single out global business interests as a major threat to the ecological future of the Aeolian archipelago. The *Società Italiana per Condotte d'Acqua* (Italian Water Works Company), which according to Legambiente Sicilia was planning a "megaport" for large cruise ships on the island of Lipari (Zanna 2011, 13), boasted €1,173,900,000 in trade in 2014. Although the Aeolian-based PU-MEX mining company went bankrupt in 2015, in 2016 it still had an active website boasting of "social capital" equaling €3,870,000, as well as offices on the island of Lipari, Milan, and London (in 2018, its website promises that it will be back online soon). Big tourism and transnational mining operations both risk undermining—and even eliminating—the islands' most precious resources, whether by overusing them or physically carrying them off to more profitable markets. UNESCO and Legambiente continue to ring alarm bells regarding what Rob Nixon (2011, 51) identifies (in his study referring to the Chernobyl and Bhopal disasters) as the "contest between the tenacity of corporeal memory and the corrosive power, over time and space, of corporate amnesia emboldened by a neoliberal regime of deregulation." Corporate greed, which carries volcanic landscapes away and leaves islanders with pulmonary disease in its wake, ignores the subtleties and vulnerabilities of volcanic landscapes. Of course, as we have seen, film productions can also disregard landscapes in their pursuit of profit, and they can suffer "corporate amnesia" or benefit from loosened regulatory and tax structures. Even though these were not the stories the islanders recalled in *Return*, some conflict between production interests and island ecology is inevitable, no matter how small the production.

In the age of the Anthropocene, however, corporate volcanic ignorance is also asserting itself on a larger scale, spinning new, incredible stories about what we have apparently *not* learned from volcanoes. In discussions about climate change, some scientists propose geoengineering a volcanic eruption, or more precisely, shooting a layer of sulfate aerosols into the stratosphere to help cool a warming planet. As Naomi Klein (2014, 258) explains, this is often called the "Pinatubo Option" after the 1991 eruption of the Philippine volcano that dropped the earth's temperatures by half a degree Celsius.[27] Some, like economists Gernot Wagner and Martin L. Weitzman (2015, 33, 71), note that a "Pinatubo Option" is "cheap"—in fact, they suggest that such a potential response to global climate emergency is "too cheap to ignore." But dimming the sun is far from a modest proposal.

As both Klein and Oppenheimer note, such a massive project of geoengineering is very likely to have unintended consequences; it will not solve the underlying causes of climate change; it cannot stop the acidification of the oceans caused by high levels of carbon dioxide in our atmosphere; and it most certainly will have "distributional consequences": some places will be impacted more than others (Oppenheimer 2011, 348).[28] One certain, evocative consequence—and not an insignificant one for the cinematic imagination—is that a fabricated volcanic eruption would change the color of the sky (348). Such a highly speculative intervention, rather than abating the risks of a climate changed planet, instead would put life on the planet at risk, not the least by further enabling forms of disaster capitalism that weaken environmental regulations and regulations of all kinds. As Klein remarks, "The ancients called this hubris; the great American philosopher, farmer, and poet Wendell Berry calls it 'arrogant ignorance'" (268).

There is one more apocalyptic-sounding concern closely related to the "Pinatubo Option," another important lesson that volcanoes may, according to some scientists, be trying to teach us. As Oppenheimer (2011, 351) explains in the final pages of *Eruptions That Shook the World*, there is the possibility that climate change might actually *trigger* more, and stronger, volcanic eruptions. Changing sea levels, thinning ice sheets, and other processes sparked by climate change alter stresses and forces on the earth's mantle, and it is possible, Oppenheimer asserts, that "deglaciation over the next century or so will modify eruptive behaviour at some volcanoes." In this scenario, perhaps volcanoes are communicating another message that Klein (2014, 285) hears: "our challenge is less to save the earth from ourselves and more to save ourselves from an earth that, if pushed too far, has ample power to rock, burn, and shake us off completely." Might volcanoes be poised to knock pesky human inhabitants right off the map?

There is much to be said about environmentalism and the apocalyptic imagination, but *Return to the Aeolian Islands* is not telling apocalyptic tales, even if such stories might lurk around its edges.[29] If you listen to the island inhabitants, to the microhistories of those who live with the volcano day by day, their emergent voices tell stories recognizing collaborative volcanic lessons, lessons of prudence, beauty, privation, and mutual respect. The pumice cliffs montage weaves together work, play, art; emotion, respiration, erosion; blue, white, flesh; rock, sand, water; 1940s, 1980s, the new millennium. As the film's title underlines, volcanoes are reasons people flee, but also reasons people settle, and in the knots of choices debated and discussed across years of celluloid and digital archives, volcanic lessons advocate against "arrogant ignorance" and for porous, open stories. Volcanic stories show us, as Braidotti (2013, 188) suggests of posthuman subjectivity, that: "Power is not a steady location operated by a single masterful owner," be it a volcano, a mining company, a paternalistic husband, or a film crew. In *Return*, volcanic knowledge is captured on camera and, like all knowledge, sutured together in the process of "give-and-take between bodies and the world" (Iovino 2014a, 103). Neither consoling nor threatening human inhabitants with apocalypse, the Aeolian volcanoes participate actively in the posthuman dance of co-constituted lives.

"Dio è dappertutto": Rereading, Recycling, and Loving the (Interdisciplinary, Inhuman) Alien

A dramatic clip from the film Vulcano *plays onscreen in black-and-white: Magnani, in the role of Maddalena, stands defiantly in front of the village church, reassuring a judgmental crowd of black-clad women that she, a woman scorned, will not enter the building. "God is not just inside there. God is everywhere," she cries in agonizing tones as she kneels on the hard volcanic stone. "Everywhere!" Cut to four women standing in front of the church, now in color, recalling the powerful scene. "Even the director cried," they said.*

At the outside edge of a crowd of women who jealously guard the church entrance (which was actually on the island of Salina, not Vulcano), Maddalena stands excluded. Throughout *Return,* many archival clips show Magnani alone, set apart from other islanders and other characters in the film. According to all accounts, the actor was suffering heartbreak while filming *Vulcano.* Mourning the loss of her beloved, Rossellini, Magnani was sad in the islanders' memories, and like her character, she suffered exile and exclusion on the volcanic islands. Barred from entering the church as a woman scorned, Magnani/Maddalena inspired pathos onscreen and on location.

Yet while the character Maddalena emotes heartbreak and despair outside of the church, her lines of dialogue underline the sacred connectedness of all things and ultimately spin tales about love. Imagining a distributive power that locates God across the landscape, Maddalena drops closer to the earth, seeking support from the stones beneath her when human empathy fails. In Taviani's film, the citation of *Vulcano* returns on location to recast

Figure 5.5. *Dio è dappertutto.* Screen capture, *Return to the Aeolian Islands* (2010), directed by Giovanna Taviani.

tragedy as something more hopeful. Here, memories of Magnani's role on the island and in front of the church draw together a sisterhood of women storytellers, in space and across time. Behind the camera and in the editing room, Taviani unites the exclusionary circle of *Vulcano* with an inclusive one in her film; the women in her documentary embrace and overturn, with their memory, the narrative of marginalization in the earlier film. Smiling as they remember their tears, these contemporary women, and the film with them, are "loving the alien," or those "subjugated and vulnerable forms of otherness" that Iovino (2013a, 182) identifies as central to new materialist understandings of our webbed bodily existence. In an essay about writer Anna Maria Ortese, and in particular treating the memorable hybrid reptilian-girl of her novel *The Iguana*, Iovino locates a subversive ontological narrative strategy that shows the sacredness of "all bodily natures" (188), and that inspires her to recall the "alien" love of a David Bowie song. Like in Ortese's gentle, rebellious novel, multiple acts of love crisscross in the stories about Magnani: Taviani's love for cinema and the volcanic islands; Magnani's love for Rossellini and the island's many dogs; the women's loving memories of ancestral stories and the island's cinematic past; a divine love that reaches outside of institutional and architectural structures to embrace the world's most forlorn creatures.[30] Here as in other moments, *Return*'s montage tells stories that are about "crossings and metamorphoses" (200), and while very different from the ones Iovino identifies in Ortese's magical realist writings, these stories similarly have generous ethical potential. Like the feminist ethic that Iovino describes in the writer's imaginative narratives, *Return* puts old and new stories together in a way that "conveys a re-enchantment made of crossings, of rediscovered proximities, of cognitive expansions" (201). The "other" here is neither "neutralized nor distanced," but instead enfolded into the film's cinematic becoming (201).

The "re-enchantment" proper to *Return* comes above all from its patient work of cinematic recycling. Taviani's role as director and screenplay writer of *Return* involved careful research, and relied on her deep archival knowledge of films about the Aeolian Islands. Preparing the screenplay meant spending long hours in the house with Chiccaredda, watching the many films, identifying geographic places, narrative tropes, characters, and historical currents, then matching those to faces, landscapes, facts, and legends. Creating the film was a prolonged project of rereading and then recycling, a project accomplished by listening to the plural island voices that were also recollecting and rereading the islands' cinematic past. Such recycling is part of the history of moving images, as Nadia Bozak (2012, 157) has emphasized: "the moving image is and has been thinking through its material life and residues since its inception. Not only is filmmaking an ephemeral art form, it is an art of repurposing—one which, outside of mainstream channels, quite often makes do with limited resources." This recycling is not, of course, an entirely innocent process. The stories of *Red Desert* in Chapter One and *Gomorrah* in Chapter Two consider the ways that cinema, too, can alter the environment: leaching toxic substances when celluloid or digital materials are discarded, consuming petroleum and other planetary resources, leaving a waste stream when films are made on location.[31] Yet a strategic engagement of cinematic recycling has at the very least the potential to create new narratives that can shift our understanding of the past and inspire visions of alternative futures.

Volcanoes participate in "recycling," too, in the etymological sense of the term. "Recycling," after all, means to "return (material) to a previous stage of a cyclic process" ("recycle, v" 2016). Through the eruption process, volcanoes in some senses make the earth new again. As Oppenheimer (2011, 46) explains, "large volcanic events effectively reset the biological clock to zero in the worst-impacted areas, providing ecologists with fascinating natural experiments on colonization and succession of flora and fauna." Forensic volcanology posits that lava and tephra (different kinds of silicate glass), ejected at extremely high temperature, "reset the radioactivity clock" (86). *Return*'s volcanic bookends, which close in on Stromboli ejecting pyroclasts into the sky, suggest that the cinematic clock has been reset in order to open the door to new films, new landscapes, new narrative and geological records.

Sinking to the ground in the film *Vulcano*, however, Magnani kneels on rocks formed when those volcanic substances returned to earth, hardened, and became landscape. The rock resembles *Return* in important ways, since, as Cohen (2015, 66) explains, "the ash from the volcano's combustion is an archive." Buried in the global volcanic archive are stories about geological, botanical, and climatic history, and human stories, too. On the nearby Italian mainland, for example, the Herculaneum scrolls from the Villa of the Papyri, constituting an entire library of classical texts buried under almost 90 feet of lava, were preserved by volcanic fires. Preserved, that is, in volcanic fashion: the charred cylinders offer a testament to the heat and pressure of pyroclastic flows, and some of the exteriors are "readable," but otherwise the precious human stories are, for the moment, locked inside. For 250 years, scholars have experimented with various methods for unrolling these fragile texts, but in the process have also destroyed a number of them. Recently, scientists posit that scanning technologies, involving a machine known as a synchrotron, may allow them to read the scrolls without unrolling them. This is another volcanic story. Brent Seales, a computer scientist working to develop a novel reading technique to interpret the data gathered in the scanning process, explains that: "It turns out there are grains of sand sprinkled all the way through the scrolls. [. . .] You can see them twinkling in the scans, and that constellation is fixed" (Jaggard 2015). The grains of sand, like stones described by Cohen, are "a catalyst for relation, a generative substantiality through which story tenaciously emerges" (33). Following tiny pieces of twinkling sand like guideposts, someday a constellation of stony fragments may lead humans to read the volcano-charred secrets of the papyri.

The painstakingly slow process of discerning these scorched stories is a labor of love requiring endless patience, not just in terms of research, but also in combatting the Olympian bureaucracies that slow scholarly access to the scrolls, or to the powerful instruments that can help read them. By now, the attempts at "reading" have been in progress for centuries, and are in fact transgenerational. The French papyrologist Daniel Delattre has dedicated much of his life to this work, even though he knows it will not suffice: "Our human scale is not the scale of the scrolls" (Seabrook 2015). In spite of the speed and drama of volcanic eruptions, volcanoes and their stories require patience and time; they present risks and mysteries; they defy and challenge the limits of one human lifespan.

Is it prudent, then, to love a volcano? Tracing "geophilia," or love of stone, Cohen (2015, 20) observes that: "Humans walk upright on the earth because the mineral long ago infiltrated animal life to become a partner in mobility. Vertebral bone is the architect of motion." Our stony centers, in turn, support us as we kneel in what Cohen figures as a "radiant carapace under which humans pray, govern, make purchases" (20): architectural bodies that enclose human bodies, united in minerality. Magnani, kneeling outside of the church, affirms that there is no outside, and her stony knees meet the stony earth in an exchange of lithic support. Volcanoes and their kin, in more than one way, hold us up and embrace us in their sometimes perilous cloaks.

Serres' (2012, 75, 74) chapter on volcanoes also lingers on the topic of love, reading love through Empedocles' writings and seeing in the early volcanic mind an ability to think in a "unified voice," or to see, "like Dante, what we don't see anymore, that love moves the Sun and the other stars." Serres' volcanoes also evoke heartbreak—pain caused not by fiery mountains, but by deep intellectual and disciplinary divisions. He cites the disjunction of our lives and our discourses as reason for despair:

> Through weakness or anxiety, to be serious or for effectiveness, we no longer know how, we are no longer capable of speaking in any but disjointed terms, in special, specialized, specious discourses, as physicists or politicians, as historians or pious believers, through equations, poems, or prayers, as scientists or those in love, in bad French or exact algebra. None of these discourses can or wants to rejoin the other, to encounter it, recognize it, yes, love it. We claim to hold colloquia, but we speak there in these dislocated terms. (74)

Serres' call to action, his desire to think, as Aldo Leopold urges, like a mountain, becomes a rousing call to interdisciplinarity, a cry to speak across specializations, borders, generations, and species, to admit a courageous and distributed love that wanders outside of bodies and bodies of knowledge and entangles us with our world. This book is a response to that cry, and although as a scholar of literature and film I know that I risk error while talking about volcanoes and dioxins, hydrocarbons and goats, I hope that this hybrid of theory, things, and stories also sparks new ideas about co-constituted lives and art forms.

Like Serres, Cohen (2015, 25) envisions Empedocles' fiery ending ("an embrace of stone that incinerated him") as connected to geophilia: "To take his theory of elementary restlessness seriously is to apprehend that the world is not centered around the human—not indifferent, not misanthropic, but *disanthropocentric*, making stories centered upon the human wobble, their trajectories veer." *Return to the Aeolian Islands* is a montage of veering stories, of narrative fragments that shift course to become a new, introspective film about Taviani and her cinematic past, but not only. Reading with stone, like watching hours of film archives, is a labor of love, one that occupies years of human time and requires intricate partnerships of humans, mountains, creatures, and celluloid. *Return*'s careful work in the cinematic archives is built on the volcanic Aeolian archive. Whereas it might seem that the lithic archive is the more solid of the two, in some cases, such as when viewing the fragile pumice cliffs as they flow to the sea, the cinema actually preserves memories of stone. In the give-and-take between film archive and geological archive, we find "confederations of the human and inhuman" (20). This chapter and this author encourage cinematic subjects to keep veering toward the disanthropocentric, to recognize that stories about humans need to wobble, to rejoin the disjointed subjects of cinematic and earthly experience in a montage born of a love for Italian cinema and love for the world that generates it.

Notes

1. Although the islands' popularity as a cinematic destination really began after the war, Genovese (2010, 22–23) also identifies several documentaries made in the early twentieth century. *Vulcani d'Italia* (*Volcanoes of Italy*, 1909), which has been lost, presumably included the Aeolian Islands; the shorts *L'eruzione dello Stromboli* (*The Eruption of Stromboli*, 1918) and *Voli sui vulcani d'Italia: l'Etna e lo Stromboli* (*Flights Over the Volcanoes of Italy: Etna and Stromboli*, 1927) (also both lost) certainly did.

2. The four friends were Alliata, Pietro Moncada, Renzo Avanzo, and Quintino Di Napoli. Avanzo was Luchino Visconti's brother-in-law and Rossellini's cousin (Genovese 2010, 25–26).

3. Nino Genovese's *Cineolie* (2010), a publication of the Centro Studi—Lipari, lists 20 fiction films and more than 60 documentaries that were filmed, from 1909 to 2010, entirely or in part on the Aeolian Islands (see the filmographies, 177–81).

4. In this chapter, "Taviani" will refer to Giovanna Taviani; I will specify other members of the Taviani family by using their first names or by referring to the "Taviani brothers."

5. Vittorio Taviani died on April 15, 2018, while this work was in progress.

6. Some legends suggest that Vulcan resided under Etna, but Etna was supposed to be connected on a subterranean level with Vulcano and Stromboli (Genovese 2010, 17).

7. In *Rising Fire*, Calderazzo (2004, 73–75) recounts that fierce "rituals of appeasement" happened in Nicaragua, where a young girl was thrown into the crater of the Coseguina volcano every 25 years; in El Salvador, girls were thrown into lakes to keep volcanoes from exploding. At Lake Ilopango, such an appeasement may have happened as recently as 1880. High-altitude graves in Peru, Chile, and Argentina reveal young girls buried ritualistically at the summit of volcanoes by Incan shamans.

8. Franco Figliodoro, interview by author, Lipari, April 20, 2013. All information from Figliodoro was collected during this interview.

9. Marco Serrecchia, interview by author, Rome, March 6, 2013. All information from Serrecchia was collected during this interview.

10. Sigurdsson (1999, 7) intriguingly suggests that it was because of the 1815 eruption of the volcano Tambora on the Indonesian island of Sumbawa that, in 1816, Mary Shelley and Percy Bysshe Shelley encountered a cold spring and had to stay inside during much of their vacation in Switzerland. "Housebound because of the miserable weather" and in search of entertainment, Mary Shelley wrote *Frankenstein.*

11. The eruption of the Campi Flegrei, known as the Campanian Ignimbrite eruption, left a massive caldera that is 30–35 kilometers across. Traces of the massive blast, "the largest in Europe for more than 100,000 years," stretch across the Mediterranean Sea, Greece and Bulgaria, and upward into Russia (Oppenheimer 2011, 209). The area was marked by a period of geological unrest from 1982 to 1984, prompting fears of another massive eruption, but the seismicity decreased to low levels. Francis and Oppenheimer (2004, 287) observe ominously: "For now, the Campi Flegrei and the city of Naples are safe. But when will the next large eruption occur, extinguishing the life and commerce of this busy part of Italy? No one can say, but fortunately it is likely that there will be precursors, which will be hard to ignore."

12. Calderazzo (2004, 86) provides a vivid description of the transformation from scorched earth into fertile soil, mentioning the early arrival of moss and lichens on volcanic landscapes and the slow erosion aided by precipitation. Visiting the Parícutin volcano in Mexico, which erupted from a field in Michoacán in 1943, he notes: "As it has many times before, this impossible geography will eventually turn into some of the most fertile earth anywhere."

13. Taviani, interview by author, Rome, March 3, 2013. All information from the director was collected during this interview.

14. For Mortimer-Sandilands (2008), situating discussions of landscape within a framework of embodied perception allows for a feminist inquiry into technological and discursive relations; or in other words, into relationships of power.

15. In April 2015, the American Civil Liberties Union called for an investigation into gender bias and discrimination in major Hollywood studios, citing studies that show that a tiny percentage of top-grossing films are directed by women (Buckley 2015).

16. This idea, articulated by Iovino (2016, 143–44), comes from Hubert Zapf's notion of "cultural ecology." In Iovino's reading of Zapf, narratives can be "counter-violent," helping to "reintegrate" the marginalized and dispossessed. Interviews in particular (she speaks of Nuto Revelli's interviews of peasants in Piedmont) can offer a mirror that allows for self-awareness and "thus a redemption for the world of the 'defeated.'"

17. Francis and Oppenheimer (2004, 17) explain, regarding geological memory of volcanoes, that: "approximately 550 have erupted within historic times, and a further 750 are known to have been active within the last 10,000 years (10kyr)."

18. Iovino (2012a, 56–57) offers an excellent synthesis of Abram's notion of world intelligence, and she contextualizes it in the wider field of material ecocriticism.

19. For more on plant intelligence, see Mancuso and Alessandra Viola's *Brilliant Green* (2015, 2), in which the scientists maintain that "arguments for denying plants' intelligence rely less on scientific data than on cultural prejudices and influences that have persisted for millennia," and that: "On the basis of decades of experiments, plants are starting to be regarded as beings capable of calculation and choice, learning and memory."

20. The scientists were subjecting plants to shortwave radiation, but they also mention stressors including adaptations to light, heat, water, salt, and resistance to pathogens. On plants and memory, see also Leopold's article on "Smart Plants: Memory and Communication Without Brains" (2014).

21. In other words, we see here, as Mortimer-Sandilands (2008, 274) explains, that "remembrance—the act of bringing experience to reflection and/or tissue, the act of embodying an act or object or place or concept in some portion of the brain or another—is not solely a question of the remembering subject."

22. As Sigurdsson (1999, 34) notes, the Mediterranean's "unique geologic structure and high level of activity" meant that the region "had already fostered an interest in volcanic phenomena and other Earth processes in antiquity."

23. Strombolian activity, which consists of "intermittent, discrete explosive bursts, ejecting basaltic pyroclasts a few tens or hundreds of meters into the air," is visually dramatic and relatively predictable, as volcanoes go (Francis and Oppenheimer 2004, 118–20). Vulcanian activity, on the other hand, sends up much higher columns when it erupts—although it does so less frequently—and is more violently explosive (120–3). Vulcano, then, is notable for its covered crater that steams sulfuric gases through many fumaroles, and it promises to be much more dangerous when it blows its top (and according to historical precedent, this could happen at any time).

24. Calanchi et al. (2007, 16–17) note that, in the eighteenth century, French geologist Déodat de Dolomieu (1750–1801) and Italian scientist and priest Lazzaro Spallanzani (1729–1799) wrote about the Aeolian Islands and the useful qualities of pumice.

25. In a 2011 Legambiente Sicilia publication, the UNESCO sites of concern are: the archaeological area of Agrigento; the Roman villa in Casale; the Aeolian Islands; the late Baroque cities in the Val di Noto (there are eight total, including Catania, Noto, and Ragusa); Siracusa and the necropolis of Pantalica; and the "immaterial patrimony" of the "opera dei pupi," or Sicilian puppet theater (Zanna 2011).

26. Here she cites theorist and philosopher Manuel De Landa and his influential book *A Thousand Years of Nonlinear History* (1997).

27. In terms of volcano pedagogy, Oppenheimer (2011, 54) notes that before April 2, 1991, several months before the massive eruption in the Philippines on June 15 of the same year, scientists did not know that Pinatubo was a potentially active volcano: "This serves as an important reminder of just how ignorant we likely remain about the volcanoes that, in the future, will produce the largest and most consequential eruptions."

28. In particular, Oppenheimer (2011, 348) suggests that Africa and Asia would experience reduced rainfall that "could significantly disrupt food production." Thus planning to geoengineer a volcanic eruption in this way would, like many other responses to "natural"

and man-made disasters, once again cause what Rob Nixon (2011, 46) identifies as a "transnational off-loading of risk from a privileged community to an impoverished one."

29. See, for example, the collection edited by Stefan Skrimshire, *Future Ethics: Climate Change and Apocalyptic Imagination* (2010).

30. Both *Return* and other chronicles of the "War of the Volcanoes" tell posthuman tales of Magnani and her love for dogs. The actor, who jokingly called herself "Anna Cagnani," traveled to Vulcano with her dog Micia and fell in love with other canines there. Reportedly, director Dieterle was annoyed by a dog that howled beneath his window at night and had it taken to the neighboring island of Lipari. Magnani was distressed at the dog's disappearance and delighted when it swam back to Vulcano and curled up at her feet (Genovese 2010, 56n32).

31. Bozak's (2012, 91) work acknowledges the disposability of cinema as well as its power to recycle: "But that the images and technology that turn nature into landscape are also located in the zone of the disposable—the terminus of throwaway commodities—foregrounds and also challenges the idea that the camera functions as a recycling implement itself."

EPILOGUE

*A*FTER A MOMENT'S HESITATION, I BEGIN BOUNDING DOWN *Vulcano's slopes through powdery volcanic ash. Along with Ed, I gladly follow in the footsteps of Pietro Lo Cascio and Flavia Grita, our knowledgeable local guides from NESOS, an association in Lipari that teaches islanders and tourists about Aeolian ecologies. Ed lingers behind to photograph the descent, and I later relive this day on my computer screen, vividly remembering the vertigo I initially felt as I launched myself down the steep incline. Then came weightless exuberance, then clouds of ash around my feet.*

When Ed hears that this memory will frame my conclusion, he reminds me of other details of the adventure: sinking down in the ash as we ran while the volcano's slopes enveloped us. Goats in the scrubby trees at the bottom of the mountain. "And our guides," he adds. "Without them, I never would have thought that descent would be possible."

Thinking through location matters. In her beautiful *Atlas of Emotion: Journeys in Art, Architecture, and Film*, Giuliana Bruno (2002, 409) suggests that the "cartography of the subjective [. . .] has implications for rethinking the placement of analytic knowledge." She maintains that the place from which research is conducted should carry weight in contemporary scholarship, although given the structure of the academic world, location is likely to be a moving target. Describing her personal pursuit of scholarly projects, Bruno writes that: "Wandering the hybrid territory of projections between home and the world, I find myself incessantly in that terrain of 'unhomely' displacements and 'border existence' that Homi Bhabha calls an 'inbetween,' a zone of cultural intersections where signification is marked by hybridity" (410).

Each chapter of this book traces a partial cartography and evokes lived experience, and this final jaunt down the volcano draws many of its threads into conversation—airborne dust particles, photogenic goats, vocal, porous earth. The hospitality of local hosts in a richly storied, hybrid landscape marked by its encounters with the cinematic apparatus and nomadic visitors. The carbon footprint of international research travel, and the physical, if here ephemeral, footprints of the walker. Evoking the image of a sculpture and performance piece by Michelangelo Pistoletto titled "Scultura da passeggio" (Walking Sculpture), Bruno (2002, 410) argues that the moving image is "a haptic 'traveling globe' that one may go strolling with." This project is my own walk with cinematic productions—and also our walk, reader. We writers and readers cannot edit ourselves out of scholarly texts, for if we do, as Bruno warns, "we end up reproducing the view from above and from nowhere" (412).

Bruno's admonition vibrates with significance in the Anthropocene, where the view from "above" and "nowhere" comes frequently into play. Think of the "Blue Marble," for example, the iconic photograph of the earth from space taken in 1972. Environmentalists initially hoped this image would show humans the fragility of our world and urge us to care about its fate. Now, increasingly, theorists of ecomedia worry that the view distances us from our home planet, reinforcing a "disembodied" perspective whereby the earth seems "lonely and immobile," little more than a "conceptual plaything" (Cohen and Elkins-Tanton 2017, 31, 42). Even more perversely, Jussi Parikka (2015, 12) suggests that the earth viewed from above is framed as a "standing reserve in Heideggerian vocabulary: a resource for exploitation, and viewed as resource, *ordered* to present itself." In this (literal) view, mediating the earth from space both enables exploitative resource geologies (as Parikka shows) and reinforces the conceptual divide that underwrote our entrance into the Anthropocene. Bruno's comments, and the scholarly concern regarding the framing of knowledge about the world, help indicate why scholarship that works to retrain our perspective is an important tool for environmentalism. Stacy Alaimo (2009, 28) has condemned the "invisible, unmarked, ostensibly perspectiveless perspective" that she finds lurking in many planet-level representations of climate change, a perspective that is abstract and potentially alienating. She argues persuasively that: "delusions of hyperseparation, transcendence, and dominance only engender denial of the many global environmental crises."

Contesting the view from "above" and "nowhere," situated knowledge hybridizes, contaminates, entangles. This is the theory at work in *Italian Ecocinema*, whose scope is more Google Street View than Blue Marble, more a long walk than a space voyage. A propos of epilogues and "thinking on foot," Franco Cassano (2012, 9) appreciates that a slow, grounded approach allows us to "love the pauses that enable us to see the road we have covered." Yet although slower and shorter and sutured to place, a walk can be vertiginous, too, as can a project in the environmental humanities.

While working in this growing field (or running down a volcano), I experience the exhilarating joys of learning new things. But I also come to intellectual impasses: I think often about how the naturalcultural world is at stake, and worry that I need more time, but that right now we have no time for slowness. As I write, now situated at home in Michigan, in the United States, the Trump Administration is pushing to open the Arctic, national parks, and protected marine areas for drilling, dismantle the Clean Power Plan, and gut the Environmental Protection Agency—and the list goes on. Scientists report that 2017 was the hottest year on record without an El Niño, and by a wide margin. There was the destruction wrought by Hurricanes Harvey, Irma, and Maria. There were devastating, deadly monsoons in India, Pakistan, and Bangladesh. There were punishing wildfires on the Iberian Peninsula and in California. The slow violence of lagging, uneven recovery efforts in the places affected by these naturalcultural disasters continues. After back-to-back years of rising seawater temperatures and increasing ocean acidification, the Great Barrier Reef was judged to be in its "terminal stages." Around the world, the front pages of newspapers reveal repeatedly that these are critical times for the planet.

Critical. Urgent. Grave. Deep breath.

The gravity of the situation makes me short of breath, reminding me to situate myself again, which brings me to gravity, which brings me to the road ahead. When we walk, Frédéric Gros (2014, 184–85) reminds us that "at every step, contact, the foot endlessly falling back down; that support every time, the perpetual sinking down to lift up again. You have to take root each time so that you can depart anew. That is how the foot takes root, through that repeated enlacement with the earth. Each step forming another knot."

Scholars face a massive task, a task that requires us to rethink so much about our relationship to the more-than-human world, and to face up, ethically and materially, to our planetary enlacement. We humanists have additional challenges. Although it seems logical that some solutions must come from a realm "that lies largely outside scientific calculation" (Holm et al. 2015, 979), we are only starting to navigate what are undoubtedly myriad, emergent ways to do research in the environmental humanities. We are still figuring out how to articulate this work for ourselves and our students. Perhaps most critically, we are still learning how to work collaboratively within disciplines that in many ways continue to favor single-authored research (tenure decisions above all). In response to these challenges, twelve engaged scholars located around the globe co-authored a manifesto, calling for environmental humanists to take up strategic positions in the fight to solve environmental problems. The manifesto cites climate scientist Mike Hulme, explaining that "'framing complex environmental changes as 'mega-problems' necessarily demands 'mega-solutions' and this 'has led us down the wrong road'" (Holm et al. 2015, 989). Instead, the international group of humanities scholars has organized a series of collaborative research "observatories." Their resounding call is ambitious and exciting; it encourages scholars to generate differentiated, specialized, localized perspectives from "history, literature, philosophy, arts, psychology, sociology, and other fields" to help formulate "culturally diverse responses" to the challenges we face (989).

The manifesto ultimately argues that at this critical moment, local thought and disciplinary specialization matter more than ever. It matters, then, that as we think towards the future, we do so by piecing together a variegated tapestry of knowledges, of human and more-than-human voices. Our individual efforts to document and respond to contemporary environmental realities may seem small and insignificant, but they never stand alone. If "Earth can never be alone," as Cohen observes, given its permeable atmospheric membrane and its role in a dynamic solar system, nothing on Earth can ever be alone either (Cohen and Elkins-Tanton 2017, 31). Work within humanistic fields is not supposed to be totalizing or definitive. It is not supposed to sit out there, alone. Scholarship that addresses the world from any perspective should acknowledge the vibrant interchange of materiality between elements of the earth system, and address its own place in that landscape. Not even a book can be alone. Not even a scholar of Italian cinema sitting at her computer in her office.

A planetary climate emergency performs the world's naturalcultural complexity. Carlo Emilio Gadda's (1965, 5) insightful Detective Ingravallo insisted that "unforeseen catastrophes are never the consequence or the effect, if you prefer, of a single motive, of *a* cause singular; but they are rather like a whirlpool, a cyclonic point of depression in the consciousness of the world, towards which a whole multitude of converging causes have contributed. He also used words like knot or tangle, or muddle, or *gnommero*, which in Roman dialect means skein." These observations, made near the beginning of *Quer pasticciaccio brutto de via Merulana* (*That Awful Mess on Via Merulana*), may sound apocalyptic, but for Ingravallo, a complex knot is an irresistible invitation to inquiry. Today, from within the Anthropocenic whirlpool of multiple converging environmental causes, the humanities must commit to finding and following the threads. Our job, the manifesto advocates, is to "refine the global picture by taking into account regional and local factors" (Holm et al. 2015, 980). Our job is to situate our knowledge and decenter ourselves, pull a thread from the entangled skein and shape new planetary stories.

This book is another knot, but a loose one, bound up in relation with the barking dog next door, lively discussions with my students in Detroit and in Abruzzo, interactions with dozens of generous, talented film crew-members, travels around Italy. It represents the way in which my understanding of Italian cinema has morphed into a view of film as a dynamic, collaborative, more-than-human hybrid. It results from my conviction that film and media are significant in many ways in the crisis at hand: as archives, as alliances, as visionary and cautionary narratives, as consumers of precious natural resources, even as discarded waste. It expresses my faith in the multiple interlocutors who populate its pages—students, friends, family, colleagues, strangers, goats, mountains, cities, dirt. Nevertheless, it is a difficult project to conclude, because in the cyclone of convergent causes, nomadic thought keeps moving beyond my reach. But what if the conclusion was right here all along, like Dorothy's home in *The Wizard of Oz*? As scholars, we must not view ourselves from "above" and "nowhere" any more than we should view the earth that way. If we zoom in to look attentively at the place from which a project is written, we see that a book is a small square in a quilt, moored to the pieces around it by intellectual and affective threads. It is a grain of sand in an hourglass, and time keeps flowing by.

One small step at a time, then, so we can depart anew.

BIBLIOGRAPHY

Abbate, Lirio, and Giovanni Tizian. 2014. "Estorsione alla produzione di 'Gomorra la serie' Ma la società non si costituisce parte civile." *L'Espresso*. November 20, 2014.

Abram, David. 1997. *The Spell of the Sensuous: Perception and Language in a More-Than-Human World*. New York: Vintage Books.

———. 2011. *Becoming Animal: An Earthly Cosmology*. New York: Vintage Books.

Adorni, Eleonora. 2015. "Bestia." In *A come animale. Voci per un bestiario dei sentimenti*, edited by Leonardo Caffo and Felice Cimatti, 27–44. Milan: Bompiani.

Adorno, Salvatore. 2010. "Petrochemical Modernity in Sicily." In *Nature and History in Modern Italy*, edited by Marco Armiero and Marcus Hall, 180–94. Athens, OH: Ohio University Press.

Agamben, Giorgio. 2004. *The Open: Man and Animal*. Translated by Kevin Attell. Stanford: Stanford University Press.

Alaimo, Stacy. 2009. "Insurgent Vulnerability and the Carbon Footprint of Gender." *Kvinder, Køn & Forskning* 26(3–4): 22–35.

———. 2010. *Bodily Natures: Science, Environment, and the Material Self*. Bloomington: Indiana University Press.

———. 2012. "States of Suspension: Trans-corporeality at Sea." *Interdisciplinary Studies in Literature and Environment* 19(3): 476–93.

Altman, Rick. 1992. "Introduction: Four and a Half Film Fallacies." In *Sound Theory Sound Practice*, edited by Rick Altman, 35–45. New York: Routledge.

Angelone, Anita. 2011. "Talking Trash: Documentaries and Italy's 'Garbage Emergency.'" *Studies in Documentary Film* 5(2–3): 145–56.

Angus, Ian. 2016. *Facing the Anthropocene. Fossil Capitalism and the Crisis of the Earth System*. New York: Monthly Review Press.

"Animali crocifissi e impiccati, La nostra denuncia contro il film 'L'Arbitro.'" 2013. www.lav.it/news, October 4, 2013.

Antonello, Pierpaolo. 2011. "Dispatches from Hell: Matteo Garrone's *Gomorrah*." In *Mafia Movies: A Reader*, edited by Dana Renga, 377–85. Toronto: University of Toronto Press.

Antonioni, Michelangelo. 1964. "Il bosco bianco." In *Il deserto rosso di Michelangelo Antonioni*, edited by Carlo Di Carlo, 15–19. Rocca San Casciano: Cappelli.

Armiero, Marco. 2011. *A Rugged Nation: Mountains and the Making of Modern Italy*. Cambridge, UK: White Horse Press.

———. 2014. "Garbage Under the Volcano: The Waste Crisis in Campania and the Struggles for Environmental Justice." In *A History of Environmentalism: Local Struggles, Global Histories*, edited by Marco Armiero and Lise Sedrez, 167–84. New York: Bloomsbury.

———, and Stefania Barca. 2004. *Storia dell'ambiente: Una introduzione*. Rome: Carocci.

———, and Marcus Hall. 2010. "Il Bel Paese: An Introduction." In *Nature and History in Modern Italy*, edited by Marco Armiero and Marcus Hall, 1–14. Athens, OH: Ohio University Press.

Arrowsmith, William. 1995. *Antonioni: The Poet of Images*, edited by Ted Perry. New York: Oxford University Press.

Barber, Jesse R., Kevin R. Crooks, and Kurt M. Fristrup. 2010. "The Costs of Chronic Noise Exposure for Terrestrial Organisms." *Trends in Ecology and Evolution* 25(3): 180–89.

———, Chris L. Burdett, Sarah E. Reed, Katy A. Warner, Charlotte Formichella, Kevin R. Crooks, Dave M. Theobald, and Kurt M. Fristrup. 2011. "Anthropogenic Noise Exposure in Protected Natural Areas: Estimating the Scale of Ecological Consequences." *Landscape Ecology* 26: 1281–95.

Barbiano di Belgiojoso, Elisa, and Livia Elisa Ortensi. 2015. "Female Labour Segregation in the Domestic Services in Italy." *Journal of International Migration and Integration* 16: 1121–39.

Barca, Stefania. 2011. "Bread and Poison: Stories of Labor Environmentalism in Italy, 1968-1998." In *Dangerous Trade: Histories of Industrial Hazard Across a Globalizing World*, edited by Christopher Sellers and Joseph Melling, 126–39. Philadelphia, PA: Temple University Press.

Barron, Patrick. 2003. "Introduction." In *Italian Environmental Literature: An Anthology*, edited by Patrick Barron and Anna Re, xxi–xxxiii. New York: Italica Press.

Barthes, Roland. 1989. "Dear Antonioni . . ." In *L'avventura. Michelangelo Antonioni, Director*, edited by Seymour Chatman and Guido Fink, 209–14. New Brunswick: Rutgers University Press.

Bauman, Zygmunt. 2004. *Wasted Lives: Modernity and its Outcasts*. Cambridge: Polity.

Belton, John. 1999. "Technology and Aesthetics of Film Sound." In *Film Theory and Criticism: Introductory Readings*, edited by Leo Braudy and Marhsall Cohen, 376–84. New York: Oxford University Press.

Bennett, Jane. 2010. *Vibrant Matter. A Political Ecology of Things*. Durham: Duke University Press.

Benvegnù, Damiano. 2018. "'Birds Who Speak My Dialect': Poetry, Birds, and Landscape in Andrea Zanzotto." *Italy and the Environmental Humanities: Landscapes, Natures, Ecologies*, edited by Serenella Iovino, Enrico Cesaretti, and Elena Past, 37–46. Charlottesville: University of Virginia Press.

Berg, Maggie, and Barbara K. Seeber. 2016. *The Slow Professor. Challenging the Culture of Speed in the Academy*. Toronto: University of Toronto Press.

Bernardi, Sandro. 2002. *Il paesaggio nel cinema italiano*. Venice: Marsilio.

Bertellini, Giorgio. 2012. "The Earth Still Trembles: On Landscape Views in Contemporary Italian Cinema." *Italian Culture* XXX(1): 38–50.

Bevilacqua, Piero. 2010. "The Distinctive Character of Italian Environmental History." In *Nature and History in Modern Italy*, edited by Marco Armiero and Marcus Hall, 15–32. Athens, OH: Ohio University Press.

Biondi, E., and S. Bagella. 2005. "Vegetazione e paesaggio vegetale dell'arcipelago di La Maddalena (Sardegna Nord-Orientale)." *Fitosociologia* 42(2): suppl. 3–99.

Bondavalli, Simona. 2011. "Waste Management: Garbage Displacement and the Ethics of Mafia Representation in Matteo Garrone's *Gomorra*." *California Italian Studies* 2(1): ismrg_cisj_8932

Bonifazio, Paola. 2014. "United We Drill: ENI, Films, and the Culture of Work." *Annali d'italianistica* 32: 329–49.

"Bovino sgozzato sul set di «Baarìa», Tornatore nel mirino della Lav." 2009. www.corriere.it. September 24, 2009.

Bozak, Nadia. 2012. *Cinematic Footprint: Lights, Camera, Natural Resources*. New Brunswick, NJ: Rutgers University Press.

Braidotti, Rosi. 2010. "The Politics of 'Life Itself' and New Ways of Dying." In *New Materialisms: Ontology, Agency, and Politics*, edited by Diana Coole and Samantha Frost, 201–18. Durham, NC: Duke University Press.

———. 2011. *Nomadic Subjects: Embodiment and Sexual Difference in Contemporary Feminist Theory*. New York: Columbia University Press.

———. 2013. *The Posthuman*. Malden, MA: Polity.

Braucci, Maurizio. 2009. ". . . a Gomorra." In the essay "Matteo Garrone: Oltre la cronaca," in *Cinema vivo: Quindici registi a confronto*, edited by Emiliano Morreale and Dario Zonta, 105–9. Rome: Edizioni dell'Asino.

Brunette, Peter. 1998. *The Films of Michelangelo Antonioni*. Cambridge: Cambridge University Press.

Bruno, Giuliana. 2002. *Atlas of Emotion: Journeys in Art, Architecture, and Film*. New York: Verso.

Buchanan, Brett, Jeffrey Bussolini, and Matthew Chrulew. 2014. "General Introduction: Philosophical Ethology." *Angelaki* 19(3): 1–3.

Buckley, Cara. 2015. "A.C.L.U., Citing Bias Against Women, Wants Inquiry into Hollywood's Hiring Practices." *New York Times*, May 12.

Buratti, Maria. 2011. "Borghi e sobborghi. Il paesaggio extraurbano tra stereotipia e perdita d'identità." In *Atlante del cinema italiano: Corpi, paesaggi, figure del contemporaneo*, edited by Gianni Canova e Luisella Farinotti, 82–105. Milan: Garzanti.

Calanchi, Natale, Pietro Lo Cascio, Federico Lucchi, Piermaria Luigi Rossi, and Claudio Antonio Tranne. 2007. *Guida ai vulcani e alla natura delle Isole Eolie*. Calenzano: Stabilimento Poligrafico Fiorentino.

Calarco, Matthew. 2009a. "Between Life and Rights." In Paola Cavalieri, *The Death of the Animal: A Dialogue*, 135–38. New York: Columbia University Press.

———. 2009b. "Toward an Agnostic Animal Ethics." In Paola Cavalieri, *The Death of the Animal: A Dialogue*, 73–84. New York: Columbia University Press.

Calderazzo, John. 2004. *Rising Fire: Volcanoes and our Inner Lives*. Guilford, CN: Lyons.

Calvino, Italo. 1996. *Prima che tu dica pronto*. Milan: Mondadori.

Caminati, Luca. 2011. "Narrative Non-Fictions in Contemporary Italian Cinema: Roberto Munzi's *Saimir* (2002), Giorgio Diritti's *Il vento fa il suo giro* (2005) and Pietro Marcello's *La bocca del lupo* (2009)." *Studies in Documentary Film* 5(2–3): 121–31.

Cardinal, Roger. 1986. "Pausing over Peripheral Detail." *Framework* 30: 112–30.

Carson, Rachel. 1994. *Silent Spring*. Boston: Houghton Mifflin.

Cassano, Franco. 2012. *Southern Thought and Other Essays on the Mediterranean*. Edited and translated by Norma Bouchard and Valerio Ferme. New York: Fordham University Press.

Cavalieri, Paola. 2001. *The Animal Question: Why Nonhuman Animals Deserve Human Rights*. Translated by Catherine Woollard. Oxford: Oxford University Press.

———. 2009. *The Death of the Animal: A Dialogue*. New York: Columbia University Press.

Celati, Gianni. 1989. "Antonioni, *L'avventura*, and Waiting." In *L'avventura. Michelangelo Antonioni, Director*, edited by Seymour Chatman and Guido Fink, 219–21. New Brunswick: Rutgers University Press.

Centemeri, Laura. 2010. "The Seveso Disaster Legacy." In *Nature and History in Modern Italy*, edited by Marco Armiero and Marcus Hall, 195–211. Athens: Ohio University Press.

Chatman, Seymour. 1985. *Antonioni Or, The Surface of the World*. Berkeley: University of California Press.

Chion, Michel. 1994. *Audio-Vision: Sound on Screen*. Edited and translated by Claudia Gorbman. New York: Columbia University Press.

Chu, Kiu-wai. 2017. "Ecocinema." In *Oxford Bibliographies in Cinema and Media Studies*, edited by Krin Gabbard. New York: Oxford University Press, March 30. http://www.oxfordbibliographies .com/view/document/obo-9780199791286/obo-9780199791286-0252.xml

Chubb, Judith. 2002. "Three Earthquakes: Political Response, Reconstruction, and the Institutions: Belice (1968), Friuli (1976), Campania (1980)." In *Disastro! Disasters in Italy Since 1860: Culture, Politics, Society*, edited by John Dickie, John Foot, and Frank M. Snowden, 186–233. New York: Palgrave.

Cocco, Sean. 2013. *Watching Vesuvius: A History of Science and Culture in Early Modern Italy*. Chicago: University of Chicago Press.

Cohen, Jeffrey Jerome. 2010. "Stories of Stone." *Postmedieval: A Journal of Medieval Cultural Studies* 1(1–2): 56–63.

———. 2015. *Stone: An Ecology of the Inhuman*. Minneapolis: University of Minnesota Press.

———, and Linda T. Elkins-Tanton. 2017. *Earth*. New York: Bloomsbury.

Corbett, Charles J., and Richard P. Turco. 2006. *Sustainability in the Motion Picture Industry*. Los Angeles: University of California, Institute of the Environment.

Corona, Gabriella, and Rocco Sciarrone. 2012. "Il paesaggio delle ecocamorre." *Meridiana* Special issue on *Ecocamorre* 73/74: 13–35.

Covino, Michael. 2009. "La Malavita. *Gomorrah* and Naples." *Film Quarterly* 62(4): 72–75.

Cox, Trevor. 2014. *The Sound Book: The Science of the Sonic Wonders of the World*. New York: W.W. Norton.

Crutzen, Paul J. 2002. "Geology of Mankind." *Nature* 415: 23.

Cubitt, Sean. 1998. *Theory, Culture, Society: Digital Aesthetics*. London: Sage Publications.

Dalle Vacche, Angela. 1996. *Cinema and Painting: How Art Is Used in Film*. Austin: University of Texas Press.

De Landa, Manuel. 1997. *A Thousand Years of Nonlinear History*. New York: Zone Books.

Deleuze, Gilles. 1989. *Cinema 2: The Time-Image*. Translated by Hugh Tomlinson and Robert Galeta. Minneapolis: University of Minnesota Press.

De Luca, Barbara. 2000. "Saper far della legna carbone. Riflessioni sui saperi dei carbonai del Cansiglio." *La ricerca folklorica* 24: 85–89.

De Luca, Tiago, and Nuno Barradas Jorge. 2016. "Introduction: From Slow Cinema to Slow Cinemas." In *Slow Cinema*, edited by Tiago De Luca and Nuno Barradas Jorge, 1–21. Edinburgh: Edinburgh University Press.

DeMello, Margo. 2012. *Animals and Society: An Introduction to Human-Animal Studies*. New York: Columbia University Press.

De Muro, Pasquale, Paola Di Martino, and Lucia Cavola. 2007. "Fostering Participation in Scampia: Let's Make a *Piazza*." *European Urban and Regional Studies* 14(3): 223–37.

Della Seta, Roberto. 2000. *La difesa dell'ambiente in Italia. Storia e cultura del movimento ecologista*. Milan: FrancoAngeli.

De Rancourt, M., N. Fois, M. P. Lavín, E. Tchakérian, and F. Vallerand. 2006. "Mediterranean Sheep and Goats Production: An Uncertain Future." *Small Ruminant Research* 62: 167–79.

De Waal, Frans. 2006. *Primates and Philosophers: How Morality Evolved*. Princeton, NJ: Princeton University Press.

Di Carlo, Carlo. 1964. "Il colore dei sentimenti." In *Il deserto rosso di Michelangelo Antonioni*, edited by Carlo Di Carlo, 25–36. Rocca San Casciano: Cappelli.

Duggan, Christopher. 2008. *The Force of Destiny: A History of Italy Since 1796*. Boston: Houghton Mifflin.

Ecomafia 2014: Le storie e i numeri della criminalità ambientale. 2014. Milan: Edizioni Ambiente.

Ecomafia 2017: Le storie e i numeri della criminalità ambientale. 2017. Milan: Edizioni Ambiente.

Engel, Larry, and Andrew Buchanan. 2009. *Code of Best Practices in Sustainable Filmmaking*. Washington, DC: Center for Media and Social Impact, February. http://archive .cmsimpact.org/sites/default/files/final_code.pdf. Accessed August 1, 2018.

Faleschini Lerner, Giovanna. 2010. "From the Other Side of the Mediterranean: Hospitality in Italian Migration Cinema." *California Italian Studies* 1(1): 1–19.

Fay, Jennifer. 2018. *Inhospitable World: Cinema in the Time of the Anthropocene*. New York: Oxford University Press.

Ferguson, John. 2013. *A Companion to Greek Tragedy*. Austin: University of Texas Press.

Forgács, David. 1996. "Post-War Italian Culture: Renewal or Legacy of the Past?" In *Reconstructing the Past: Representations of the Fascist Era in Post-War European Culture*, edited by Graham Bartram, Maurice Slawinski, and David Steel, 49–63. Keele: Keele University Press.

Frammartino, Michelangelo. 2011. "Le quattro volte." Interview. In Andrea Lavagnini e Giuseppe Zito S.I., *Parlare di cinema: schede tecniche e percorsi interpretativi dei migliori film dell'anno*, 145–50. Milan: San Paolo.

Francis, Clinton D., Nathan J. Kleist, Catherine P. Ortega, and Alexander Cruz. 2012. "Noise Pollution Alters Ecological Services: Enhanced Pollination and Disrupted Seed Dispersal." *Proceedings of the Royal Society B* 279: 2727–35.

Francis, Peter, and Clive Oppenheimer. 2004. *Volcanoes*. Oxford: Oxford University Press.

Gabrys, Jennifer. 2011. *Digital Rubbish: A Natural History of Electronics*. Ann Arbor: University of Michigan Press.

Gadda, Carlo Emilio. 1965. *That Awful Mess on Via Merulana*. Translated by William Weaver. New York: George Braziller.

Garrard, Greg. 2004. *Ecocriticism*. New York: Routledge.

Garrone, Matteo. 2009. Interview. "Oltre la cronaca: Incontri con Dario Zonta e con Maurizio Braucci." In *Cinema vivo: Quindici registi a confronto*, edited by Emiliano Morreale and Dario Zonta, 93–121. Rome: Edizioni dell'Asino.

Genovese, Nino. 2010. *Cineolie: Le Isole Eolie e il cinema*. Lipari: Edizioni del Centro Studi.

Ghirardo, Diane. 2013. *Italy: Modern Architectures in History*. London: Reaktion Books.

Gilbert, Christopher J. 2013. "Toward the Satyric." *Philosophy and Rhetoric* 46(3): 280–305.

Gilebbi, Matteo. 2014. "Animal Metaphors, Biopolitics, and the Animal Question: Mario Luzi, Giorgio Agamben, and the Human-Animal Divide." In *Thinking Italian Animals: Humanism and Posthumanism in Modern Italian Literature and Film*, edited by Deborah Amberson and Elena Past, 93–107. New York: Palgrave Macmillan.

Gilfillan, Daniel. 2016. "Of Parrots, Behaviours, and Moods. Thinking about Sound in the Anthropocene." Online video. Vimeo, Nov. 20.

Ginsborg, Paul. 1989. *Storia d'Italia dal dopoguerra a oggi*. Turin: Einaudi.

González, Alice Elizabeth. 2014. "What Does 'Noise Pollution' Mean?" *Journal of Environmental Protection* 5: 340–50.

Gorfinkel, Elena, and John David Rhodes. 2011. "Introduction: The Matter of Places." In *Taking Place: Location and the Moving Image*, edited by Elena Gorfinkel and John David Rhodes, vii–xxx. Minneapolis: University of Minnesota Press.

Gros, Frédéric. 2014. *A Philosophy of Walking*. Translated by John Howe. New York: Verso.

Grossman, Elizabeth. 2006. *High Tech Trash: Digital Devices, Hidden Toxins, and Human Health*. Washington: Island Press.

Handzo, Stephen. 1985. "Glossary of Film Sound Technology." In *Film Sound. Theory and Practice*, edited by Elisabeth Weis and John Belton, 383–426. New York: Columbia University Press.

Haraway, Donna. 2003. *The Companion Species Manifesto: Dogs, People, and Significant Otherness*. Chicago: Prickly Paradigm Press.

———. 2004a. "Cyborgs to Companion Species: Reconfiguring Kinship in Technoscience." In *The Haraway Reader*, 295–320. New York: Routledge.

———. 2004b. "Otherworldly Conversations; Terran Topics; Local Terms." In *The Haraway Reader*, 125–50. New York: Routledge.

———. 2008. *When Species Meet*. Minneapolis: University of Minnesota Press.

———. 2015. "Anthropocene, Capitalocene, Plantationocene, Chthulucene: Making Kin." *Environmental Humanities* 6: 159–65.

Harvey, David. 2014. *Seventeen Contradictions and the End of Capitalism*. Oxford: Oxford University Press.

Hempton, Gordon, and John Grossman. 2009. *One Square Inch of Silence: One Man's Quest to Preserve Quiet*. New York: Free Press.

Hinson, Joy. 2015. *Goat*. London: Reaktion Books.

Holm, Poul, Joni Adamson, Hsinya Huang, Lars Kirdan, Sally Kitch, Iain McCalman, James Ogude, Marisa Ronan, Dominic Scott, Kirill Ole Thompson, Charles Travis, and Kirsten Wehner. 2015. "Humanities for the Environment—A Manifesto for Research and Action." *Humanities* 4: 977–92. doi:10.3390/h4040977

Huber, Matthew T. 2013. *Lifeblood: Oil, Freedom, and the Forces of Capital*. Minneapolis: University of Minnesota Press.

Iovino, Serenella. 2006. *Ecologia letteraria. Una strategia di sopravvivenza*. Milan: Edizioni Ambiente.

———. 2009. "Naples 2008, or, the Waste Land: Trash, Citizenship, and an Ethic of Narration." *Neohelicon* 36: 335–46.

———. 2010a. "Ecocriticism and a Non-Anthropocentric Humanism." In *Local Natures, Global Responsibilities: Ecocritical Perspectives on the New English Literatures*, edited by Laurenz Volkmann, Nancy Grimm, Ines Detmers, and Katrin Thomson, 29–53. Amsterdam: Rodopi.

———. 2010b. "The Human Alien. Otherness, Humanism, and the Future of Ecocriticism." *Ecozon@* 1(1): 53–61.

———. 2011. "The Wilderness of the Human Other: Italo Calvino's *The Watcher* and a Reflection on the Future of Ecocriticism." In *The Future of Ecocriticism: New Horizons*, edited by Serpil Oppermann, Ufuk Özdağ, Nevin Özkan and Scott Slovic, 65–81. Newcastle upon Tyne: Cambridge Scholars Publishing.

———. 2012a. "Material Ecocriticism: Matter, Text, and Posthuman Ethics." In *Literature, Ecology, Ethics*, edited by Michael Sauter and Timo Müller, 51–68. Heidelberg: Winter Verlag.

———. 2012b. "Stories from the Thick of Things: Introducing Material Ecocriticism." *Interdisciplinary Studies in Literature and Environment* 19(3): 449–60.

———. 2013a. "Loving the Alien. Ecofeminism, Animals, and Anna Maria Ortese's Poetics of Otherness." *Feminismo/s* 22: 177–204.

———. 2013b. "Toxic Epiphanies: Dioxin, Power, and Gendered Bodies in Laura Conti's Narratives on Seveso." In *International Perspectives in Feminist Ecocriticism*, edited by Greta Gaard, Simon C. Estok, and Serpil Oppermann, 37–55. London and New York: Routledge.

———. 2014a. "Bodies of Naples: Stories, Matter, and the Landscapes of Porosity." In *Material Ecocriticism*, edited by Serenella Iovino and Serpil Oppermann, 97–113. Bloomington: Indiana University Press.

———. 2014b. "Le voci di dentro (e quelle di fuori)." In *Teresa e le altre*, edited by Marco Armiero, 147–54. Jaca Book.

———. 2016. *Ecocriticism and Italy: Ecology, Resistance, and Liberation.* New York: Bloomsbury Academic.

———, and Serpil Oppermann. 2014. "Introduction: Stories Come to Matter." In *Material Ecocriticism*, edited by Serenella Iovino and Serpil Oppermann, 1–20. Bloomington: Indiana University Press.

"Isola Budelli." 2014. www.vladi-private-islands.de/en/objects/europe-mediterranean-sea /italy/buy/isola-budelli/. Accessed September 22, 2014.

"Isole Eolie (Aeolian Islands)." 2016. *UNESCO World Heritage Centre.* UNESCO, n.d. https:// whc.unesco.org/en/list/908. Accessed August 1, 2018.

Ivakhiv, Adrian J. 2013. *Ecologies of the Moving Image: Cinema, Affect, Nature.* Waterloo, Ontario: Wilfrid Laurier University Press.

Jaffe, Ira. 2014. *Slow Movies: Countering the Cinema of Action.* London: Wallflower Press.

Jaggard, Victoria. 2015. "Ancient Scrolls Blackened by Vesuvius are Readable at Last." www .Smithsonian.com. January 20, 2015.

Jordan, Randolph. 2010. *The Schizophonic Imagination: Audiovisual Ecology in the Cinema.* Diss. Concordia University.

Kirkham, Victoria. 2004. "The Off-Screen Landscape. Dante's Ravenna and Antonioni's *Red Desert*." In *Dante, Cinema, and Television*, edited by Amilcare A. Iannucci, 106–28. Toronto: University of Toronto Press.

Klein, Naomi. 2014. *This Changes Everything: Capitalism vs. the Climate.* New York: Simon and Schuster.

Kohn, Eduardo. 2013. *How Forests Think: Toward an Anthropology Beyond the Human.* Berkeley: University of California Press.

LaRoche, Scott W., David J. Roy, and John S. Brand. 1999. Method of Manufacturing Gelatin. Eastman Kodak Company, assignee. Patent US5908921 A. 1 June. Print.

Laino, Giovanni, and Daniela De Leo. 2002. "NEHOM: Le politiche pubbliche per il quartiere Scampia a Napoli." Naples: Dipartimento di Urbanistica della Facoltà di Architettura dell'Università di Napoli Federico II.

Lam, Stephanie. "It's About Time: Slow Aesthetics in Experimental Ecocinema and Nature Cam Videos." In *Slow Cinema*, edited by Tiago De Luca and Nuno Barradas Jorge, 207–18. Edinburgh: Edinburgh University Press.

Latini, Giulio. 2011. *L'energia e lo sguardo: Il cinema dell'Eni e i documentari di Gilbert Bovay.* Rome: Donzelli.

Leake, Elizabeth. 2014. "Cesare Pavese, Posthumanism, and the Maternal Symbolic." In *Thinking Italian Animals: Humanism and Posthumanism in Modern Italian Literature and Film*, edited by Deborah Amberson and Elena Past, 39–56. New York: Palgrave Macmillan.

LeMenager, Stephanie. 2014. *Living Oil: Petroleum Culture in the American Century*. New York: Oxford University Press.

Leopardi, Giacomo. 2010. *Canti*, edited and translated by Jonathan Galassi. New York: Farrar Straus Giroux.

Leopold, A. Carl. 2014. "Smart Plants: Memory and Communication Without Brains." *Plant Signaling & Behavior* 9–10: e972268.

Lestel, Dominique. 2014. "Hybrid Communities." Translated by Brett Buchanan. *Angelaki: Journal of the Theoretical Humanities* 19(3): 61–73.

Lim, Song Hwee. 2014. *Tsai Ming-Liang and a Cinema of Slowness*. Honolulu: University of Hawaii Press.

Lippit, Akira Mizuta. 2000. *Electric Animal: Toward a Rhetoric of Wildlife*. Minneapolis: University of Minnesota Press.

———. 2002. "The Death of an Animal." *Film Quarterly* 56(1): 9–22.

Lioi, Anthony. 2007. "Of Swamp Dragons: Mud, Megalopolis, and a Future for Ecocriticism." In *Coming into Contact: Explorations in Ecocritical Theory and Practice*, edited by Annie Merrill Ingram, Ian Marshall, Daniel J. Philippon, and Adam W. Sweeting, 17–38. Athens, GA: University of Georgia Press.

Lucretius. 1995. *On the Nature of Things: De rerum natura*. Edited and translated by Anthony M. Esolen. Baltimore, MD: Johns Hopkins University Press.

Lugli, Francesca, and Assunta Alessandra Stoppiello. 2000. "Le strutture abitative dei carbonai delle Serre (Vibo Valentia, Calabria)." *Archeologia Postmedievale* 4: 41–51.

Lundblad, Michael. 2009. "From Animal to Animality Studies." *PMLA* 124(2): 496–502.

MacDonald, Scott. 2004. "Toward an Eco-Cinema." *Interdisciplinary Studies in Literature and Environment* 11(2): 107–32.

———. 2013. "The Ecocinema Experience." In *Ecocinema Theory and Practice*, edited by Stephen Rust, Salma Monani, and Sean Cubitt, 17–42. New York: Routledge.

MacHugh, David E., and Daniel G. Bradley. 2001. "Livestock Genetic Origins: Goats Buck the Trend." *PNAS* 98(10): 5382–84.

Macfarlane, Robert. 2012. *The Old Ways: A Journey on Foot*. New York: Penguin.

Malamud, Randy. 2012. *An Introduction to Animals and Visual Culture*. New York: Palgrave Macmillan.

Mancino, Anton Giulio. 2008. "Da Rosi a Garrone: L'ombra delle vele di Scampia." *Cineforum* 475: 12–14.

Mancuso, Stefano, and Alessandra Viola. 2015. *Brilliant Green: The Surprising History and Science of Plant Intelligence*. Translated by Joan Benham. Washington, DC: Island Press.

Manes, Christopher. 1996. "Nature and Silence." In *The Ecocriticism Reader: Landmarks in Literary Ecology*, edited by Cheryll Glotfelty and Harold Fromm, 15–29. Athens: University of Georgia Press.

Marchesini, Roberto. 2009. *Il tramonto dell'uomo: La prospettiva post-umanista*. Bari: Edizioni Dedalo.

———. 2011. *Il galateo per il cane. Manuale di educazione sociale per una buona convivenza*. Florence: De Vecchi.

———. 2014. "Foreward: Mimesis. The Heterospecific as Ontopoietic Epiphany." In *Thinking Italian Animals: Humanism and Posthumanism in Modern Italian Literature and Film*, edited by Deborah Amberson and Elena Past, translated by Elena Past with Deborah Amberson, xiii–xxxvi. New York: Palgrave Macmillan.

———. 2015. "Ospite." In *A come animale. Voci per un bestiario dei sentimenti*, edited by Leonardo Caffo and Felice Cimatti, 177–90. Milan: Bompiani.

———. 2015. *Etologia filosofica: alla ricerca della soggettività animale.* Milan: Mimesis.

Marcus, Millicent. 1986. *Italian Film in the Light of Neorealism.* Princeton, NJ: Princeton University Press.

———. 2016. *"Gomorra* by Matteo Garrone: 'La normalità dello sfacelo.'" In *Italian Political Cinema: Public Life, Imaginary, and Identity in Contemporary Italian Film,* edited by Giancarlo Lombardi and Christian Uva, 302–16. Bern: Peter Lang.

Marino, Giorgia. 2014. "EcoMuvi: è italiano il primo disciplinare ambientale per il cinema." http://www.greenews.info/progetti/ecomuvi-e-italiano-il-primo-disciplinare -ambientale-per-il-cinema-20140619/. June 19, 2014. Accessed July 30, 2018.

Marks, Laura U. 2000. *The Skin of the Film: Intercultural Cinema, Embodiment, and the Senses.* Durham, NC: Duke University Press.

Massey, Doreen B. 1999. *Space, Place, and Gender.* Minneapolis: University of Minnesota Press.

Maxwell, Richard and Toby Miller. 2012a. "Film and the Environment: Risk Offscreen." In *Film and Risk,* edited by Mette Hjort, 271–90. Detroit, MI: Wayne State University Press.

———. 2012b. *Greening the Media.* Oxford: Oxford University Press.

"memory, n." 2015. *OED Online.* Oxford University Press, www.oed.com. Accessed August 1, 2018.

Menely, Tobias, and Margaret Ronda. 2013. "Red." In *Prismatic Ecology: Ecotheory Beyond Green,* edited by Jeffrey Jerome Cohen, 22–41. Minneapolis: University of Minnesota Press.

Metz, Christian. 1999. "Aural Objects." In *Film Theory and Criticism: Introductory Readings,* edited by Leo Braudy and Marhsall Cohen, 356–59. New York: Oxford University Press.

"Michelangelo Antonioni." 1967. Interview by Jean Luc Godard. In *Interviews with Film Directors,* edited by Andrew Sarris, 3–11. Indianapolis: Bobbs-Merrill.

Miranda-de la Lama, G.C., and S. Mattiello. 2010. "The Importance of Social Behaviour for Goat Welfare in Livestock Farming." *Small Ruminant Research* 90: 1–10.

Molinier, Jean, Gerhard Ries, Cyril Zipfel, and Barbara Hohn. 2006. "Transgeneration Memory of Stress in Plants." *Nature* 442(31): 1046–49.

Montanari, C., P. Prono, and S. Scipioni. 2000. "The Study of Charcoal-Burning Sites in the Apennine Mountains of Liguria (NW Italy) as a Tool for Forest History." In *Methods and Approaches in Forest History,* edited by M. Agnoletti and S. Anderson, 79–91. Wallingford: CABI Publishing.

Montgomery, David R. 2007. *Dirt: The Erosion of Civilizations.* Berkeley: University of California Press.

Mortimer-Sandilands, Catriona. 2008. "Landscape, Memory, and Forgetting: Thinking Through (My Mother's) Body and Place." In *Material Feminisms,* edited by Stacy Alaimo and Susan Hekman, 265–87. Bloomington: Indiana University Press.

Morton, Timothy. 2010. *The Ecological Thought.* Cambridge, MA: Harvard University Press.

———. 2013. "Treating Objects Like Women: Feminist Ontology and the Question of Essence." In *International Perspectives in Feminist Ecocriticism,* edited by Greta Gaard, Simon C. Estok, and Serpil Oppermann, 56–69. New York: Routledge.

Nawroth, Christian, Jemma M. Brett, and Alan G. McElligott. 2016. "Goats Display Audience-Dependent Human-Directed Gazing Behaviour in a Problem-Solving Task." *Biology Letters* 12: 1–4.

Nicolini, Flavio. 1964. "Diario." In *Il deserto rosso di Michelangelo Antonioni,* edited by Carlo Di Carlo, 37–84. Rocca San Casciano: Cappelli.

Nixon, Rob. 2011. *Slow Violence and the Environmentalism of the Poor.* Cambridge, MA: Harvard University Press.

Oppenheimer, Clive. 2011. *Eruptions that Shook the World.* Cambridge: Cambridge University Press.

Oppermann, Serpil. 2013. "Feminist Ecocriticism. A Posthumanist Direction in Ecocritical Trajectory." In *International Perspectives in Feminist Ecocriticism*, edited by Greta Gaard, Simon C. Estok, and Serpil Oppermann, 19–36. New York: Routledge.

Parati, Graziella. 2014. "Mountain Fish, Occitan Borders, and Literary Representations." *Italian Studies* 69(3): 311–27.

Parikka, Jussi. 2015. *A Geology of Media.* Minneapolis: University of Minnesota Press.

Past, Elena. 2013. "'Trash Is Gold': Documenting the Ecomafia and Campania's Waste Crisis." *ISLE: Interdisciplinary Studies in Literature and Environment* 20(3): 597–621.

———. 2014. "(Re)membering Kinship: Living with Goats in *The Wind Blows Round* and *Le quattro volte*." In *Thinking Italian Animals: Humanism and Posthumanism in Modern Italian Literature and Film*, edited by Deborah Amberson and Elena Past, 233–50. New York: Palgrave Macmillan.

———. 2016a. "Documenting Ecomafia." In *Nuovo Cinema Politico: Public Life, Imaginary, and Identity in Contemporary Italian Film*, edited by Giancarlo Lombardi and Christian Uva, 81–92. New York: Peter Lang (Italian Modernities).

———. 2016b. "Mediterranean Ecocriticism: The Sea in the Middle." In *Handbook of Ecocriticism and Cultural Ecology*, edited by Hubert Zapf, 368–84. Berlin: De Gruyter.

Petitti, Giovanni. 2014. "Intervista a Matteo Garrone. «Gomorra», gangster movie rosselliniano." *Chiacchiere culturali.* June 14, 2014. Originally published in *Frame OnLine*.

Petrini, Carlo. 2007. *Slow Food Nation: Why Our Food Should Be Good, Clean, and Fair.* Translated by Clara Furlan and Jonathan Hunt. New York: Rizzoli.

Pick, Anat. 2011. *Creaturely Poetics: Animality and Vulnerability in Literature and Film.* New York: Columbia University Press.

———, and Guinevere Narraway. 2013. "Introduction: Intersecting Ecology and Film." In *Screening Nature: Cinema Beyond the Human*, edited by Anat Pick and Guinevere Narraway, 1–18. New York: Berghahn.

Pinkus, Karen. 2011. "Antonioni's Cinematic Poetics of Climate Change." In *Antonioni: Centenary Essays*, edited by Laura Rascaroli and John David Rhodes, 254–75. London: British Film Institute.

Pinna, Alberto. 1999. "All'asta l'isola di Budelli: Prezzo base 2 miliardi, ma il terreno non è edificabile." *Corriere della Sera*, December 13, 1999: 22. http://www.archiviostorico.corriere.it. Accessed August 1, 2018.

Pratesi, Fulco. 2010. *Storia della natura d'Italia.* Soveria Mannelli: Rubbettino.

Rascaroli, Laura, and John David Rhodes. 2011. "Interstitial, Pretentious, Alienated, Dead: Antonioni at 100." In *Antonioni: Centenary Essays*, edited by Laura Rascaroli and John David Rhodes, 1–20. London: British Film Institute.

Rath, John R. 1964. "The Carbonari: Their Origins, Initiation Rites, and Aims." *The American Historical Review* 69(2): 353–70.

"recycle, v." 2016. *OED Online.* Oxford University Press. www.oed.com. Accessed March 10, 2016.

Renga, Dana. 2013. *Unfinished Business: Screening the Italian Mafia in the New Millennium.* Toronto: University of Toronto Press.

Restivo, Angelo. 2002. *The Cinema of Economic Miracles: Visuality and Modernization in the Italian Art Film.* Durham: Duke University Press.

Rhodes, John David. 2007. *Stupendous, Miserable City: Pasolini's Rome*. Minneapolis: University of Minnesota Press.

———. 2011. "Antonioni and the Development of Style." In *Antonioni: Centenary Essays*, edited by Laura Rascaroli and John David Rhodes, 276–300. London: British Film Institute.

Riedweg, Christoph. 2005. *Pythagoras: His Life, Teaching, and Influence*. Translated by Steven Rendall. Ithaca, NY: Cornell University Press. ProQuest ebrary. October 23 2014.

Rust, Stephen, and Salma Monani. 2013. "Introduction: Cuts to Dissolves—Defining and Situating Ecocinema Studies." In *Ecocinema Theory and Practice*, edited by Stephen Rust, Salma Monani, and Sean Cubitt, 1–14. New York: Routledge.

Sarris, Andrew. 1972. *Interviews with Film Directors*. Indianapolis: Bobbs-Merrill.

Saviano, Roberto. 2007. *Gomorrah*. Translated by Virginia Jewiss. New York: Picador.

Schafer, R. Murray. 1977. *The Tuning of the World*. New York: Alfred A. Knopf.

Schaumann, Caroline, and Heather I. Sullivan. 2011. "Introduction: Dirty Nature: Grit, Grime, and Genre in the Anthropocene." *Colloquia Germanica* 44(2): 105–9.

Schoonover, Karl. 2011. "Antonioni's Waste Management." In *Antonioni: Centenary Essays*, edited by Laura Rascaroli and John David Rhodes, 235–53. London: British Film Institute.

Seabrook, John. 2015. "The Invisible Library." *The New Yorker*. November 16, 2015.

"sedimentary rock." 2013. *A Dictionary of Geology and Earth Sciences*, edited by Michael Allaby. Oxford: Oxford University Press. *Oxford Reference*.

Seger, Monica. 2014. "*Le quattro volte*, All At Once." *The Italianist* 34(2): 292–97.

———. 2015. *Landscapes in Between. Environmental Change in Modern Italian Literature and Film*. Toronto: University of Toronto Press.

Serres, Michel. 2012. *Biogea*. Translated by Randolph Burks. Minneapolis: Univocal.

Settis, Salvatore. 2012. *Paesaggio costituzione cemento: La battaglia per l'ambiente contro il degrado civile*. Turin: Einaudi.

Sigurdsson, Haraldur. 1999. *Melting the Earth: The History of Ideas of Volcanic Eruptions*. New York: Oxford University Press.

Sisto, Antonella C. 2014. *Film Sound in Italy: Listening to the Screen*. New York: Palgrave Macmillan.

Sitney, P. Adams. 1995. *Vital Crises in Italian Cinema: Iconography, Stylistics, Politics*. Austin: University of Texas Press.

Skrimshire, Stefan, ed. 2010. *Future Ethics: Climate Change and Apocalyptic Imagination*. London: Bloomsbury.

Slovic, Scott. 2008. *Going Away to Think: Engagement, Retreat, and Ecocritical Responsibility*. Reno: University of Nevada Press.

Small, Pauline. 2011. "No Way Out: Set Design in Mafia Films." *Italian Studies* 66 (1): 112–27.

Sobchack, Vivian. 2005. "When the Ear Dreams: Dolby Digital and the Imagination of Sound." *Film Quarterly* 58(4): 2–15.

"Società Italiana per Condotte D'Acqua S.p.A. fondata il 7 aprile 1880." 2014. Società Italiana per Condotte D'Acqua S.p.A.

Solnit, Rebecca. 2000. *Wanderlust: A History of Walking*. New York: Penguin.

Starosielski, Nicole, and Janet Walker, eds. 2016. *Sustainable Media: Critical Approaches to Media and Environment*. New York: Routledge.

"State of Conservation." 2007. *UNESCO World Heritage Center*. UNESCO. https://whc.unesco .org/en/soc/1068. Accessed August 1, 2018.

"State of Conservation." 2010. *UNESCO World Heritage Center.* UNESCO. https://whc
.unesco.org/en/soc/540. Accessed August 1, 2018.

Steimatsky, Noa. 2008. *Italian Locations: Reinhabiting the Past in Postwar Cinema.* Minneapolis: University of Minnesota Press.

Steffen, Will, Wendy Broadgate, Lisa Deutsch, Owen Gaffney, and Cornelia Ludwig. 2015.
"The Trajectory of the Anthropocene: The Great Acceleration." *The Anthropocene
Review* 2(1): 81–98.

Sullivan, Heather I. 2012. "Dirt Theory and Material Ecocriticism." *Interdisciplinary Studies
in Literature and Environment* 19(3): 515–31.

Théberge, Paul. 2008. "Almost Silent: The Interplay of Sound and Silence in Contemporary
Cinema and Television." In *Lowering the Boom: Critical Studies in Film Sound,* edited
by Jay Beck and Tony Grajeda, 51–67. Urbana: University of Illinois Press.

Thwaites, Thomas. 2016. *GoatMan: How I Took a Holiday from Being Human.* New York:
Princeton Architectural Press.

Trombini, Claudio, Daniele Fabbri, Marco Lombardo, Ivano Vassura, Elisabetta Zavoli, and
Milena Horvat. 2003. "Mercury and Methylmercury Contamination in Surficial Sedi-
ments and Clams of a Coastal Lagoon (Pialassa Baiona, Ravenna, Italy)." *Continental
Shelf Research* 23: 1821–31.

Tuana, Nancy. 2008. "Viscous Porosity: Witnessing Katrina." In *Material Feminisms,* edited
by Stacy Alaimo and Susan Hekman, 188–213. Bloomington: Indiana University Press.

Tulli, Stefania. 2008. "Produzione, promozione, distribuzione." In *Il vento fa il suo giro:
Sceneggiatura originaria di Giorgio Diritti e Fredo Valla,* 21–23. Mantua: Publi Paolini.

Vecchio, Bruno. 2010. "Forest Visions in Early Modern Italy." In *Nature and History in Modern Italy,* edited by Marco Armiero and Marcus Hall, 108–125. Athens: Ohio University
Press.

Verdicchio, Pasquale. 2011. "Documentary on the Verge of Progress." *Studies in Documentary
Film* 5(2–3): 107–119.

Verona, Marzia. 2006. *Dove vai pastore? Pascolo vagante e transumanza nelle Alpi Occidentali
agli albori del XXI secolo.* Scarmagno: Priuli & Verlucca.

Wagner, Gernot, and Martin L. Weitzman. 2015. *Climate Shock: The Economic Consequences
of a Hotter Planet.* Princeton, NJ: Princeton University Press.

Weil, Keri. 2012. *Thinking Animals: Why Animal Studies Now?* New York: Columbia University Press.

Wolfe, Cary. 2008. "Learning from Temple Grandin, or, Animal Studies, Disability Studies,
and Who Comes After the Subject." *New Formations* 64: 110–23.

———. 2009a. "Human, All Too Human: 'Animal Studies' and the Humanities." *PMLA*
124(2): 564–75.

———. 2009b. "Humanist and Posthumanist Antispeciesism." In Paola Cavalieri, *The Death
of the Animal: A Dialogue,* 45–58. New York: Columbia University Press.

Yaeger, Patricia. 2010. "Editor's Column: Sea Trash, Dark Pools, and the Tragedy of the Com-
mons." *PMLA* 125: 523–45.

Zanna, Gianfranco, ed. 2011. *UNESCO alla Siciliana: i siti in sofferenza della bella Sicilia.*
Palermo: Luxograph.

Zavattini, Cesare. 1952. "Diario." *Cinema nuovo* 1(1): 8.

———. 1954. "Il neorealismo secondo me." *Rivista del cinema italiano* 3(3): 18–26.

INDEX

Abram, David, 10–11, 20n5, 21n18, 34; on intelligence, 172, 174, 188n18
Abruzzo, 8, 119n12, 194
acousmatics, 137–38, 150n23, 150n24. *See also* Pythagoras
acoustic ecology, 3, 13, 18, 128, 140. *See also* "ear cleaning"; noise pollution; soundscape
acoustic footprint, 135–38, 140, 143. *See also* acoustic ecology; carbon footprint; noise pollution
actors (human): as activists, 13; global marketplace for, 7; as guests, 107; non-professional, 12, 105, 108, 113; as part of the film production process, 48–49, 115–16, 174; in posthuman cinema, 28, 72, 89, 110. *See also* film production crew; nonhuman actors
Adriatic Sea: filming in, 34–38; petrochemical industry in, 29, 45
Aeolian Islands, 153–56; cinematic history of, 164, 182–83; ecology, 159–61, 179, 186n1, 186n3, 188n24, 188n25, 190; learning from, 177–78; in the mid-twentieth century, 167; in mythology, 158; resources of, 163, 176–77. *See also* Lipari; *Return to the Aeolian Islands*; Salina; Stromboli (island)
aesthetics, 12, 22n26; architectural, 66; and the environment, 25, 65, 94; as political, 14; and sound, 127, 148n7. *See also* Antonioni, Michelangelo; ecocinema; Garrone, Matteo; Rossellini, Roberto
Africa, 65, 120n16, 135, 161, 188n28
Agamben, Giorgio, 92, 101
AGIP *(Azienda Generale Italiana Petroli)*, 31, 34, 49. *See also* Paguro platform
agriculture: in Campania, 78, 85n13; and "cementification," 10; history of, 97–98; loss of, 93; spaces of, 106, 108; violence, 99–100; and volcanoes, 60, 163. *See also* animals; goats

Alaimo, Stacy, 17, 26–27, 38, 47, 72, 81, 191. *See also* trans-corporeality
Alicudi (film), 156
Alicudi (island), 161
Allais, Giacomino, 96
Alliata, Francesco, 154, 186n2
Alps, 93, 96, 98, 102; herding in, 104; walking in, 4. *See also* Ussolo; Valle Maira
American Civil Liberties Union, 187n15
American Humane Association (AHA) Film and Television Unit, 111–12, 116, 122n35
analytical philosophy, 90–91, 118n5
angrisano, nicol*, 77
ANIC *(Azienda Nazionale Idrogenazione Combustibili)*, 31–32, 52n3, 53n12
"animal question," 90–92, 110, 113, 118n5
animal rights activists, 112
animals: buffalo, 59; cattle, 97, 99–100, 110, 113, 117, 118n4, 122n35, 136; chickens, 14, 105; horses, 91, 97, 112, 151n36; pigs, 18, 89, 97, 108, 113, 117; sheep, 18, 89, 97–99, 107, 113, 121n28, 122n34, 135; snails, 18–19, 146–47. *See also* dogs; goats; more-than-human world; nonhuman actors; nonhuman animals; nonhuman world
animal studies, 17, 20n3, 90–91, 94, 120n19
Anthropocene, 5, 15, 20n9, 54n20; acoustic footprint of, 140; birdsong in, 125; and human bodies, 46; and human separation, 191; landscapes of, 43, 177; lessons of, 179
anthropocentrism: and the "animal question," 90; challenges to, 43; and film, 15, 42–43, 127; hubris of, 92; and time, 6. *See also* ecocriticism; humanism
anthropogenic noise. *See* noise pollution
"anthropological machine" (Agamben), 101
Anti-Vivisection League (LAV), 122n35
Antonioni, Michelangelo, 2; aesthetics of, 35; cinematic legacy of, 23–24; director, 11, 26, 29–31, 40, 43–44, 47–48, 50–51, 54n26;

influence of, 53n14, 54n23, 55n31; style, 63, 154. See also *L'avventura*; *Red Desert*

Aquino, Gennaro, 56–58, 69, 71, 78–79. *See also Gomorrah* (film)

AranciaFilm, 87

archaeology, 177; cinematic, 178

architecture, 113; industrial, 37; modern, 66, 68, 85n23, 85n28; rural, 98, 105; theater, 127

archives: cinematic, 18, 23, 102, 156–57, 171, 181, 186; of oral histories, 90; volcanic, 184. *See also* memory

Aristotle, 41, 175

Associazione Protezione Animali (APA-Association for the Protection of Animals), 119n12

Atria, Benni, 150n18, 154

audience. *See* spectators

Avatar (Cameron), 22n27

Baarìa (Tornatore), 122n35

Baby Needs Some Fresh Air, The (Prudente), 77

Barthes, Roland, 50, 54n22, 55n30

Bazin, André, 119n9

Bellissima (Visconti), 153

Benvenuti, Paolo, 18, 123, 128–30, 140; recollections of, 145; recording strategies of, 131, 133, 135, 142, 146–47, 149n14, 150n17. See also *Le quattro volte*

Bergman, Ingrid, 155, 160, 164–65; on Stromboli, 167

Bianche Eolie (1948), 156

Biasi, Pierangela, 87, 108–9

Bindé, Jérôme, 20n7, 77

biodiversity, 98, 125

biopolitics, 18, 90, 92, 94

Biùtiful cauntri (2008), 71, 77

"Blue Marble, The", 191

Bonfini, Paolo, 13, 56, 71, 78, 81, 86n37

borders, 6–8; crossings, 53n14, 102–5, 121n28; disciplinary, 185; of the human body, 140. *See also* global capital; globalization; neoliberalism

Bovay, Gilbert, 34

Braidotti, Rosi: on breaking down anthropocentrism, 54n20, 144, 159; posthuman perspectives of, 17, 21n14, 28, 118n5, 151n34,

181; on postmodern labor, 109–10, 114. *See also* nomadism; posthumanism

Brass, Tinto, 53n12

Braucci, Maurizio, 79–80, 86n36

Budelli Island, 30, 54n23; pink rocks sequence, 17, 40–42, 44–45. See also *Red Desert*

Cacciatori sottomarini (Underwater Hunters–Genovese*)*, 154

Calabria, 129, 137, 149n10, 150n20, 151n26; human and nonhuman populations of, 8, 141, 145, 147; soundscape of, 18, 131, 135, 139–40, 146, 148. See also *Le quattro volte*

Calabria, Esmeralda, 77

Calarco, Matthew, 92, 110–11, 113, 116, 118n5

Calvino, Italo, 42, 44, 54n19

cameras. *See under* cinematic apparatus

Cameron, James, 22n27

Camorra, 83n12; construction business of, 69–70, 85n30; eco-, 84n14; in *Gomorrah*, 63–65, 68, 76–79, 81; violence of, 71; waste disposal business of, 61, 75, 86n33. *See also* ecomafia; *Gomorrah* (book); *Gomorrah* (film); Garrone, Matteo; Le Vele; language; organized crime

Campania: earthquake, 67, 69–70; eco-criminality in, 17, 62, 71, 83n12, 84n13, 85n31, 86n32; environmental justice movement in, 77–79; fertility of, 60–61; pollution of, 2, 72, 76, 82. *See also* Camorra; ecomafia; *Gomorrah* (book); *Gomorrah* (film); Irpinia earthquake; Land of Fires; Legambiente; Le Vele; Naples; Scampia

Campi Flegrei, 187n11

Cannes, 150n20

carbonai. See charcoal burners

Carbonari, 141

Carbon Black (company), 32, 48. *See also* petrochemical industry

carbon black (material), 48–50, 54n29. *See also* toxic waste

Carboneria, 138–39, 141–42, 144–45, 151n27, 151n28. *See also* charcoal

carbon footprint, 136; of film production, 12, 15, 48, 58; of scholarship, 190. *See also* acoustic footprint

Cardinal, Roger, 14–16
Caro Diario (1993), 156–57
Carson, Rachel, 25, 38, 123–25, 128. See also
  Silent Spring
Carta, Roberto, 87, 109, 114
celluloid: animal by-products in, 18, 54n27,
  93, 116, 119n8; as archives, 181, 186; chemi-
  cal composition of, 12, 50, 54n27; decay
  of, 46, 54n26; exposure to pollution, 37;
  format, 28, 43, 72–74, 126, 156, 165, 171,
  173; toxicity of, 15, 73–74, 183. *See also* cin-
  ematic apparatus; digital filming formats
Center for Environmental Filmmaking, 58,
  83n4
Center for Media & Social Impact, 58, 83n4
*Centro Studi e Ricerche di Storie e Problemi
  Eoliani* (Center for Study and Research on
  Aeolian History and Problems), 178, 186n3
Cerchio, Fernando, 53n12
charcoal, 18, 129, 139–44, 150n20, 151n26,
  151n32. *See also* charcoal burners
charcoal burners, 18, 139–42, 146–48. See also
  Carboneria
Chemello, Mario, 87, 108–9, 115, 121n29
Chersogno. *See* Ussolo; *The Wind Blows
  Round*
Chionetti, Carlo, 24
Ciano, Edda, 163, 165
"cinema muto," 126
cinematic apparatus, 7, 190; cameras, 12, 39,
  41–44, 119n9, 143, 150n17, 154, 181, 189n31;
  encounters with, 75, 81, 190; functioning
  of, 92–93, 126, 149n8; waste created by,
  34–35, 48, 57. *See also* celluloid; cinematic
  machine; digital filming formats; film
  industry; film production crew; sound;
  technology
cinematic machine, 93, 115, 147, 167–68. *See
  also* film industry
cinematic recycling, 14, 154, 183, 189n31. See
  also *Return to the Aeolian Islands*
citizenship: ecological, 21n12, 80; "thwarted," 81, 86n42
class, 62, 85n27, 91, 109, 159
climate change, 6, 83n9, 179–80; in Antonioni's films, 29; emergency, 193; solutions,
  179; and volcanoes, 158, 162

"Code of Best Practices in Sustainable
  Filmmaking" (Center for Media & Social
  Impact), 58, 83n4
"cognitive zooanthropology," 91. *See also*
  Marchesini, Roberto; *Scuola di Interazione Uomo-Animale* (SIUA)
collaboratrice domestica. See domestic collaborators
commercials, 130, 132, 149n13
conservation, 25. *See also* Filmmakers for
  Conservation
consumption: capitalist, 4, 24; of cinema, 48,
  58, 83n7, 117, 119n8; of resources, 42, 44, 96;
  and sound, 149n13; and waste, 86n41
Corpo forestale dello Stato (State Forestry
  Corps), 56
Corsale, Ivana, 77
Criterion Collection, 30, 39, 57, 69–70
Crutzen, Paul, 20n9
"cultural ecology," 187n16
Cuneo, 5, 90
cyborgs, 12, 146

Dallamano, Massimo, 34
D'Ambrosio, Andrea, 77
Damiano, Caterina, 109–10
deforestation, 9, 83n9, 98, 120n15, 144
De Lazzaris, Greta, 56, 59, 71; on Garrone,
  83n3, 86n36, 86n37; on location filming,
  75, 78–79, 81
Deleuze, Gilles, 138, 150n17, 150n25
Del Giudice, Raffaele, 71
Del Grande, Anamaria, 87
De Rerum Natura (Lucretius), 155
De Re Rustica (Varro), 60
Derrida, Jacques, 91–92, 117
Descartes, René, 132, 149n16
Deserto rosso. See Red Desert
dialetheic logic, 41–42, 46–47, 50
dialogue: absence of, 18, 102, 123, 128, 130;
  audio/visual, 41, 73; dubbing of, 127;
  mixing of, 126, 132, 148n4; with the
  nonhuman, 88, 107
Di Carlo, Carlo: book on *Red Desert*, 31–33;
  interview with, 16–17, 23–24, 48. *See also*
  Nicolini, Flavio; *Red Desert*
Dieterle, William, 155, 189n30

digital filming formats: animal by-products
in, 93, 116, 119n8; obsolescence, 54n26,
86n35; toxicity of, 73–74; use of, 156, 171.
See also cinematic apparatus; digital technology; technology
digital technology, 46, 86n35; effects, 132;
photography, 72; problems of, 73–74,
86n35; storage, 181; streaming, 73; waste,
7, 15, 183. *See also* archives; digital filming
formats; DVDs; technology
dioxins, 14, 17, 72–73, 186. *See also* Seveso
dioxin disaster; toxic waste
Diritti, Giorgio, 2, 87, 118n1. See also *The
Wind Blows Round*
dirt, 59–62; as an actor, 2, 14–15; connectedness with, 27, 76–78, 81, 83n9, 194; and
crime, 85n31; pollution of, 72; and poverty,
65; suburban, 64, 66–69; as transnational,
6. *See also* "dirt theory"; "dirty" cinema;
ecocriticism; *Gomorrah* (film); landscapes; nomadism; toxic waste
"dirt theory," 17, 46, 49, 59–60, 76. *See
also* dirt; "dirty" cinema; ecocriticism;
Gomorrah (film)
"dirty" cinema, 17, 56–57, 59, 62, 79–82, 84n20.
See also ecocriticism; *Gomorrah* (film)
disability studies, 120n19
Di Salvo, Franz, 66
disease. See environmental illness
documentary: "backstage," 109; industrial,
33–34; narrative, 18, 156, 165–66, 176
dogs, 18–19; companion species, 1, 91, 97,
107, 119n6, 121n25, 133, 144, 189n30; in *Le
quattro volte*, 131, 134–38, 149n14, 150n20,
183; in *The Wind Blows Round*, 100, 104–5,
131. *See also* animals; nonhuman actors;
nonhuman animals; Vuk
domestication, 94, 104–7, 120n24, 121n28
domestic collaborators, 109–10, 121n32,
121n33. *See also* labor; immigrants
domesticity, 104–5, 108, 113–14. *See also*
nomadism
DVDs, 73–74. *See also under* specific films

"ear cleaning," 13, 22n25, 128. *See also*
acoustic ecology; soundscapes
ecocamorristi. See *ecomafia*

ecocinema, 1–3, 6, 12, 20n6. *See also* ecocriticism
ecocinema studies, 20n6, 119n9, 125. *See also*
ecocriticism
ecocriticism, 16, 20n5; and anthropocentrism, 127, 132, 145; and dirt, 59–60;
feminist, 19, 159; material, 2, 6, 14, 30, 142,
157, 171, 188n18. *See also* "dirt theory";
ecocinema; environmental humanities;
Iovino, Serenella; natureculture; nonhuman world; posthumanism; slowness;
technopoiesis; trans-corporeality
ecological footprint, 2, 136. *See also* acoustic
footprint; carbon footprint
ecology, 42, 60; of the Aeolian Islands,
178–79; of cinema, 21n19, 127; history, 157.
See also acoustic ecology; "cultural
ecology"; Italy; landscapes; place
ecomafia, 8–10, 17, 61–62, 84n14; construction industry, 70, 83n11; films about, 71;
opposition to, 77. *See also* Camorra;
organized crime; toxic waste
Ecomafia reports, 82, 84n13, 86n33
ecomedia studies, 15, 191
EcoMuvi, 58
"economic miracle." *See under* Italy
8 1/2 (Fellini), 170
Empedocles, 175–76, 185–86. *See also* volcanology
ENEL *(Ente Nazionale per l'Energia
Elettrica)*, 32
ENI *(Ente Nazionale Idrocarburi)*, 25, 33, 50,
53n13; film production division, 34, 52n10,
52n11, 53n12
environmental history, 8, 97, 176
environmental humanities, 3, 14, 191–94. *See
also* ecocriticism; posthumanism
environmental illness (EI), 27, 52n4, 52n5, 72,
125. *See also* multiple chemical sensitivity
(MCS); tinnitus
environmentalism, 5, 7, 180, 191. *See also* Italy
environmental justice, 4, 17, 62, 72, 77, 79
Environmental League. See *Legambiente*
ethics: affirmative, 5, 116; environmental,
21n18; labor, 109; posthuman, 47, 110,
120n23, 150n20. *See also* Calarco, Matthew; Iovino, Serenella

Etna, 161, 187n6; writings about, 175. *See also* volcanoes
European Union, 7, 67

Fascist regime, 1, 99, 127; political prisoners of, 163, 165
Felicetti, Gianluca, 122n35
Fellini, Federico, 170
feminism, 52n7, 119n6, 187n14; ethics, 183; geographies, 165; ontology, 41, 46; theory, 19, 148n6, 159, 187n14
feminist ecocriticism. *See under* ecocriticism
Figliodoro, Franco, 153–54, 159, 170, 178
film industry: consumption of, 23, 44; fuel of, 17, 29, 35; and location, 166; market, 21n10; waste created by, 33, 58, 72, 79. *See also* celluloid; cinematic machine; digital filming formats; filmmaking; film production crew; gender; global capital; Hollywood film; location filming; oil; petroleum; pollution; technology
Filmmakers for Conservation, 58, 83n4
filmmaking: and environmental awareness, 59; environmental impact of, 93; and film interpretation, 2; practice, 74, 81, 83n4, 108, 110–11, 157, 183; reciprocity with the world, 12–13, 18; toxicity of, 14–15. *See also* film industry; film production crew; Hollywood film; nomadism; nonhuman world; technology
film production crew, 117; assistant directors, 32, 87, 105, 109, 154; camera operators, 2, 17, 56; collaborations, 13, 81, 87–88, 113–14, 117, 146, 150n18, 178; directors, 2, 13, 131, 142, 156, 159, 174, 178; dog trainer, 149n14; exposure to danger, 69; exposure to toxins, 32, 62, 71–72, 74–75; as guests, 78–81, 86n36, 107–10; location manager, 2, 17, 56, 79; makeup artist, 87, 108, 115; as nomadic, 105, 164; posthuman, 145; (co-)producers, 7, 37, 58, 87, 108, 114–15, 131; production designers, 13, 17; production managers, 13, 87, 117, 123, 147, 149, 159; production secretaries, 13, 15, 108; on site, 12, 34, 47, 59, 88–89, 151n36, 155, 164; sound recordists, 2, 18, 123, 130–31, 142–43, 146, 150n18; waste generated by, 15, 57. *See also* cinematic

apparatus; film industry; filmmaking; hospitality; location filming; nomadism
film studies, 14–15, 127, 148n6, 155
film technology. *See* technology
Foley sound, 135, 137–38
fossil fuels. *See* hydrocarbons; oil; petrochemical industry; petroleum
Frammartino, Michelangelo, 2, 123, 146–47; decentering the human, 150n17; on filmmaking and the environment, 13; on goat behavior, 134; on location, 151n35; recording strategies of, 132, 137. *See also Le quattro volte*
Fughe e approdi. See Return to the Aeolian Islands

Gadda, Carlo Emilio, 193
Garrone, Matteo, 2, 56; aesthetics of, 63, 84n16; depiction of Camorra, 68, 76, 83n3, 85n28; relationship with crew, 81; working style of, 86n36, 86n37. *See also Gomorrah* (film)
gaze, 148n5, 155; disanthropocentric, 15; in films, 38, 132, 157; and invisibility, 72–73, 80; more-than-human, 9, 40; panoptic, 71; socio-political, 65
gender, 62, 90–91, 106, 159, 165–66; and the film industry, 187n15
geoengineering, 19, 179–80, 188n28. *See also* climate change; "Pinatubo Option"
geography, 139, 157, 165, 187n12
geology, 42–43, 50, 90, 166, 177; archive, 186; teaching of, 177. *See also* time
"geophilia," 185–86
German forces in World War II, 97, 99
Giant of Ravenna, The (Cerchio), 53n12
Giornata d'uno scrutatore (Calvino), 54n19
Gli uomini del petrolio. See The Oil Men
global capital: disaster capitalism, 180; and environmental destruction, 7, 21n12, 26, 45, 64; and filmmaking, 53n14; flows of, 65; and organized crime, 84n15, 84n19. *See also* globalization; neoliberalism
globalization, 7–8; and cinema, 6–7; of sound, 149n13
goatherds, 18, 104–5, 129; fear of, 134; in *Le quattro volte*, 140, 143; as nomadic, 107. *See also* goats; herding

goats: as actors, 14–15, 93–96, 101–6, 108, 129–31, 137, 147–48, 150n20; behavior of, 119n14, 133–34; collaboration with, 18–19, 89–90, 110–13, 117–18, 147, 151n35, 159, 194; environmental impact of, 119n12, 120n15, 135; in human history, 97–100, 107, 119n11, 119n13, 122n34. See also herding; Le quattro volte; more-than-human world; nonhuman actors; nonhuman animals; The Wind Blows Round
Goldoni, Katia, 13, 87, 108–9, 114
Gomorra (Garrone). See Gomorrah (film)
Gomorra (television series), 79
Gomorrah (book, Saviano), 73–75, 81–82, 83n3, 85n29. See also Saviano, Roberto
Gomorrah (film, Garrone), 2, 7; collaboration on, 56, 75; depiction of dirt, 17, 61–62, 68–69, 81, 84n20; depiction of organized crime, 78–79, 83n3; depiction of toxic waste, 14, 63–64, 69–75, 86n41, 183; DVD, 57, 70, 73; location filming, 59, 62–65, 71–72, 75–76, 80, 86n36; as slow cinema, 77–78; theme of invisibility, 72–73, 86n34. See also Camorra; dirt; "dirty" cinema; Gomorrah (book); Le Vele; Naples; organized crime; Scampia; Saviano, Roberto
Great Acceleration, 5–6, 8, 20n9
Great Barrier Reef, 192
Gros, Frédéric, 4–5. See also slowness
Guerra, Tonino, 23, 33
gunpowder, 143, 151n32

Happy as Lazzaro (Rohrwacher), 58
Haraway, Donna: on collaboration across species, 8–9, 91, 108, 116–17, 147, 151n36, 152n37; on companion species, 78, 94, 114, 120n17, 120n24, 133, 135; posthuman perspectives of, 20n8, 21n14, 113, 118n5, 119n6; on sacrifice, 92, 118. See also "animal question"; more-than-human world; natureculture; posthumanism
Harris, Richard, 7, 24, 34, 36
Hawaii, 158
hearing, 140, 145–46, 148n5. See also listening; sound; soundscapes
Herculaneum, 184–85

herding, 89, 96, 99, 104–5, 107; relationship to animals, 121n28; and wolves, 119n12. See also goatherds; goats; nomadism; transhumance
History for Energy, A (Pontecorvo), 53n12
Hollywood film, 111, 116, 132, 176, 187n15. See also cinematic machine; film industry
Holocene, 5, 161
hospitality, 16; across human-nonhuman worlds, 94, 103–4, 114, 116; conditional, 103–4, 107, 120n22; of Le Vele, 75, 78, 80–81; of local hosts, 190. See also actors; film production crew; Gomorrah; location filming; Marchesini, Roberto; nomadism; Ussolo; The Wind Blows Round
Hulme, Mike, 192
humanism, 52n6, 88, 90, 146
humanities, 15, 193–94. See also environmental humanities
hurricanes, 81, 85n26, 192
hydrocarbons: cinema's dependence on, 2, 14–15, 17, 23; and Italy's "economic boom," 29–30, 33–34, 52n4; landscapes of, 49–50; and modernity, 36–37, 45. See also oil; petrochemical industry; petroleum; Red Desert

ICMESA, 52n3
Iguana, The (Ortese), 182–83
Il gigante di Ravenna (Cerchio), 53n12
Il Postino (Radford), 7, 156
Il vento fa il suo giro (Diritti). See The Wind Blows Round
immigrants, 109, 120n22, 157, 164, 166. See also domestic collaborators; hospitality; labor
INA-Casa, 66, 70, 85n22
industry: and cinema, 33–35, 47, 51; cosmetics, 120n13; development, 99; disasters, 49–50; food, 89, 117; landscapes of, 31, 36–38, 52n10, 63, 84n16; mining, 176–77; pollution caused by, 5, 17, 25–26, 46, 60–61, 64–65, 70, 124; and society, 40–41, 52n4. See also film industry; Italy; modernity; petrochemical industry; Ravenna
"interactionism," 35, 52n7. See also "vital materialism"

International Geosphere-Biosphere Programme, 20n9
"interstitial spaces," 32, 52n9, 129. *See also* natureculture
Iovino, Serenella: ecocriticism of, 3, 7–8, 54n19; on human relationships with the world, 13, 21n12, 38, 101, 120n19, 142–43, 182–83; on memory, 169, 173; on Naples, 62, 66, 80, 82, 86n42; on Piedmont violence, 89–90, 99; on situated knowledge, 81, 178, 181, 187n16; on slowness, 4–6. *See also* ecocriticism; Piedmont; posthumanism; slowness
Irpinia earthquake, 67, 69; and organized crime, 69–70, 76, 85n26, 85n30, 85n31. *See also* Campania
Isola d'Acciaio. *See* SAROM island
Isole di Fuoco (1955), 156
Istituto Luce, 154
Istituto Nazionale delle Assicurazioni. *See* INA-Casa
Istituto Nazionale della Previdenza Sociale, 121n32
Italia Nostra, 25, 52n2
Italian Water Works Company, 179
Italy: animal laws of, 98–99, 122n35; cinema, 6, 14, 18–19, 154, 165; ecology of, 8–9, 144; "economic miracle," 24–25, 28, 30–33, 44, 47, 50, 52n4, 53n14; environment, 9, 21n15, 25, 82, 123; history, 141–42, 151n27; mapping of, 15–16; social housing, 85n23; volcanoes of, 161–63. *See also* Abruzzo; Aeolian Islands; agriculture; Alps; Calabria; Campania; industry; modernity; petrochemical industry; Piedmont; Ravenna
Italy Is Not a Poor Country (Ivens), 53n12
Ivens, Joris, 53n12

Kaos (Taviani brothers), 153–54, 156–57, 174, 176
Kilauea volcano, 158
Klein, Naomi, 179–80
Kodak, 7, 73, 93

La bambina deve prendere aria (Prudente), 77
labor, 54n14, 64, 81, 109–10, 122n37. *See also* domestic collaborators; nomadism

"La ginestra o, il fiore del deserto" (Leopardi), 172–73, 176
Land of Fires, 71, 73–74, 86n33. *See also* Campania; Scampia
landscapes, 4; acoustic, 131, 136, 141, 150n18; dirty, 64, 71–75, 79, 81; industrial, 24–28, 43–44, 47–50, 84n16; and memory, 157–59, 162, 172–74; more-than-human, 6, 8–9, 18, 21n16, 28, 69, 89, 124, 152n37; as protagonist, 29–32, 35–38, 40–41, 189n31; rural, 96, 98–99; urban, 59; volcanic, 19, 154–55, 160, 163–66, 169, 175–79, 183–84, 187n12. *See also* Anthropocene; hydrocarbons; memory; petrochemical industry; soundscapes
language: of the Camorra, 64; of charcoal burners, 141–43; of cinema, 155; digital, 46; Fascist, 127; more-than-human, 175; in philosophy, 120n21, 121n26, 128; in *The Wind Blows Round*, 96–97, 102–4. *See also* Occitan; Piedmont; *rueido*; UNESCO
"La pompa di benzina" (Calvino), 42–44
L'avventura (Antonioni), 154, 156, 165
Lazzaro felice (Rohrwacher), 58
Legambiente, 9, 21n17, 60; in Campania, 72; mafia categories of, 83n11; in Sicily, 177, 179, 188n25; on toxic waste, 71, 84n18. *See also* *Ecomafia* reports
Leopardi, Giacomo, 158, 172–73, 176
Leopold, Aldo, 164, 185
Le quattro volte, 2, 11, 18, 20n3; black screens, 139, 141, 150n25; credits, 150n20; DVD, 137, 145, 150n20; engagement of deep space, 150n17; making of, 59, 145, 147; more-than-human histories, 142–43, 145–48; sound recording for, 7, 123, 128–38, 142, 144, 150n18, 150n22; space in, 130. *See also* Benvenuti, Paolo; dogs; goatherds; metempsychosis; Olivero, Simone Paolo; Serrecchia, Marco; sound; soundscapes; soundtracks
Le Vele, 17, 65–71, 85n24, 85n37–85n38; hospitality of, 59, 75–76, 78–80. *See also* Camorra; *Gomorrah* (book); *Gomorrah* (film); hospitality; Scampia
Lipari, 153–54, 156; filming on, 167, 174; industrial development of, 179; political prisoners on, 165; pumice cliffs of, 163, 174, 176–78. *See also* Aeolian Islands; NESOS

listening: anthropocentric, 127–28, 148; attentive, 3, 142; importance of, 124, 148n5; passive and receptive, 138, 178; reciprocal, 133. *See also* acoustic ecology; hearing; sound; soundscapes

L'Italia non è un paese povero (Ivens), 53n12

Lobosco, Rocco, 87, 117

location filming, 2–3; connection with residents, 75, 81–82, 115; dangers of, 50, 72; embeddedness in, 10, 12, 24, 28, 47, 166; environmental impact of, 15, 57–59, 115, 183; film crew's relationship to place, 18, 75, 78–79, 164; sound recording, 129, 135, 146, 149n14. *See also* Aeolian Islands; Budelli Island; Calabria; Campania; hospitality; Le Vele; location scouting; Naples; place; Ravenna; Scampia; Ussolo

location managers. *See under* film production crew

location scouting, 2, 57, 71, 155

Lucretius, 155

Maddalena Archipelago, 30, 44–45. *See also* Budelli Island; Santo Stefano Island

Magnani, Anna, 153, 155, 165, 167; on the Aeolian Islands, 181–82, 184–85; love of dogs, 189n30

Manfredonia poisoning, 25, 49, 52n3

Marchesini, Roberto: on collaboration, 147; on domestication of animals, 121n25; on hospitality, 16, 104, 107, 113–14; posthuman theories of, 17–18, 21n14, 88–89, 91, 103, 116, 118n3, 118n5, 119n6, 119n7, 121n26; on technology, 144, 146. *See also* "cognitive zooanthropology"; posthumanism; technopoiesis

Marshall Plan, 54n24

material ecocriticism. *See under* ecocriticism

material histories, 142, 144

Mattei, Enrico, 33. *See also* ENI

Mazzini, Giuseppe, 151n29

Mediterranean Sea: commerce of, 163; geology of, 161, 187n11, 188n22; pollution of, 8, 19; flows of, 64; as setting for films, 34, 39–40, 84n5

memory, 19, 168–73; cinematic, 154, 156–57, 167, 174; corporeal, 179; functioning of, 98,

188n21; in plants, 188n19; and sound, 150n22; of volcanoes, 162, 176, 188n17. *See also* Iovino, Serenella; landscapes; montage; place; *Return to the Aeolian Islands*

"Metanopoli" (Methane City), 34

metempsychosis, 18, 129

military-industrial complex, 44–45

mimesis, 103, 146–47

mining. *See* resource extraction

modernity, 4; advance of, 96; industrial, 17, 25, 27–30, 36–37, 42–43, 45, 50; in *Red Desert*, 35; rhythms of, 154; speed of, 77. *See also* hydrocarbons; industry; Italy; petroculture

Monopoli, Franco, 154

montage, 13–14, 42; and memory, 169, 171, 173–74; storytelling through, 159, 164–65, 180, 183, 186. See also *Return to the Aeolian Islands*

Monti, Attilio, 53n12. *See also* SAROM

more-than-human world: and cinema, 14–15, 194; dangers to, 71–72; disanthropocentric, 186; disregard for, 64, 138; future of, 19; human entanglements with, 6, 8, 21n12, 21n14, 27, 50, 90, 157–59, 176–77; human reliance on, 2; intelligence of, 173; landscape, 28; listening to, 123–29, 134, 144, 148, 149n11, 178; and petroleum, 38–39; scholarship, 11, 20n5, 192–93; stories of, 143. *See also* Abram, David; animals; ecocriticism; Haraway, Donna; Iovino, Serenella; landscapes; nonhuman actors; nonhuman animals; nonhuman world; posthumanism; trans-corporeality

Moretti, Nanni, 156

Morton, Timothy, 41, 45–47, 53n16

Mountain of Lies, A (angrisano), 77

Mount Vesuvius. *See* Vesuvius

multiple chemical sensitivity (MCS), 27, 52n5

Murch, Walter, 149n15

music, 33, 53, 126, 131, 148n4, 174. *See also* sound; soundscapes

Naples: crisis in, 80, 84n14, 86n42; dirt of, 17, 60, 71, 76–77; earthquake, 67; organized crime in, 61–62, 85n31; volcanic activity around, 8, 158, 162, 169, 187n11. *See also*

Campania; *Gomorrah* (film); Land of
Fires; Le Vele; Scampia; Vesuvius
National Institute of Social Security, 121n32
natural gas, 30, 42, 49. *See also* hydrocarbons; petroleum
"natura morta," 43–44
natureculture, 4, 9–10, 20n8, 192–93; in film,
12, 133; "interstitial spaces" of, 32, 52n9.
See also Haraway, Donna
neoliberalism, 7, 61, 64, 179. *See also* global
capital
neorealism, 20n1
NESOS, 178, 190
NGOs, 7, 9, 61. *See also* Legambiente
Nicolini, Flavio, 17, 36; production diary of,
23, 31–32, 44, 47–50. See also *Red Desert*
Nigeria, 34, 84n18
Noiret, Philippe, 7
noise pollution, 124–25, 135–36, 146, 148n2.
See also acoustic footprint; sound
nomadism: convergence with domesticity,
113–14; of dirt, 60; of filmmaking, 53n14,
58, 108, 159, 190; of herders, 98, 104–7; and
labor, 109–10; of scholarship, 80. *See also*
Braidotti, Rosi; domesticity; goats; hospitality; labor; location filming
nonhuman actors, 2–3, 7–8, 14–16, 20n5;
agency of, 40–41; anthropomorphic qualities of, 43–44; in cinematic space, 18, 28,
59, 89, 129, 131, 134, 137, 142; harm to, 112;
human relationships with, 90, 108; inclu-
sion in politics, 47. *See also* animals; *Le
quattro volte*; more-than-human world;
nonhuman animals; nonhuman world;
The Wind Blows Round
nonhuman animals, 2, 20n5; companion
species, 97, 114; death, 18, 52n3, 88, 92–94,
100, 103, 112–13, 116–17; domestication
of, 94, 104–7; exploitation of, 92–93, 100,
120n17, 122n35; human hybridization with,
88–89, 91, 98, 101–2, 110; listening, 136;
and noise, 125. *See also* animals; animal
studies; dogs; goats; Haraway, Donna;
more-than-human world; nonhuman actors; nonhuman world
nonhuman world, 20n5; and cinema, 93,
138; in filmmaking, 13; human debt to, 92;

human participation in, 10, 46, 97, 120n17,
145; interaction with human bodies,
26–27; limits of, 100–101; noise effects on,
148n2; soundscape of, 18, 138; voices of,
142. *See also* ecocriticism; more-than-human world; nonhuman actors; nonhuman
animals; trans-corporeality

Occitan, 20n3, 96, 102, 120n20. *See also*
language
oil: in capitalism, 36–37, 54n24, 70; in the
film industry, 119n8; and the more-than-
human world, 38, 42–44; spill, 45–46;
transport of, 40. *See also* hydrocarbons;
petrochemical industry; petroculture;
petroleum
Oil Men, The, 34–35, 49–50
Olivero, Simone Paolo, 18, 123, 128–30,
140; recollections of, 145; recording
strategies of, 131, 133, 135, 143, 146–47,
149n14, 150n17
organized crime, 9; in Calabria, 147; in
Campania, 83n12; in cinema, 57, 59; in
construction, 85n30, 85n31; daily activities
of, 78; and global capital, 84n15; toxic
waste trafficking, 61–62, 64, 70. *See also*
Camorra; ecomafia; global capital;
Gomorrah (film); Naples
Orsini, Valentino, 33, 53n12
Ortese, Anna Maria, 182–83
Osservatorio Vesuviano (Vesuvian Observatory), 158. *See also* Vesuvius

Paguro platform, 31, 34–35; accident, 49–50,
55n30. *See also* AGIP; petrochemical
industry
Panària Film, 154, 167, 186n2
partisans, 5, 90, 99. *See also* Revelli, Nuto
patriarchy, 90, 118n4. *See also* gender
Pavese, Cesare, 118n4
pedagogy: cinematic, 174; volcanic, 19,
177–78, 188n27; "zooanthropological," 91
"pedinamento," 1, 20n1. *See also* "slow cinema";
walking
"peripheral detail," 12, 14–16, 52n6, 78, 132
"Petrol Pump, The" (Calvino), 42–44
Petrini, Carlo, 4–6, 20n7, 77–78

petrochemical industry, 24–25, 33, 43, 45, 48–49; landscapes, 47, 50. See also AGIP; ENI; hydrocarbons; Manfredonia poisoning; modernity; oil; petroculture; petroleum; plastic; Ravenna; SADE; SAROM; Seveso dioxin disaster

petroculture, 17, 29, 33–35, 53n14

petroleum: composition of, 42, 44, 53n18; connection to the more-than-human world, 38–39, 51; and the film industry, 33, 37, 54n28, 183; as fuel, 4, 24, 30, 45, 136; and the Marshall Plan, 54n24; pollution, 27, 32, 48, 64. See also hydrocarbons; natural gas; oil

Piedmont, 4–6, 118; language of, 120n20; rural, 96, 187n16; violence in, 89–90, 99. See also Cuneo; Revelli, Nuto; The Wind Blows Round; Ussolo; Valle Maira

pigs. See under animals

Pinatubo, 188n27

"Pinatubo Option," 19, 179–80, 188n28. See also geoengineering

place: in cinema, 2, 7–8, 10, 12, 19, 57; connections to, 76–78, 165–66; disposability of, 82; knowledge of, 86n36, 159; and memory, 1, 169–72, 188n21; and scholarly research, 190, 194; sonic characteristics of, 127, 130, 149n14. See also acoustic ecology; dirt; ecology; hospitality; "interstitial spaces"; Le Vele; location filming; trans-corporeality; walking

plant world, 171–73, 188n19, 188n20

plastic, 17, 25, 30, 45, 54n28; parts, 74, 86, 119; in oceans, 45; waste, 15, 57, 62

pollution: in ecocriticism, 60; effect on celluloid, 37; fight against, 25–26, 123–24; and the film industry, 47–48, 83n7; industrial, 5, 66. See also dirt; noise pollution; toxic waste

Pompeii, 158, 169, 173, 176

Pontecorvo, Gillo, 53n12

posthumanism, 14–18, 21n14; and the animal question, 118n5, 120n19; breaking down boundaries with the nonhuman, 9–10, 28–29, 52n7, 88–91, 103, 145, 181, 189; and cinema, 92–94, 105, 110, 145; and memory,

171; and mind-body distinction, 149n16; and technology, 146. See also Haraway, Donna; Marchesini, Roberto; more-than-human world; nonhuman actors; nonhuman animals; nonhuman world; technopoiesis; trans-corporeality

Pratesi, Fulco, 60, 83n10

production crew. See film production crew

production designers. See film production crew

production managers. See film production crew

production secretaries. See film production crew

Prudente, Barbara Rossi, 77

pulsatile tinnitus, 140–41

PUMEX, 177, 179

pumice, 156, 163, 174, 179, 186, 188n24; mining of, 176–77. See also Lipari; PUMEX

Pythagoras, 18, 129, 137, 148, 149n10; school of, 150n23; teaching from behind a curtain, 132. See also acousmatics; metempsychosis

Quer pasticciaccio brutto de via Merulana (Gadda), 193

race, 91, 159

Radford, Michael, 7

Radiotelevisione Italiana (RAI), 53n12

Rancière, Jacques, 22n26

Ravenna, 17; on film, 53n12; hydrocarbon culture of, 29; industrial landscape of, 23–25, 31–37, 40, 44–45, 50, 64. See also petrochemical industry; Red Desert

recycling, 57, 59

Red Desert (Antonioni), 2, 7, 16–17; Budelli island sequence, 39–45; color, 54n28; ecological footprint of, 46–48, 183; and industry, 24–34, 49–51, 52n10, 53n13, 54n19, 63–64; making of, 23; SAROM island sequence, 35–39; the white forest, 48. See also ENI; petrochemical industry; petroculture; Ravenna; SAROM; SAROM island

refugees, 8

resource extraction, 4, 7, 93, 124, 191; on the Aeolian Islands, 163, 177, 179. *See also* hydrocarbons; oil; petrochemical industry; pumice

Return to the Aeolian Islands (Taviani), 7, 14, 18–19, 153, 156; as a bildungsroman, 174–75; locatedness of, 166; making of, 159–60, 171, 174; and memory, 157–58, 171, 173–74, 179; oral history telling, 164, 167–68, 180–83, 186; and pedagogy, 178; pumice cliffs sequence, 176; title translation, 20n3; women in, 164–65. *See also* Aeolian Islands; cinematic recycling; memory; montage; pumice; volcanoes

Revelli, Nuto, 5, 90, 99, 187n16

Roma, 67, 85n22, 85n27

Roman Empire, 60, 83n9, 163

Rome, 1, 23, 25, 56, 123, 153, 169

"room tone," 130, 139, 149n11, 149n14. *See also* sound; soundscapes

Rosi, Francesco, 85n28

Rossellini, Roberto, 181–82, 186n2; aesthetics of, 35; filming on the Aeolian Islands, 154–55; *Stromboli*, 162, 167, 173–74; on Stromboli, 168

rueido, 97–99, 103–4, 116

Ruggiero, Peppe, 77

SADE *(Società Adriatica di Elettricità)*, 31–32, 49–50

Salina, 153, 156, 161, 170–71; agriculture on, 163; as film set, 167, 181; library, 178. *See also* Aeolian Islands

SalinaDocFest, 168

Santo Stefano Island, 45

Sardinia, 30, 44

SAROM *(Società Azionaria Raffinazione Olii Minerali)*, 31–32, 48, 53n13. *See also* Monti, Attilio; petrochemical industry

SAROM island, 29–30, 34–40, 49. See also *Red Desert*

Saviano, Roberto: on the Camorra, 61, 70, 85n29; on illegal waste system, 74–75, 84n18; writing of *Gomorrah* (book), 57, 73, 81–82, 83n3. *See also Gomorrah* (film); organized crime

Scampia, 59, 65–67; classes of, 85n27; dirt of, 84n21; on location in, 79–81, 86n36. *See also* Le Vele; Naples

Schafer, R. Murray, 22n25

School of Human-Animal Interaction, 91. *See also* Marchesini, Roberto

screens, 10–11, 16

Scuola di Interazione Uomo-Animale (SIUA), 91. *See also* Marchesini, Roberto

Serra San Bruno, 129, 139, 143. *See also* charcoal burners

Serrecchia, Marco, 123; production manager for *Le quattro volte*, 59, 146–47, 149n14, 151n35; production manager for *Return to the Aeolian Islands*, 154, 159

Seveso dioxin disaster, 25, 49, 52n3

Shelley, Mary, 187n10

Sicily, 18, 122n35, 154–55, 177. *See also* Aeolian Islands; Legambiente

"silent cinema," 126

Silent Spring (Carson), 25, 123–25

situated knowledge, 81, 191

"slow cinema," 11, 14

Slow Food movement, 4–5, 77. See also Petrini, Carlo

slowness, 3–6, 11, 192; of geological time, 43

"slow violence," 4, 65, 192

Società Italiana per Condotte d'Acqua, 179

SOJA, 31

sound: in cinema studies, 148n6; cinematic, 14, 18, 126–27, 135–38, 146–47, 148n3, 148n7, 149n8, 149n12, 149n15; and environmental health, 124–25, 148n2; in *Le quattro volte*, 130–34; material effects of, 140–44; mixing of, 150n18; nonhuman, 15, 41; perception of, 128–29, 149n13; recording, 2, 7, 149n11, 149n14; in space, 132. *See also* acousmatics; acoustic ecology; acoustic footprint; "ear cleaning"; Foley sound; noise pollution; "room tone"; "silent cinema"; sound effects; soundscapes; soundtracks

sound effects, 126, 132, 148n4. *See also* Foley sound; soundtracks; surround sound

sound recordists. *See under* film production crew

soundscapes, 147; anthropogenic, 136; cinematic, 18, 126; horizontal, 134, 146; of *Le quattro volte*, 129, 131, 133–34, 139–40; in nature, 124; preservation of, 128. *See also* acoustic ecology; Benvenuti, Paolo; noise pollution; Olivero, Simone Paolo; "room tone"

soundtracks, 14, 19, 148n3; *Le quattro volte*, 18, 129, 131–33, 135, 138, 142; limitations of, 132–33; post-synchronization, 148n7; of *Red Desert*, 36, 38, 41, 45, 51; of *Return to the Aeolian Islands*, 157, 173–74; space replacement of, 127; of *The Wind Blows Round*, 94. *See also* sound; sound effects; soundscapes

spectators, 11–12, 115–16, 126–27; nonhuman, 28; and reception, 15, 52n10, 129, 132–34, 140, 149n12

Spinoza, Baruch, 144, 149n16, 151n34

State Forestry Corps, 56, 71

"still life," 43–44

Storia della natura d'Italia (Pratesi), 60

Stromboli (island), 162, 164, 166, 168–69; films about, 186n1. *See also* Aeolian Islands

Stromboli (volcano), 14, 19, 154, 159, 161–63, 187n6; eruption, 157, 164, 177, 184, 188n23; writings about, 175

Stromboli: Terra di Dio (Rossellini), 155–56, 160, 162, 164–66, 176; filming of, 166–67; memories of, 168–69, 173–74

Summers, Lawrence, 65

surround sound, 126, 132–33, 137

Tahiti, 158

Taviani, Giovanna, 2, 19, 153; archival approach to filmmaking, 156–57, 159, 164–66, 171, 178, 183; as a director, 168, 174–75, 183, 186; and memory, 169–71, 173. *See also* cinematic recycling; montage; *Return to the Aeolian Islands*; SalinaDocFest

Taviani brothers, 53n12, 153–54, 156, 170; Vittorio, 157, 174, 176, 187n5

technology: cinematic, 6, 12, 18, 33, 35, 73–74, 126–28, 148n3, 167–68, 189n31; and filmmaking, 59; human interactions with, 21n14, 27–28, 88–89, 144, 146–47, 152n37;

157; media, 15; and nonhuman animals, 93; politics of, 80, 149n13; toxicity of, 73. *See also* cinematic apparatus; digital filming formats; digital technology; technopoiesis

technopoiesis, 88–90, 110, 152n37; of cinema, 18, 92–93; learning from the nonhuman, 146. *See also* Marchesini, Roberto; posthumanism

Tempesta Film, 58, 83n5. *See also* EcoMuvi

Terra dei fuochi. See Land of Fires

That Awful Mess on Via Merulana (Gadda), 193

Thwaites, Thomas (GoatMan), 98

time: anthropocentric, 6; dead, 43–44, 150; geological, 24, 38, 42–44, 53n18, 154, 160–61, 163, 165–66, 169, 175; nonhuman, 11; volcanic, 159, 161, 185

tinnitus, 125, 140. *See also* environmental illness

Tizzoni, Piero, 44

Tornatore, Giuseppe, 122n35

Toscan, Thierry, 104–5, 108

tourism, 94, 116, 119n12, 178–79

toxic waste, 6, 8; and cinema, 74–75; depictions of, 2, 17; dumping of, 61, 65, 70–71, 76, 84n18; of filmmaking, 57, 183; trafficking in, 72–73, 86n32. *See also* dirt; film industry; global capital; *Gomorrah* (film); industry; organized crime; petrochemical industry; pollution

tragedy, 113, 118, 122n35

trans-corporeality, 26–29, 38, 49, 52n7, 81; of cinema, 17, 81; and place, 71, 75, 173. *See also* ecocriticism; posthumanism

transhumance, 104, 107. *See also* herding

Trump administration, 192

Tunisia, 122n35

"turbocapitalism," 4–5

Una montagna di balle (angrisano), 77

Una storia per l'energia (Pontecorvo), 53n12

UNESCO, 20n7, 77; *Atlas of the World's Languages in Danger*, 120n20; World Heritage Sites, 176–77, 179, 188n25

United Nations, 7, 176. *See also* UNESCO

United States, 8, 20n3, 38, 53n14; animal safety on film sets, 111; consumption of resources, 136; environmental policy, 192; military, 45 urban sprawl, 9–10. *See also* dirt

Ussolo, 87, 90; depopulation of, 99; domestic life of, 94, 117; and goats, 97; guests in, 107–8, 110. *See also* Cuneo; Piedmont; Valle Maira; *The Wind Blows Round*

Vajont Dam disaster, 49
Valla, Fredo, 100, 115
Valle Maira, 17, 89, 96, 104, 118; history of, 120n16. *See also* Ussolo; *The Wind Blows Round*
Varro, Marcus Terentius, 60
Vesuvius, 60, 161; eruption of, 86n32, 158; memories of, 169, 172–73; and Naples, 162. *See also* volcanoes
Villa of the Papyri, 184–85
vital materialism, 52n7, 53n17. *See also* "interactionism"
Vitti, Monica, 25, 34, 165
volcanoes, 3, 8, 14–15, 19, 151n32; as archives, 184–86; eruption of, 179–80, 187n11, 188n23; in films, 153–55, 157, 159–60, 186n1, 189n30; in history, 158, 161–63, 187n10; human relationships with, 164–65; memory of, 168–70, 173–74, 188n17; recycling function of, 183–84; rituals, 187n7; as teachers, 174–81, 188n27. *See also* archives; Etna; geology; landscapes; Naples; Stromboli (volcano); time; Vesuvius; volcanology; Vulcano (volcano)
volcanology, 3, 175, 177, 184
Vuk, 136–38, 147, 149n14, 150n20–150n21. *See also* dogs

Vulcano (Dieterle), 155–56, 165, 181–82, 184
Vulcano (island), 19, 154, 156, 161, 165, 181, 189n30
Vulcano (volcano), 161–62, 175, 187n6, 188n23, 190

walking, 1–2, 3–5, 19, 190–92; and mindfulness, 10; in a volcanic landscape, 160
Watcher, The (Calvino), 54n19
Wind Blows Round, The, 2, 8, 12, 17–18, 87–88; animal question in, 92, 117–18; dead goats sequence, 94–95, 100–101, 113, 117–18; distribution of, 114–15, 122n35; DVD, 109; hospitality, 107; making of, 93–94, 110–14, 121n29, 145; production crew of, 87, 108–9, 154; species boundaries, 96; title translation, 20n3; on violence, 115–16. *See also* goats; nonhuman actors; nonhuman animals
Wolfe, Cary, 91, 101–2, 116–17, 118n5, 120n19, 120n21, 120n23
World Bank, 7, 65
world intelligence, 171–72; plant, 173; world, 188n18. *See also* Abram, David
World War II, 32, 54n24, 97, 99; films of, 154
World Wildlife Fund, 83n10, 119n12

YouTube, 15, 43, 53n12, 73, 86n37

Zanna, Gianfranco, 177. *See also* Legambiente
Zavattini, Cesare, 1, 20n1. *See also* "pedinamento"

ELENA PAST is Associate Professor of Italian at Wayne State University. She is the author of *Methods of Murder: Beccarian Introspection and Lombrosian Vivisection in Italian Crime Fiction*. She is editor (with Deborah Amberson) of *Thinking Italian Animals: Human and Posthuman in Modern Italian Literature and Film* and editor (with Serenella Iovino and Enrico Cesaretti) of *Italy and the Environmental Humanities: Landscapes, Natures, Ecologies*.

CPSIA information can be obtained
at www.ICGtesting.com
Printed in the USA
BVHW041927240220
573171BV00009B/119

9 780253 039484